IGNITE YOUR SPIRIT

– ENERGY HEALING –

Realise Your Highest Potential

Includes over 150 testimonials from those who have experienced the IYS Energy Healing modality.

IGNITE YOUR SPIRIT

– ENERGY HEALING –

Realise Your Highest Potential

BY SHAKTI DURGA (KIM FRASER)

To know, to love,

To be free,

To understand,

To progress, to have gratitude,

To appreciate beauty,

To relate harmoniously

Such is the richness of life.

5th edition, revised and reprinted 2026 by
Higher Guidance Pty Ltd
PO Box 211, Cooranbong NSW 2265 Australia
Phone: 02 4905 0216 www.shaktidurga.org
Shanti Mission
213 Martinsville Rd, Cooranbong NSW 2265 Australia
Ph: 02 49773300
Email: info@shantimission.org www.shantimission.org
First published 2004 by Higher Guidance Pty Ltd 2nd edition 2007 by Findhorn Press.
3rd edition (revised), published 2010 by
Higher Guidance Pty Ltd

Other Publications by the same author:

Empowering Relationships, 2012

Child of God, 2006

Dimensions of Wealth 2009, 2nd edition 2016

Spiritual Mastery 2008, 2nd edition 2016

National Library of Australia Cataloguing-in-Publication Creator: Durga, Shakti, 1961- author.
Title: Ignite Your Spirit Energy Healing: Realise Your Highest Potential / Shakti Durga (Kim Fraser).
Edition: 4th edition
ISBN: 978-0-987-1091-6-3 (paperback) 613.7046
Notes: Includes bibliographical references.
Cover artwork by Michelle Bennett, michelle@bennettdesign.net.au Illustrated by Sava Pinney and Melanie Claire Purcell
Internal design and typesetting Bungoona Technologies P/L, www.bungoona.com.au, Set in 11/13.8 Cambria
Printed in Australia by Griffin Press

CONTENTS

INDEX OF EXERCISES

INDEX OF TESTIMONIALS

Introduction

RE you bursting with energy and enthusiasm? Do you wake up in the morning and think, *life is so great, I feel amazing?* Does your love life sizzle? Do you enjoy a zest for life, loads of energy and good health? Do you have passion for your work and hobbies? Do you sleep well? Is your mind able to stop at night and allow you peace, inner harmony and wellbeing? Do money and opportunities flow easily to you?

If you answered yes to all or most of these questions, then you may have already ignited your spirit and be optimising your energy. If not, chances are your spirit is still under wraps and your energy could do with some rebooting.

Nothing is as painful as living in disharmony with your authentic (Higher) self. The longer you do this the worse things get. You experience feelings of emptiness, separation, alienation, dissatisfaction, loneliness and depression, as well as self sabotage, poor relationships with others, exhaustion and premature death. No wonder you feel like you need to reboot your life and access some new energy! This denseness clogs up our energy field and can make a person feel droopy, like an indoor plant that hasn't been watered for too long. Energy healing can be an effective way to help move through these issues, and regular maintenance of your own essential, vital energy can be learned and added to your wellness regime. How to go about that is the subject of this book.

We know when we feel in good spirits, and when we don't. When we ignite our spirit and reboot our life, it is like re-igniting an inner fire that gives us a glow of wellbeing. We feel more peaceful, have more energy, life is easier and we are in the flow. If you are interested in spirituality, you can also experience some amazing states of higher consciousness with continuous practice of energy healing.

It is easier to be more aligned with your Higher Self (Soul), and to be grounded and practical in your life with a strong and clean energy body. The Higher Self (Soul) is like an unseen frequency, which is there all the time, though it often remains undetected by us. Our body knows about it and reacts and responds to it, yet our minds often miss the connection. It's literally a case of out of sight, out of mind. This is a shame because our Higher Self (Soul) loves us unconditionally, has only our best interests at heart and can guide us like no one else.

No matter what is happening in your life, you can find a way to make your heart sing and put a sparkle in your smile. This might seem impossible from your present circumstances and point of view, but as you read on you will be pleasantly surprised at what you can do to change that. A number of testimonials have been included at the back of this book, to give you some idea of the scope of IYS Energy Healing. The basic techniques given here will enable you to lighten your load and do a lot of simple healing work. However, like anything there are many layers which add up to mastery of a subject. It takes two transformative, exciting and fulfilling years to become a fully qualified IYS Energy Healing therapist who work at a much deeper level to assist more profound healing. This book is designed to help with self-care of the etheric body and accessing more of your spiritual energy to create a better life.

Back to your Higher Self (Soul), which really knows what is best for you. Wouldn't it be good if we had an antenna through which we could clearly hear the voice of the soul? Well, we do. It is called the etheric body, or energy anatomy. Previously only highly trained mystery school initiates knew about it, but this book makes it easily understandable and accessible to all who are open to learning.

The etheric body refers to the body's chakras and meridians, as well as the aura in which our body resides. The chakras are whirling vortices of energy and information which infuse our body, mind and spirit with energy. Meridians are lines of energy that join up the chakras, and the aura is the bubble of energy in which it all happens. Other modalities which work with the etheric body includes Acupuncture, Reiki, Pranic Healing, Kinesiology and Chiropractic.

Like the Higher Self (Soul), the etheric body is not visible to the ordinary eye, and is obviously not made out of physical stuff. However, it is very real and often very messy in most people.

When we want to get healthier, happier and feel better about ourselves and solve issues in our lives, by accessing higher consciousness this becomes easier. The accessing of higher consciousness, which already exists inside our Higher Self (Soul), takes practice. It also requires that we have the strength of being to do it. This strength is mostly to be found in our energy body. The energy body can be likened to the hardware of your computer, whereas the consciousness we get access to is like software. We cannot use advanced software programs on the kinds of computers that were around in the 1980's when a 250-megabyte computer was seen as huge! Now we measure computer capacity in terabytes, and who knows what the future holds. These upgrades have enabled us to store, learn and undergo much more complex kinds of information than ever before in known history.

The Higher Self (Soul) is like the software, and the electricity which makes it go, combined together.

In order to make effective use of the Higher Self (Soul), the etheric or energy body needs to be in reasonable condition. Like our computers, if the hardware (etheric body) is small or faulty, big programs (the Higher Self (Soul)) will not run on it. In other words, if our etheric hardware is small and dirty, we are likely to experience illness, difficulties and blockages, and we are unlikely to be as successful in life as we might like to be until we deal with the blockages and rev up our etheric body.

Spiritual development: it's about tuning in, not tuning out

Spiritual development is not about sitting in a cave and meditating 24/7. It's about real people leading dynamic and satisfying lives and having the tools to help them through when the going gets tough. It's about living better than you have before and enjoying yourself more. It's about wholesomeness and personal empowerment. When that happens, there is a natural tendency to want to help others. The process of self-healing does not stop, but continues and transforms us into shining beings of love. Obstacles are still there, but we have many more tools to deal with them.

When we ignite our spirit, we remove the limitations and obstacles that stand between the separate physical 'me' that lives in a physical body and our Higher Self (Soul). We become aware of the non-physical world. This inner world is just as real as the outer world, and just as obvious when we know what to look for and how it operates. By understanding the inner world, we can more readily understand the seemingly random events of our physical lives, which take on a much more coherent shape. Hence, life makes more sense and because we understand more, we can make positive changes more quickly, and live with greater ease and grace.

While this book gives an understanding of the processes involved in igniting the spirit and rebooting your life, it is recommended that you also take part in the seminars 'Ignite Your Spirit, Centres of Consciousness' and 'Ignite Your Spirit, Energy Healing Made Easy'. Experience is far more powerful as a catalyst for change than mere concepts. Understanding is good, but experience brings wisdom.

I affirm, I visualize and still nothing happens

By now most people will be familiar with the use of positive self-talk, or affirmations, to assist in bringing about desired change. I have found using affirmations and visualization to be amazing tools for self-transformation. However, I have also found that you can use affirmations and visualize what you want until you are blue in the face, but there are times when it just doesn't work. Even more frustrating, it seems that I can easily employ affirmations in some areas of life, but not others.

There is a reason for this. Some of our chakras are clearer, bigger and more efficient than others. When they are big and clear, affirmations are generally effective. When they are congested and slow, relying on affirmations to work is like walking in quicksand. There is no progress and, if anything, things get worse.

Every area of our life is influenced by what is stored in our chakras. This is where a lot of our 'unconscious self' resides. If the chakra primarily concerned with the area we are trying to change is healthy, change will be relatively easy to achieve. If the area requires information from a chakra that is unhealthy, then it is going to be difficult to effect change until the basic problem is addressed, which is that the chakras are caked with garbage and not capable of powering change in the area we want. The clearer we get, the easier and faster change is able to be made in our lives. Miracles start to happen, and serendipitous events occur all around us.

Sally was a high-powered lawyer with a wonderful ability to make money and have fun. Her base chakra, which holds the energy of security and money making, was in fabulous shape. Sally found affirmations around new levels of income very effective but had no luck whatsoever with affirmations around relationships.

Despite being gorgeous and vivacious, Sally could not hold down a relationship. Love eluded her. That was because her heart chakra was relatively closed. When she learned to open her heart and ignite her spirit, her relationship affirmations were successful.

Where are you at?

Before we proceed, why not do a stocktake of your life right now and focus on which areas might need work, because here we will find the kindling to really ignite your spirit.

Get a pen and choose an adjective (or expletive if you must) to describe how you feel about the following areas of your life.

STOCKTAKE OF YOUR LIFE

Area	Wonderful	Good	Average	Poor	Abysmal
Feeling of personal security					
Relationship with parents					
Finances, level of abundance generally					
Membership of groups or clubs					
General health & vitality					
Expression of creativity					
Sex life					
Relationship with children					
Personal power					
Self esteem					
Relationships					
Body image					
Body weight					
Love					
Relationships					
Personal freedom					
Playfulness					
Stress management					
Career					
Mental processes					

Clarity of mind			
Spiritual life			
Sense of adventure			
Sense of responsibility			
Living now, not in the past			
Living now, not in the future			

As you read this book, remain aware of what you have identified as issues in your life, as this will give you a clue as to the main areas of your etheric body that might need help. When the spirit is ignited, energy flows cleanly through every facet of our life, bringing resolution to seemingly impossible situations and circumstances.

Don't like the life you have? Then grow the life you want

Our etheric body extends around and penetrates our physical body. It infuses us with and holds reservoirs of life force energy. Life force energy is also known as subtle energy, prana or chi.

Chakras are meant to rotate back and forth like washing machine agitators, spinning energy in and out of our bodies. If they are full of etheric garbage, they block up. Then, clean energy cannot get into the body through the chakras and dirty energy cannot get out. In this way chakras are like lungs; they bring to us something we need and get rid of stuff that is used up or dirty.

When they are looked after and work the way they were designed to work, we have lots of energy and we feel and look great. Life is good. Our mind is clear. Problems are easier to deal with, as are difficult people and stressful circumstances. However, too much unresolved negative energy causes chakras to shrink and slow down, eventually even stop, and while we might be ignorant of the effect on our chakras, we will not fail to notice the resultant sluggishness of our bodies and minds. Clear conscious connection with our Higher Self is unlikely when we are carrying a truckload of dirt in our etheric bodies. Our internal guidance system is likely to be screwy, and this leads to struggle, effort and disappointment.

When our energy centres or chakras are blocked, we do not have the required energy to pull what we want into our lives. If our aura is ragged and bent out of shape, we are not centred and are not fully present in our own energetic power.

Often emotional and energetic blockages build up over time, preventing people from functioning, let alone relating to others, in an optimal way. These emotional blocks build up in our etheric body, which in turn lead to physical blockages such as ill health, tiredness, weight gain, depression, stress, anxiety, strained marriages, appetite changes, loss of libido, workplace disputes and so on. Medical intuitives have shown how specific emotional blockages create disease and lack of wellbeing in predictable ways.

The good news is, when effective energetic healing and self-care is implemented, the negative effects and potentials are often reversible. (See *You Can Heal Your Life* by Louise L. Hay or *Your Body is the Barometer of Your Soul* by Annette Noontill for detailed descriptions of the effects negativity and emotional blockages can have on parts of the body specifically and on illness in general.) You can start to understand how your energy anatomy works and begin to use it more consciously and effectively. You can heal yourself and start to grow the life you would like, using very simple energy healing techniques combined with meditation.

Throughout the book are various anecdotes from my clinical practice as a healer. Names have been changed and all of the stories are composites to protect the confidentiality of those who have come for healing.

It's now time to begin an adventure of discovery to find out how our aura and chakras affect our personality, life experiences and potential for success. First, we look at the aura and reveal some of its secrets and then we move onto the chakras, which are described generally before the specific information and illustrations of how each major chakra operates. At the end of each chapter on the individual chakras, there are easy exercises which specifically work on that chakra and strengthen it.

The last part of the book describes the basic steps of IYS Healing Energy, which is about how to bring change, develop your own multisensory awareness and effect healing by working directly with the aura and chakras. The method set out is simple and can be used on yourself or others.

For those who want to know more, an entire 2-3 year immersion program to be an accredited Ignite Your Spirit Therapist is available which is deeply transformational and will Ignite Your Spirit in ways you could not imagine. Rich friendships form, consciousness expands, horizons grow and abilities you never knew you had rise to the surface and enrich your life. You can find out more about that via our website www.igniteyourspirit.com

PART

Chapter

1

THE MULTIDIMENSIONAL YOU

THE physical world we see around us is obviously not the entirety of life. There are many important parts of our world that we cannot classify as physical. Things such as feelings, premonitions, the energy body, will and our spirit; these things are real but are not physical. Many old spiritual books talk about the outer world of form (the physical dimension) and the inner world of the spirit. However, the inner world is not just a big space with stuff floating around in it. It is separated into different dimensions, and each dimension has different fundamental rules. There is sufficient evidence available today to say with certainty that energy healing works. People in their thousands are turning to alternative therapies for healing and wellbeing, and in many medical schools, including our local universities, medical students are required to study an alternative healing module.

Energy healers do not work on the physical body, or in the physical dimension. They work in the etheric dimension. Waves of energy are felt

14

there as they treat their clients. Manipulation of these etheric waves creates rapid, tangible change in the wellbeing of a patient.

An ancient esoteric truth says things are created on the inner plane first, and then they take form on the outer plane, in the physical world. My observations confirm that this is so. Change our inner world and miracles seem to occur in our outer life.

Energy healing, when performed by a powerful healer, can do things that defy the physical laws of matter. I have personally witnessed energy healing where physical tissue was regenerated as we watched. A badly burnt finger was regenerated over a period of hours by several healers working non-stop; at the end of the healing period the finger did not even have a blister. If we consider only physical reality, such a thing could not occur.

Whilst there are countless dimensions, and each dimension has countless sub-dimensions, we can talk sensibly about five definite and discrete dimensions that humanity at this point in our evolution is heavily engaged with. What is more, we each have five bodies, each corresponding to one of the five dimensions.

These dimensions (and bodies) are:

1. The physical dimension
2. The etheric dimension
3. The astral dimension
4. The soul dimension
5. The Divine void

In an effort to make this simple, one could say that, vibrationally speaking, the physical dimension is the densest or lowest body that we have. The etheric body is above it. On top of that is the astral dimension, which is vibrationally lower than the soul dimension, and the Divine void is the highest and lightest body.

To see this in a diagram it would look something like this:

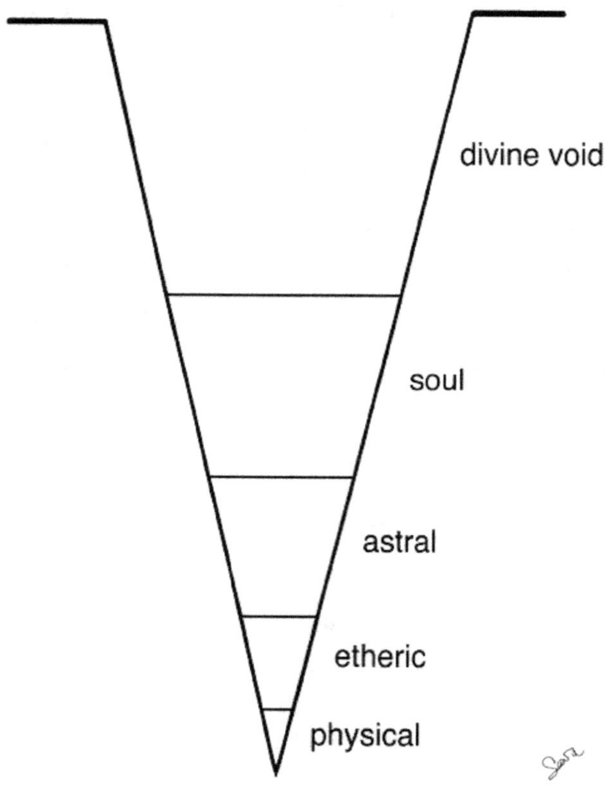

The physical dimension, the physical body

It goes without saying that this is the most noticeable part of who we are. Countless industries exist around how to look after the physical body, and our mainstream medical fraternity has done an amazing job, developing physical, surgical and chemical forms of healing which have alleviated a great deal of suffering in the world.

When we ignite our spirit, we do not ignore our physical body. We honour it. The difference is we understand that it is not ALL of who we are.

Our ability to love, be affectionate and happy and have fun are not physical things that medical science can teach us about. These things are the province of the soul and our astral bodies. The rate at which our physical bodies are able to recover from illness or injury is only partially a physical matter. Extraordinary recoveries occur when the etheric body is treated as well.

We can look after our etheric bodies until we are blue in the face, but if we are still pumping toxins into our body, either through food, drugs (legal and illegal), environmental factors and so on, or consistently not getting enough sleep, we are likely to suffer an effect eventually. Living on fast food and neglecting exercise is not, unfortunately, going to be remedied by cleaning our etheric body.

Our physical bodies definitely work better when the energy body is in good shape. For example, if the base chakra is clogged up, the lower back might feel sore. Remove the dirt and the back feels better. If the throat chakra is clogged up, the thyroid might begin to malfunction. Remove the garbage and energy flows to the thyroid again, often leading to a resolution of the problem. Each part of the physical body has a chakra or combination of chakras that feed it energy.

In my clinic, I have treated some very good athletes. One man was a road bike racer who competed in high-level competitions. After his first healing he experienced a surge in energy that was so great, he was able to outclass his training buddies the next day. They were amazed, and wanted to know what he had taken. He hadn't taken anything, he had had his etheric body cleaned out which ignited his spirit.

Another man I saw regularly was a lifelong swimmer who competed in the State and National Masters competitions. After several sessions devoted to cleansing and energizing his various bodies, he broke his own record in the 400 metre medley by an incredible seventeen seconds. In the future it is inevitable that serious athletes and sports teams will have an energy healer on staff to boost the performance of the team naturally.

Some ailments are so advanced that nothing short of surgery will help. I have had many patients come to me with serious medical conditions. The energy healings have been of great assistance and alleviated a lot of pain and stress. In every case where surgery has been necessary, the results with patients who had energy healing first have been outstanding. One woman, Rose, had serious brain surgery. Her prognosis without the surgery was certain death, and the prognosis with the surgery was probable death. She had about a twenty-five percent chance of recovery without significant side effects such as partial paralysis or inability to speak, or brain damage. This remarkable woman was only in her early thirties and had two small children.

Rose saw me about six times before the surgery, and we also sent energy to the surgical team and operating theatre. We dealt with all manner of energies and dimensions that related to her condition but ultimately this heavy physical condition required surgical care. We energized all the drugs she would be taking and I gave her absent healing immediately after the operation. She was fully cognizant as soon as the general anaesthetic wore off. She had no side effects, and her surgeon could not believe the speed of her recovery and the completeness of the cure. We could.

Our entire body is regenerated regularly. Our skin is new every five months. Our skeleton, seemingly so solid and rigid, is entirely new every three months. "Every year, fully 98% of the total number of atoms in your body are replaced, this has been confirmed by radioisotope studies at the Oak Ridge Laboratories in California."[1] How is it then that this does not put an end to any disease that might be present?

Our physical body contains cells, each of which has its own memory. At a basic level, this involves the knowledge of how to reproduce themselves. They also reproduce the energy that is inside the parent cell, thereby replicating our storehouse of attachments, energies and memories.

Large build ups of negative cellular memory can cause emotional, psychological and medical problems. These are not easily removed by just working on a physical level. When we know how to work on our etheric and astral bodies, these things can be more effectively dealt with.

Sometimes these cellular memories leak through from past lives. Our physical body is the temple which anchors our soul into this dimension. Our soul contains an overview of all our various incarnations, and soul energy pervades our being. It is not all that surprising that old memories would occasionally surface; it is more surprising that we have forgotten so much that we think this is strange.

---

[1] Deepak Chopra MD, *Perfect Health,* Bantam Books, 1990, p.12.

Like it or loathe it, our physical body is the only one we have this lifetime. We might as well look after it and enjoy it. We will never have the opportunity to live this very life again.

The etheric body

The etheric body is larger than the physical body and has a habit of partly joining up with the people we interact with and have relationships with. In this way, energy and information flows between us, and we get a greater sense of oneness than when we place our awareness just in the physical dimension.

The etheric body is the dimension in which most energy healers work. Physical problems manifest in this dimension first as disturbances in a person's energy body; as the energy gets denser the disturbances then trickle down into the physical dimension. This is similar to the way energy builds in the sky and causes a thunder storm. When energy builds up and cannot easily flow away, it has to go somewhere. In nature, storms release energy through lightning strikes. From the etheric body, a build up of stuck energy is usually released by the physical body through illness.

The range of illnesses a person ultimately succumbs to can be predicted based on which chakras get clogged due to a build up in energy that has not been cleaned out. Many experienced healers, including myself, can sometimes detect illnesses before they occur because of the changes in a person's etheric body. What is more, we are often able to detect the underlying cause of the imbalance because the energy body is full of pictures that depict your most dominant beliefs about yourself and the world. All we do is read them.

The etheric body is like a transfer station, through which we flow back and forth between our various other bodies, the physical, astral and soul bodies. It is happening every day. Whenever you fall asleep you flow out of your physical body, through the etheric body and into the astral or soul body. You float around and have dreams, sometimes you can even remember them. Some people jerk when they fall asleep. This is the moment when they actually leave their physical body. It is how we are built. It is natural.

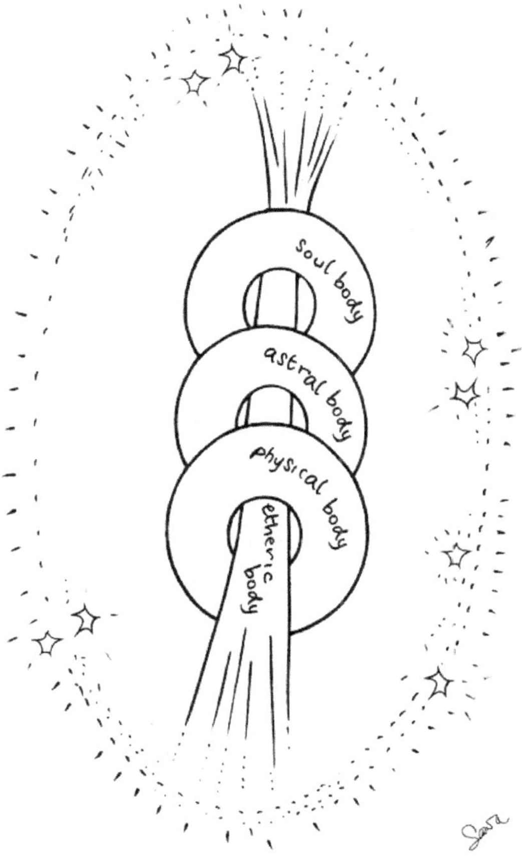

The etheric body is like a transfer station

The astral body

Between the soul body and the physical body, and interpenetrated by the etheric body, is the astral body. The astral body contains thoughts, emotions, beliefs, imagination, memory and so on, and is very watery in nature. It flows inside and around us. We are even more connected astrally with everyone else than we are physically or etherically. Thoughts and emotions have a fluid quality which allows for partial telepathic communication. This happens to all of us from time to time. Have you ever known who is on the phone before you pick it up? Have you ever known that a loved one was in danger, or had a dream that contained some kind of premonition? Telepathic communication becomes more refined and more conscious as we work on our etheric body. While this type of awareness is astral in nature, we have to develop our etheric selves if we want to have a powerful apparatus through which the information can be sent and received.

In a nutshell, the astral body comprises the thoughts and emotional messages that we send and receive, and the etheric body is the hardware through which this takes place.

Most people are largely unaware of what they send and receive, but their lives will in large part reflect this. When one develops even partial clairvoyance, it is clear that people wear big energy signs around their necks that read "I am successful" or "I am worthless, just use me". We all receive these messages about people, though usually the message is subconscious. We can learn to become conscious of these powerful astral signals, which we and everyone else carry in our etheric bodies, and if we don't like our signs, we can learn to change them. This is such a big subject, I am writing a separate book about it. (Watch out for my book *Yoga of the Mind.*)

The soul dimension

Our Higher Self is our soul (in this book we use the terms soul and Higher Self interchangeably). Our soul is a huge, intelligent body that is much larger than our physical body. The physical, etheric and astral bodies are all a part of our soul, like toes are part of our feet. We are really souls on Earth having human holidays. The soul dimension is home, and when we are able to contact this in a conscious way, our whole outlook changes.

Life becomes a huge revelation.

Take away the soul and the body dies. When the body dies, the soul does not. It just extracts information and energy from our physical and etheric bodies and recycles it. (For more information about this process, see *Meditations for Soul Realization* by Master Choa Kok Sui.) This process takes place at a level of vibration that is too high for a normal physical brain to comprehend at this point in our evolution and, let's face it, when you are dead, your brain is not much use anyway.

The extracted information is placed within the etheric body of the next baby we become. We do not remember it because it all happens at a vibrational level that is way off the vibrational Richter scale of our awareness. Some say that we swim in the river of forgetfulness between lifetimes, which is another way of saying the same thing.

When we incarnate, part of our soul enters the physical realm. This gives us life and animates our being. Most of our soul does not enter the physical plane but remains outside our usual focus, and this, the largest part of ourselves, we call the Higher Self. Union with our Higher Self brings access to endless wisdom, the ability to be telepathically in contact with our guides and spiritual teachers, a heightened sense of intuition and a vastly more pleasant life.

The Higher Self is not bounded by space or time, and has an enormous overview of life, including awareness of things that we, with our physical consciousness, have no idea about.

If we want to become more conscious of the voice of the soul, certain parts of our etheric body need to be developed. They also need to be clean, energetically speaking. We can then get glimpses, and eventually a full picture, of what we experienced before we entered the current physical body that we inhabit. Accessing that type of information, which at a soul level is always available, inevitably has to do with the level of development and clarity of the etheric body.

The Divine Void

At our very core, we are in fact comprised of very essential stuff. This stuff we refer to as Divine, and call God, Universal Energy or the Great Spirit. In fact it is known by many names and is recognized in all cultures as the eternal omnipotent being, God/ Goddess.

Quantum physics might seem like a strange place to learn about divinity, but it appears that science has begun to prove many ancient mystical teachings. Fasten your seatbelts, you are about to have the briefest and most simplified quantum physics lesson in the history of man.[2]

---

[2] The author is not a scientist: you are invited to explore this fascinating area further yourself. For (relatively) simple information about our reality and the quantum field see *Dancing Wu Li*

It used to be thought that atoms were the smallest things in creation. That was until the late 1800s when finally our scientists found a way to split the atom. Then they found that there were indeed more levels of reality than had previously been considered possible. What is more, most of the physical laws do not apply when examining the goings-on at these levels. When we speak of the sub-atomic field, we speak of really small stuff. Millions of atoms can fit on a pinhead. According to Gary Zukav in his book *The Dancing Wu Li Masters,* to see the atoms in a baseball bat, the bat would need to be the size of Earth. The atoms would then look the size of grapes.

Inside the atom are protons, electrons and other things with strange names. Actually, although names have been given to the stuff that has been discovered by quantum physicists, it is not correct to think of this field as containing 'things'. There are just waves of energy that resemble tracks. Thus the quantum field is not full of things, it is actually more like a void. The tracks that are left by sub-atomic energy fields have had scientists assume that something has in fact been there.[3] This is the closest they have come to proving the existence of 'things' in the quantum field. No one has ever actually seen things in the sub-atomic field. Whilst this seems fairly strange, it is true.

Quantum field theory basically says that Earth, in fact the entire universe, is made of the same substance. This substance is non-material. If the essential substance of the universe is nonphysical, what is it?

In his book *The Tao of Physics,* Fritjof Capra quotes Deepak Chopra: *"This invisible nothingness [within the atom] silently orchestrates,*

Masters, by Gary Zukov (1979 Rider, London) and *Taking the Quantum Leap* by Fred Alan Wolf (1989, Harper and Row, New York).
[3] See *Dancing Wu Li Masters,* by Gary Zukov (1979 Rider, London) p.38.

instructs, governs and compels nature to express itself with infinite creativity, infinite abundance and unfaltering exactitude, into a myriad of designs and patterns and forms." Everything, including a piece of human brain tissue, a bit of quartz rock, a flower, a piece of metal or plastic, has the same basic (non) material inside. Mankind (well, Western man anyway) has become confused in its belief that humans are made of a special substance and everything else isn't. Quantum physics tends to disprove this myth.

The quantum field can be described as organic and aware; it is not dead or inorganic. Thus physical objects, of which atoms form a part, cannot really be said to be dead or inorganic either. Almost every shamanic faith through recorded history acknowledges the sacredness of all things, particularly everything in the natural world. The Tao, the Celts, the Native American Indians, the Australian Aboriginals, all treat everything as sacred. They cannot understand the Western lack of perception of the divinity in all things.

In the quantum field, protons and electrons display gestalt intelligence. Gestalt intelligence refers to the complete understanding of a problem or situation without the need for any linear deductive or logical thought.

Sub-atomic energy waves know things not after they happen, but as they happen, and amend their own behaviour accordingly. This has been shown in various experiments and, without getting too technical, protons and electrons seem to make decisions about what they are going to do *before* consequences from events are incurred. They already know what is going to happen. Human intelligence can't do that. Divine intelligence can.

Probably the weirdest thing of all about the quantum field is that in an experiment, it responds to the scientists' expectations. This means that two scientists can do the very same experiment, one expecting result A and the other expecting result B, and each will get what they expect. This will happen every time they do it, and won't change until they change their expectation. This calls into question the idea of objectivity.

"The constituents of matter and the basic phenomena involving all are interconnected, interrelated, and interdependent... they cannot be understood as isolated entities, but only as integrated parts of the whole."[4]

From a metaphysical point of view, it appears that science is validating the most basic propositions of mysticism.

As we Ignite our Spirits, we start to recognise that everything is part of the one whole, and holy. Everything is made out of the same stuff, which is Divine energy or love, different names for God/Goddess. Inside us are lots of atoms, and inside them is God. God in things or people is God made manifest, and God not in things is unmanifest God, or Holy Spirit. As we think about things, quanta start to pop in and out and cause our thoughts to affect energy, and eventually our physical lives.

True oneness comes from the Divine core which gave life to our soul in the first place. Divine energy, or love, is the essential building block of life and creation. Looked at from the perspective of our Divine selves, we are in truth all one and each one of us really is Divine.

---

[4] See *The Tao of Physics,* by Fritzof Capra (1975, Shambhala Publications, Boston) p.131.

Chapter

2

NEED AN ENERGY FIX?

Scientists used to think of the world as a big machine made of physical matter that operated in predictable and controllable ways. Modern scientists tell us that this is not really true. Everything is comprised of energy. Even something as solid as a wooden table is actually made of energy.

When we have too little energy we feel run-down and tired, even depressed or ill. When we have too much energy we become stressed, anxious and restless. When our energy becomes congested and heavy, we do not feel so good. Our thoughts become negative, our spirit droops and we often undersell ourselves and fail to achieve what we are really capable of. However, when our energy is clean and light, we feel refreshed and happy.

Mainstream culture still does not recognise the value of keeping our energy in balance as an effective means of alleviating a lot of physical, mental and emotional discomfort. However, as more people try energy healing, increasing numbers are finding to their delight and relief that they can change their energy levels, their perceptions and their lives.

Subtle energy is also called aether, life force energy or prana. It is an ocean of subtle substance, the building blocks from which matter and form take shape. Subtle energy can come from a number of sources. These include:

1. The natural physical world: what we eat and drink.
2. The elemental world: fire, Earth, air and water.
3. The astral world: energy inherent in our thoughts, beliefs and emotions.
4. The soul dimension: energy flowing to us from our own eternal being, which is vast, and from our spiritual guides, angels and teachers who are enlightened and live in a different dimension to us.
5. The Divine dimension: This is the ultimate source of all energies, and everything that is part of the manifest and unmanifest cosmos. (The dimensions and their properties are discussed at length in my book *Dimensions of Wealth*.)

Energy and the natural physical world

We get energy from food, water and sunlight. Even the air we breathe contains loads of subtle energy. Subtle energy is everywhere, but it is very concentrated in forests, the mountains and the sea. Thus, when we visit these places, we feel different. Notice how energy can feel dissimilar in various geographic locations. People generally choose to live in areas that match their vibration. As you drive from one suburb to another, even in the same city, they feel different. Start to notice why that is. It is more than just the physical attributes. As you move from one region to another, or from country to country, the difference is very pronounced.

The more natural the surroundings, the more subtle energy there is likely to be present. Subtle energy is much less prevalent in manmade fabrics, fibres and products. When we are in a city we usually feel less energy than when we are in the countryside. Natural building materials such as wood and stone hold far more energy than artificial materials, and natural light is more energizing than artificial light, as anyone working in an office tower will tell you.

Professor Ron Laura, a brilliant philosopher, claims that as we 'progress' and become an increasingly technology-driven society, able to create more and more stuff, we gain more and more control over a deader and deader world. (Professor Laura has written numerous books on this theme including *Empathetic Education,* co-authored with Matthew Cotton.) When nature is excluded or when our lives are not lived in natural rhythms, but are forced into artificial timetables, humans start to suffer. This suffering can be physical, mental or emotional. As our food and environment become more and more artificial, the natural energy that should be there, and which we require for good health and wellbeing, is missing. We become partially deadened as a reflection of our deadened surroundings. So much for progress.

One very simple way of getting an amazing hit of energy is by hugging a beautiful big healthy tree. Trees are a rich source of energy. One can simply sit under a tree to soak in its vitality. Many sanitariums, where people go to convalesce after a serious illness, are set in pristine natural environments with lots of trees. This is because the effect of trees upon the patients is very noticeable.

The following exercise can intensify the energy you get from trees.

BLESSING AND RECEIVING ENERGY FROM TREES

1. *Choose a healthy largish tree.*

2. *Invoke (see Part III)*

3. *Raise your hands towards the tree and ask that the Divine of your understanding bless the tree and its subtle bodies. Imagine the tree's healthy branches, leaves and roots, its strength and beauty.*

4. *Ask that the tree bless you with energy, and breathe in.*

5. *To make the exercise stronger, you can actually bless the tree. Focus on the top of your head, breathing in energy through the crown chakra and letting some of it flow from your raised hands to the tree.*

6. *Relax, breathe in and thank the tree for the energy it shares with you.*

7. *Sit for a few minutes and be aware of the waves of energy that flow to you from the tree. notice how you feel.*

Just for the experience, you can try the same exercise with a man-made structure like a concrete pillar. The difference is staggering. We don't recommend that you do this more than once. No wonder so many Holy men and women retreated to the country to live.

The elements and energy

Fire, Earth, air and water are the building blocks of our reality. Each of these elements holds energy differently, and each is required for a healthy functioning body. Ayurvedic medicine is based upon attaining the appropriate elemental balance within us.

Certain parts of our etheric body resonate strongly with particular elements. To see how this feels, meditate in a natural setting where each element is represented. The Earth beneath you, the sun above, clean air. Do it near the sea, or a clean river, stream or dam. If you do not live near a body of water then have a bowl of fresh water beside you.

MEDITATION ON THE ELEMENTS

1. *Invoke (see Part III).*
2. *Focus on one element at a time. Imagine you can breathe it in, and that it is distributed in a healthy way throughout your body. Be aware.*
3. *Notice how you feel, and get a sense of the energy and how it enters your energy anatomy.*
4. *Go to the next element and do the same thing.*
5. *Notice how the body registers each element differently.*
6. *Give thanks for the experience.*

Energy through sound

Music soothes the savage beast. If we want to rev ourselves up, we can listen to any popular forms of 'up' music from rock to pop to rap to dance music. Some people find this very energizing, and this accounts for the popularity of dance parties, discos and so on. If you have had a hard day at the office and come home stressed, you can play soothing music to reduce your level of tension.

A Japanese scientist, Dr Emoto, performed a number of experiments on water. He used Tokyo tap water, and filled a number of test tubes with the water. Then he subjected the water to various sounds. He froze the water and then examined it under a high powered microscope to see if the sound had any effect on the formation of the ice crystals. What he found was truly amazing. Certain types of music such as heavy metal caused the crystals to fragment and become deranged. Prayer and words of love resulted in magnificent crystals, whole and geometric. (You can see the images of this at www.hado.com)

As humans, water is the largest component of our physical selves. It makes up about seventy per cent of our body mass. If sound makes water in a test tube do crazy or magnificent things, what is it doing to us?

Esoterically, sound is considered to be the basis of everything and existed before light did. The Bible tells us that in the beginning was the word; that is, sound. In the East, the sound or word of God is considered to be OM.

The sound of OM has a cleansing effect on people, places and things. Have you ever walked into a room and thought, someone has been having an argument in here? There may be no visual cues, and you may not have heard anything, but the feeling in the room is very tense. This is because the subtle energy that exists in the room is impregnated with the emotional energy of the people in it. If they are strong emotions, they will linger long after the people have left. Chanting OM can have an incredibly soothing and healing effect on us and our surroundings. If you put on an OM CD and let it play in the room, when you come back the dirty energy will have dissipated.

Even though I live in a happy household, I still regularly play an OM CD. I put it on as I am taking the kids to school and when I come back, the house is clear, serene and ready for the new day. It has been OM'd! Thought forms lingering from television programs, which are often very disturbing and negative, can also be cleaned out this way. After you watch the evening news, you should definitely OM the house. If your kids are having a hard time at school, OM their bedrooms because they bring that energy home with them and it accumulates in their room. It compounds their problems. Get rid of it. (Turn to the back of the book for information about my OM Your Every Day Life soundtrack available on streaming platforms.)

Energy from thoughts

We are nearly always thinking thoughts and/or feeling feelings.

Thoughts are a way in which we put form to energy.

When we think something a lot, it becomes a clearly identifiable form in our aura. That thought contains energy, and the more we think it, the more energy we direct to it. Once it is in our aura, it takes a while to come out again. Often it will float around and attract to it similar thoughts from other people. We will gravitate towards those people and they to us, for shared experiences that match our thoughts.

When a lot of people think the same thing, a huge mass of energy stamped with the pattern of that thought is formed. It floats around and gains strength from other people who are thinking thoughts of the same kind. In the end the big thought form has so much energy that it is like a beacon which passes over us and causes us to think a thought of the same nature as the thought form. This is how mass hysteria operates, and public opinion in general.

Thoughts, and the energy trapped in them, provide us with a certain amount of energy whether we like it or not. If we are around healthy and positive people, the energy transfer is good. However, most of the time we are in a mixture of thought forms, which tend to have an unsettling effect and do not really assist us. In my book *Yoga of the Mind,* and the corresponding seminar, we show you how to recognize and minimize the negative effects of this and create your own reality. For now, if it feels like you are in a dirty thought form soup, put on your OM CD. This dirty thought form energy is a source of energy that you do not want to work with.

Energy from the soul dimension

Subtle energy is also given to us by and from Divine sources such as the Divine Mother, as well as various non-physical beings such as angels, Ascended Masters and spiritual 'helpers'.

Through our crown chakra and the chakras above it, we access the energy of the Divine and spiritual realm. When this occurs it feels like being in a shower of light. *Yoga of the Mind* discusses this in more detail.

If we want to be blessed (receive energy) by loving Divine beings, we first have to ask for that blessing.

Because we live in a free will zone, we are free to live in love and light, or pain and despair. There is no point having free will if you have to do only one thing, or have to have only certain experiences. A vast range of possibilities exist, and we are free to experience them all. Naturally, all of our choices have consequences, but we do not wish to discuss that rather huge topic here. The point is, any truly loving being will honour your free will, even to the point of allowing you to suffer so that you can experience the consequences of *your* choices. This is not a punishment but the natural order of things (God) at work. When we are ready to stop banging our heads against a brick wall, all we have to do is ask for help. That help is immediately forthcoming. Many humans fail to notice the help straightaway, but it is there nonetheless. When you genuinely ask for blessings and assistance, that is what you get, straightaway.

When we ask for assistance from beings who love us, such as Jesus, Buddha and others, they send us energy. That energy can enter our etheric body provided we are receptive and in a fit etheric state to receive it. By cleansing and clearing your etheric body, you become prepared for conscious Divine union. Talk about ignite your spirit!

When we invoke, the aura expands

Positive and negative energy

Energy can simply be divided up into positive and negative energy. No matter which dimension the energy is flowing in, it is still either positive or negative.

Positive energy makes our aura and chakras bigger and stronger. In the end, through a great deal of positive energy, we are able to grow and grow and eventually merge with all-that-is (God).

Negative energy makes our aura and chakras smaller and weaker. It separates us from everything else and makes us insular and alone.

When we speak or are spoken to in a positive manner, we grow in energy and so do the people to whom we are speaking. This feels good. When we speak to or are spoken to in a negative manner, we shrink and so do the people with whom we are speaking. This does not feel good.

Positive and negative are not the same as good and bad. There is no value judgment attached to these terms, just an understanding of the energy effect. When there is a build-up of positive energy, things that we find pleasurable tend to occur in the physical world. When there is a build-up of negative energy, things we don't like tend to occur.

Energy discharge tends to happen in a big way. Built-up energy, eventually needs to be discharged, like lightning discharges the energy of a storm. When a big dirty lump of energy is released, we either get a disease or have an 'accident' that uses it up. When you understand more about the subtle world, terms such as 'accident' and 'coincidence' stop having very much meaning. Just about everything can be understood in terms of the behaviour of subtle energy and our personal relationship to it.

Positive and negative can be tested for in various ways. Some people use a pendulum, others use muscle testing, as in kinesiology. We are going to show you how to use your hand to scan for positive and negative, as they show up in your energy in a way that you can actually feel.

Energy with a 'zing'

Subtle energy is all around us and inside us, and comes from various sources. It is meant to flow freely in through our chakras and aura, and be distributed around our body by meridians and many tiny chakras. Our physical bodies need subtle energy to function, and when the chakras, meridians or aura become blocked, this is not able to happen properly. When blockages become severe, this creates a series of negative experiences within and in the outer physical life of the person concerned.

When we ignite our spirit we clean out the negative energy and put in heaps of positive energy. In this way, we change our vibration and attract into our lives more positive outcomes in all areas.

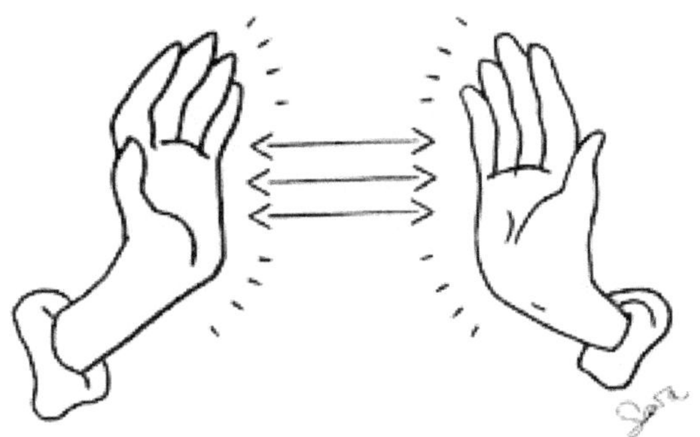

Feeling subtle energy

Many people are able to perceive their subtle energy on their first try. Some like me take a bit longer. Keep trying and you will soon start to realise that you can feel the energy.

CREATING AND BREATHING IN BUBBLE OF ENERGY

Rub your hands together for a minute or two, and then put them together in the prayer position. Slowly pull them apart and move them back and forward. As you do this, you may see lines of light between your hands or fingers. you may feel a slight resistance between your hands, more than just air, heat or tingles.

Allow the energy to build up between your hands until it forms a ball of energy. Make it as big as you feel comfortable with. Pack the energy in. Feel it coming in through the top of your head and the front of your throat. Every time you breathe in, imagine the energy of the breath goes straight into the bubble.

Drop the bubble of energy in through the top of your head, right down to the base of your spine, then into the Earth. Breathe in as you do this. Feel the 'zing' go through you? You can do this whenever you need a burst of energy!

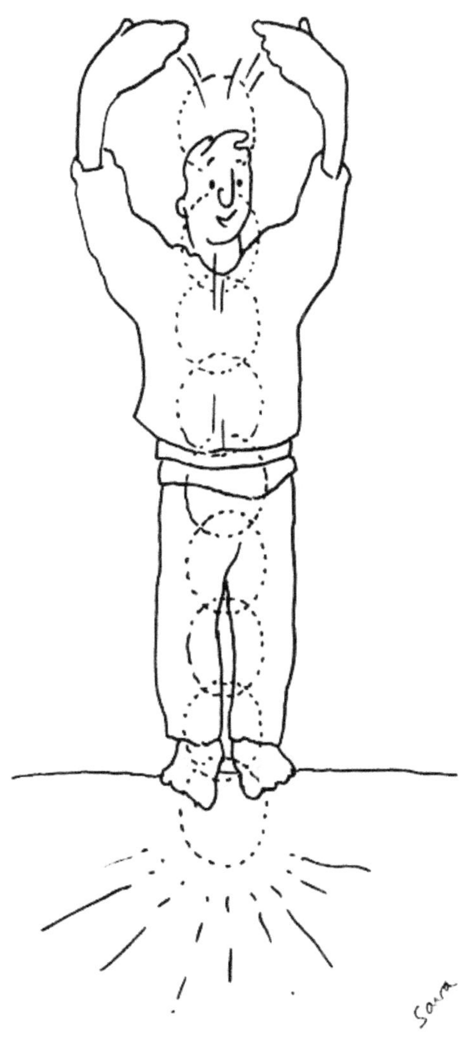

Chapter

3

IT'S ALL ABOUT THE VIBES

VIBRATION is the periodic motion about a line of equilibrium, such as in the creation of sound. Sound notes at a low or slow vibration are low or base notes, and the vibration is slower. Sound notes at a high or rapid vibration are high or treble notes, and the vibration is faster. To illustrate, on the graph below, the high vibration is the top wiggly line, and the low vibration is the lower, flatter line.

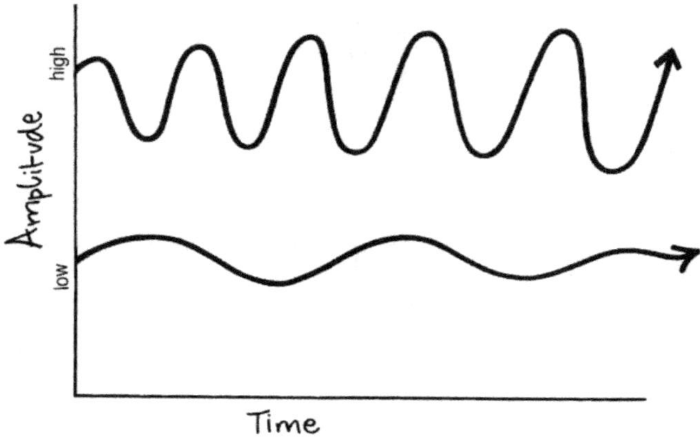

Our etheric bodies vibrate. The chakras in particular are subject to changes in vibration, which affect them in a cumulative manner. Each chakra is a storehouse of memories, experiences and perceptions about different aspects of the life experience.

Some can vibrate much faster than others.

Negative emotions have a low vibration and positive emotions have a high vibration. The highest vibration is love and the lowest is fear. When we experience fear, separation from the Divine, or strong negative emotions, our vibration slows down. This can happen really fast. If it happens a lot, it can slow down our general rate of vibration.

When we experience love, joy, happiness, connectedness to the Divine or peace, our vibration speeds up. People who experience these feelings a lot tend to have a high vibration. They are good to be around.

The main thing that tends to pull vibrational resonances into our energy system is the quality of our thoughts. When we think negative thoughts, critical, judgmental, pessimistic thoughts, our vibration slows down. When we think loving and happy thoughts, our vibration speeds up. Our thoughts become receptacles for certain emotional vibrations, and this potent combination of thought and emotion can create wonders or havoc in our lives.

Life seems to get easier as our vibration increases. Eventually, we can access the path of ease and grace. A fair bit of work is required to achieve this. Every bit helps, however, and every try is rewarded and recorded in the annals of heaven. These annals are the akashic records, which are the individual library of events, vibrations and karma for each soul. (This is further discussed in my Ignite Your Spirit seminars.) From the perspective of the soul, how you do something and why is as important as what you do. The idea is to do everything with love and for the good of all. This raises everyone's vibration. It can also be tricky to do.

During periods of rapid self-transformation, I have experienced my whole body vibrate for a couple of minutes, then stop. It is like a wholesale change in the vibration of all bodies which even finds expression in the physical body.

One of the functions of our aura is to keep our multidimensional bodies together in a neat bundle, and to keep other people's bodies more or less out. Sometimes we make agreements which bind us to other people, and if this happens, we end up stuck together even after we die. This is often done through love, like a Mum who dies young but promises her kids she will not leave them. By the time the kids are in their forties with their own kids, Mum is still with them, even though they cannot see her.

They pray for guidance, and the voice in their head, that they think is their soul, is actually Mum. No doubt Mum loves them and wants what is best for them, but this desire is from her perspective and blocks the soul's perspective. The vibration of her astral perspective is not likely to be as high as her child's own higher soul. As such the quality of the advice may not be as encompassing and accurate, because the vision is not so large.

I once had a wonderful client, Sophia. Her mother, with whom she had been very close, had passed away a couple of years previously. The grief and loss started her on a path of self-realisation and spiritual awakening. By the time she came to see me she was meditating regularly and opening her mind. However, she was very confused about how she felt, and about what she should do. She had a frequently recurring thought about opening a plant nursery which she believed to be Divine guidance. Sophia loved plants, so it didn't seem so weird, but she felt there was something fundamentally out of balance about it.

Upon close questioning it occurred to her that her mother had always wanted to have a plant nursery but had never had the opportunity to do it. We had a talk with Mum, who was still with her beloved daughter, and explained that she was stuck in her daughter's energy field. She was very attached (literally) to her daughter, fearful that her daughter would not be okay by herself. We explained that her presence had a controlling effect on her daughter and was interfering with her free will. Sophia thought she wanted the plant shop, but all along it was really Mum who wanted it! With a lot of love and gratitude, we were able to help Mum transition to the right place, and thereafter, Sophia never even considered opening a plant nursery. She went on to run one of the best healing clinics I have known, and helped a great many people with her love, warmth and light.

In Ignite Your Spirit seminars and healing, we help people to reach love-filled closure with such relationships so that the stillness inside can be revealed. Into this stillness the voice of the soul can flow.

HOW TO RAISE YOUR VIBRATION

To raise our vibration, there are several key ingredients to keep in mind:

1. *Avoid negative thinking, and going over old troubles again and again like a broken record playing. It will make matters worse.*

2. *Avoid getting caught up in a downward spiral of negative emotion. There is nothing wrong (and everything right) about feeling such emotions, but the trick is to let them flow through. They can then harmlessly transmute into happiness again. Have you watched a young child? One minute they are screaming because they cannot have twenty chocolates, the next minute they are laughing and have forgotten about their outburst. Adults tend to harbour resentment and cling on to upsets for a plethora of reasons. Let it go.*

3. *Meditate, using meditations which have a positive effect on your energy.*

4. *As the Indian saint Sai Baba used to say: "Help ever. Hurt never!" Helping others opens our hearts, makes us happy, feels good and is good. Harmlessness in thought, word and deed is the ambition of the spiritual aspirant who seeks to raise his or her vibration so as to commune through golden bliss with the inner teachers and Great Ones.*

Our vibration affects our essential energy. If you want to ignite your spirit, treat your vibration as one of your most precious resources.

Chapter

4

THE ETHERIC BLUEPRINT

WE have an etheric blueprint which is the same shape as the physical body. People who have had serious accidents which result in the loss of a limb, often report that they are still able to feel the amputated part/s. That is because the etheric blueprint for it still exists. They can still experience pain, itching, tingling and other sensations because their etheric limb was not amputated. Such people would be well served to learn about their etheric body and how to do self-healing to remove the unpleasant sensations.

Our etheric blueprint is the plan for our physical body. This may have interesting implications for those who wish to change their body shape. It is probable that lasting change to the physical body, short of having surgery, is only achieved when change (conscious or unconscious) is made to the etheric self.

We can see our etheric blueprint by doing a simple exercise.

MICROCOSMIC ORBIT

1. *Put your hands in front of you with fists clenched.*
2. *Extend your index fingers, and turn your hands so the index fingers are pointing at each other, almost touching.*
3. *Relax the focus of your eyes and look into the space between the tips of the extended fingers.*
4. *Breathe, relax.*
5. *Intend to see your etheric body. What do you see? Most people will see a shiny white nimbus of light both between the fingers and running along them. This is it, this is part of the etheric body.*

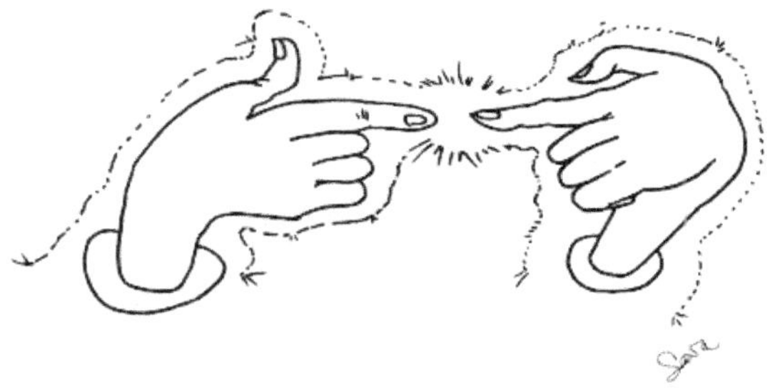

Let's now look at another important part of the etheric body, the meridians.

The meridians

The meridians are like a spider's web of energy currents which run through the etheric body and join up the energy centres, or chakras. This allows for communication within the etheric body. Meridians are similar to the physical nervous system, but operate in a different dimension.

Acupuncturists work on meridians. A good, classically trained acupuncturist can tell what is wrong with you just by feeling the 'pulse' of the meridians in your wrist. From this, they know what meridians are blocked and the spots that have to be needled to release the blockages.

If there is no blockage, acupuncture is completely painless. If there is a blockage present, the pain can be amazing. It passes quickly, however, as the energy blockage is released. Normally, I enter a state of deep peace when I receive this type of treatment, and as the meridians are stimulated, I can feel the harmonious flow of energy around my body.

Shiatsu massage works in the same way. This is a deep tissue style of massage which massages along the meridians to work blockages out of the body. Again, if the energy is blocked, it is very painful and there is no pain when it is not blocked.

By looking at the irises of the eyes, iridologists are able to diagnose the state of health of the body. Meridians join the eyes etherically to all parts of the body. Similarly, by working on the meridians of the feet, reflexologists can treat the whole body.

Two great big ones

The main meridians I wish to bring to your attention are the micro-cosmic orbit and the pillar of light.

The micro-cosmic orbit

The micro-cosmic orbit flows from your mouth down the front of your body to the perineum, which lies between the anus and the sex organs. Another part of the meridian flows from the perineum, up the back, past the base of the spine to the neck, back of the head and crown, then down the forehead to stop at the roof of the mouth.

Energy circulates through this channel. However, the channel only operates fully when the gap between the two parts of it are joined. This is achieved by rolling the tongue and putting the underside of it against the roof of your mouth. This greatly strengthens the micro-cosmic orbit and allows it to be used for many purposes, including tantric practices and advanced yoga practices involving the activation of the kundalini. Kundalini is a sacred, fiery energy which resides at the base of the spine. Activation of the kundalini creates seemingly miraculous qualities in the yogi who has mastered it.

However, certain risks are inherent in the activation of the kundalini before multidimensional development is properly established. I strongly suggest that you exercise caution in the awakening of this sacred force within you, and that you do so under the guidance of a highly developed spiritual teacher who can monitor and guide you.

It is safe to activate the micro-cosmic orbit. Simply join the two ends of it together by putting the tongue on the palate. It is recommended that you adopt this mudra (body posture) as often as possible to strengthen your energy.

Micro-cosmic Orbit

The pillar of light

The other big meridian we have is the central pillar of light which flows from the Divine-source-of-all, through thousands of energy centres, diluting energy and vibration to a level that we can use in our physical existence. This central column runs down into our body through the crown chakra on top of the head then out through the base chakra into the core of the Earth. When we activate this column of light, we look like a big pillar of light that joins heaven (the inner world) to Earth (the outer world). The expression 'pillar of the church' comes from the spiritual pillar that exists within all of us.

One of the most profound meditations that I know involves building this pillar by strengthening both ends of it. This is discussed below.

In most people, the pillar of light is pretty hard to distinguish, and can resemble threads of cotton rather than a pillar. Through the practices of healing, prayer and meditation, the pillar is built up strand by strand over many incarnations. It is similar to optic fibre cable. Fragments of optic fibre will not give us a signal on our TV. When we have the full formation of a cable, light can run through it properly. When this occurs we get full sight and sound on our TV.

Contact with our Higher Self is like this. When we build a pillar of light connection, we become conscious of our Higher Self. Building this connection takes a lot of practice but in the end a clear picture and full sound can be achieved, so we can clearly perceive higher guidance and the realities of the non-physical world.

The ability to distinguish between the voice of the soul and the voice of the mind takes a bit of training, trial and error and a big pillar of light. (For those interested in this field, the art of spiritual discernment is covered in the Ignite Your Spirit seminar. This in turn is part of the Path of Ease and Grace seminar series designed to help us live effective, loving and peaceful lives through integrating the 5 dimensions of our being into everyday life.)

PILLAR OF LIGHT MEDITATION

The pillar of light meditation is a powerful meditation that:

- *Strengthens the core of our energy anatomy.*
- *Connects us to Earth (outer world) and heaven (inner world).*
- *Brings balance to auras that are either too big at the top or the bottom.strengthens the aura and our energy field in general.*
- *Strengthens and develops the pillar of light meridian.*
- *Centres you very quickly.*
- *Develops the crown chakra and the base chakra.*

Follow these steps to practise the pillar of light meditation:

1. *Place your tongue on your palate so that the underside of the tip of the tongue is against the roof of the mouth, joining up the micro- cosmic orbit.*

2. *Breathe in, and as you release the breath, imagine it leaving your body through the base chakra and going deep into the Earth.*

3. *With the next in-breath, breathe in through the base chakra and into the pillar of light meridian. Imagine the healthy pure Earth energy coursing up through the core of your body, out through the top of your head (crown chakra) and up through the many chakras that exist between the crown chakra and the Supreme Being. Imagine it travelling through all of your subtle bodies and all dimensions. Feel the energy move.*

4. *With the next in-breath, breathe in energy from God/Goddess, bring it down through the many chakras above your head, in through the crown chakra, down through the pillar of light meridian, and out through the base chakra into the Earth.*

5. *Repeat the cycle (steps 2, 3 and 4) between three and seven times.*

6. *End the practice by bringing energy up from the Earth to the heart chakra.*

7. *Say either out loud or to yourself: "I am grounded and connected to the Earth. I am one with the Infinite and one with all. I am a Divine being of love. Through Divine grace, so be it."*

Chapter

5

HOW'S YOUR AURA?

THE aura is like an energy bubble in which we live. Its appearance has a lot to do with the strength of our autoimmune system. Our aura is an instrument of sensation and a container that houses our subtle bodies (which can be thought of as a series of Russian dolls of which the physical body is the smallest and the Higher Self the largest).

The aura functions on physical, etheric, mental, emotional and spiritual levels, and through the corresponding bodies of each of these levels. What is happening in one of our bodies affects all of the others. Thus, a physical injury will affect the etheric body, which will affect the other bodies.

A large upset will affect the astral body, which will affect the etheric body, which may then clog up with other unresolved astral material and be the cause of disease. Handled correctly, it is unlikely to do so. Handled correctly means we have dealt with the issue thoroughly so that there is no negative residue surrounding it. Most people do not have the skills to handle prolonged or serious conflict and other upsets in a manner that is healthy for their etheric and physical bodies. These skills can be learned.

Because the aura is like a bubble of light energy around us, it can be photographed through Kirlian photography. Kirlian photography was developed in Russia and is so sensitive it can photograph subtle energy. It captures amazing colour spectrums in our auras. You can find the specialized equipment of Kirlian photography at most Body Mind Spirit festivals or by enquiring at New Age centres.

To my observation, the colours in people's aura change frequently and relate to transient as well as long-term factors. Because of this, I do not place too much importance on the colours in the aura at this stage, unless the colours are murky, brownish or black. These colours are associated with disease and negativity. Through thorough and regular cleaning of the aura, these drab colours can be removed.

A healthy aura will be vibrant and bright, no matter what colours swirl through it. From the perspective of a higher dimension, each being is able to be recognized and identified by their colour frequency. It is like our name or our signature. The development, achievements, and strengths of the individual are discernible through the colour and vibrational spectrums.

We are not going to deal with the colour spectrum any further here, other than to say that gold is the colour of Christ or Lakshmi consciousness. If you see someone with a lot of gold in their aura, this person is quite developed. People with golden auras have actually done the inner work of transformation, which is necessary to do before the Christ light can shine through. Such a person is worth their weight in gold and can show you how to progress. It is one thing to understand the *theory* of how to do it, it is another thing to actually master it and to have the light shine through. The golden light portrayed as a nimbus around old images of saints was put there because those who commissioned the paintings understood this concept.

Bright strong aura

Droopy weak aura

When the aura is big, bright and bouncy, we appear healthy and well. When it is droopy and greyish, we become unwell and have little energy. A healthy aura is attractive to others, whether they can see it or not, and proclaims our zest for life, vitality and energy.

As well as being able to be seen, the aura can be felt with the hand. This, for most people, is quite easy to do, and in our seminars over ninety per cent of people are able to do it to some degree on the first day. If, like me, you are a slow learner, you can still come to feel energy if you are willing to practise. I was not able to feel auras until I had practised for several months. Despite my own slow start, I am now acutely sensitive to auras and energy through my hands, because I have spent thousands of hours doing it. This ability is called clairsentience or scanning.

The aura is our personal space. When people crowd us, it can feel uncomfortable. People with powerful auras who stand close to us infuse us with their energy. If their energy is light, it is a nice feeling. If their energy is full of stress, conflict or negative emotions, it feels horrible. We feel a compulsion to move back from them.

Angry exchanges cause the aura to bend. So does passive aggression. When we are closed off from the energy of another person, even a family member, it is visible in the aura. Barbara Brennan in her book *Light Emerging* has wonderful illustrations of the way in which the aura bends around people if they are being aggressive, defensive, controlling, receptive, and so on.

Bent out of shape

The aura is meant to be an ovoid shape in which our physical body is centred in our own energy. When we get bent out of shape, we literally do get bent out of shape. What gets bent is our aura and chakras.

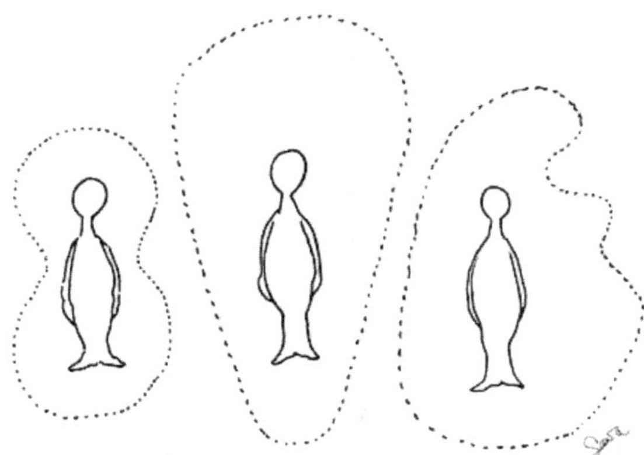

The aura and chakras are moving all the time in response to our feelings and external stimuli. When they get pushed and pulled in the same direction regularly, they have a tendency to grow in that direction, a bit like training a plant to grow a certain way for a certain effect. The plant adapts to the constraints imposed on it by the gardener and finds the easiest path to get the energy it needs. Its shape is thus affected. The same thing is happening with us all the time, except that it is an unconscious process, and the factors which affect us are multifaceted.

Many people are out of balance and this imbalance shows up in their aura. You can learn to have more control over this process, and over the shape of the you to come. Broadly speaking, we have found the following easily perceived imbalances in the aura.

Yin and yang

In Taoism, everything is seen as a balance between two opposing forces, yin and yang, female and male energy. These energies have been stereotyped as belonging primarily to men (yang) or women (yin), but this is not the reality. Every person has both characteristics, no matter what sex they are.

Yin energy is called feminine energy, the energy of being. It is soft, receptive, conceptual, empathetic, intuitive, submissive, process oriented, accepting, cool, gentle and nurturing. Yin energy is most noticeable in our right brains and the left-hand side of our body, which is controlled by the right brain.

Yang or masculine energy is the energy of doing. It is active, initiating, out there, language oriented, logical, overtly strong, result oriented, dominant, warm and expansive. Yang energy is most noticeable in our left brains and the right-hand side of our body, which is controlled by the left brain.

We have found that many people have big imbalances in their yin/yang energy. This shows up in the aura. Interestingly, such people often attract to themselves people who have the opposite imbalance to achieve between them a kind of yin/yang harmony.

Of course, relying on another person to achieve this balance is fraught with problems and inherently unstable. It causes co-dependency, and can get to be like a seesaw, swinging wildly up and down. It is far better to achieve internal balance and then find a partner who is also balanced.

<table>
<tr><td>If the aura is too yin (feminine) it leans to the left.</td><td>If the aura is too yang (masculine) it leans to the right.</td></tr>
</table>

Too yin

A person who is too yin will often have an aura that billows out on their left-hand side and is rather small on the right-hand side. Such a person may have a receptive rather than an initiating nature. They may find it really hard to go out and make things happen, and be very physically attuned, empathetic, and sensitive emotionally. Such a person may be very artistic and imaginative, but lack the more assertive yang characteristics. They do not know how to go about creating the structure through which the things or circumstances they desire can come to them. Their yang has up and vanished, leaving them vulnerably yin. Such a person may have a definite tilt to the left in their aura.

If the aura is too yin (feminine) it leans to the left.

Too yang

A person who is too yang will often have an aura that billows out on their right-hand side and is small on the left-hand side. A very yang person is one who is a real go-getter, logical, rational and pro-active. Often such people find feelings, relationships, spirituality, empathy and so on, either challenging or irrelevant. Yang types are often good at making money, running a business, doing things. Yang energy is good at initiating things and is interested in worldly power. It creates structure and judges things by results. The ends can justify the means in those with a big yang imbalance and an insufficiently developed heart chakra. The focus is on the form, but not so much on the essence of life. Such a person may have a definite tilt to the right in their aura.

Either form of imbalance is limiting; it is good to restore the balance.

Living in the past or the future

Some people are always brooding over things that upset them a long time ago. The weight of this literally topples them backwards. Too much time spent living in the past causes the back of the aura to be heavy and blow out.

Very often I see people in the clinic who have suffered greatly in their earlier years in one way or another. Some people are able to let go of their problems, forgive those who have hurt them and move on. In such people, old trauma is not so evident in their energy anatomy, and they do not exhibit the 'tilting backwards' effect that we are referring to.

In other cases, people might still be really hooked into old disputes, even twenty or thirty years after the event. They will talk about their divorce, their ex-husband or wife, as though the breakup was last week or last year. They are unable to energetically disconnect from it, so it plays on their mind and in their energy. Little do they know, it also reduces the amount of energy they have available to them to deal with their lives in present time. Their power circuits are partially plugged into very tired old stories. The amount of stuck emotional energy they have stored in their bodies is huge and pulls them backwards.

Worrying about the future all of the time is equally disempowering and causes a build-up of energy pushing the aura way out in front.

The point of power is actually in the present moment. When we call back our energy into the now, we become much more able to lead balanced and successful lives.

Ice cream cone or bell shaped?

Some people have auras that are shaped like a bell, small at the top and big at the bottom. These people are mainly focused in the physical world. They have developed the lower energy centres and as a result the aura is large at the bottom, but this needs to be balanced by development up top so to speak. Only then can they truly ignite their spirit. Such people are practical and good at making money; they believe if you can touch it, then it is real. Many of the highly successful barristers that I associated with whilst practising law had very large lower auras and chakras.

Other people have auras shaped like ice cream cones. They are big at the top but tiny at the bottom. This comes from a great deal of Divine focus without a balance of worldly focus. These people generally have no problem connecting spiritually, feeling or seeing energy, believing in fairies or angels; but they forget to balance the chequebook and may find it hard to get things done. They are not very good at making money and prefer to transcend the physical realm whenever they can. Many traditional spiritual teachings have preached that the physical side of life contains temptations and evils, and so the transcendent approach has been encouraged.

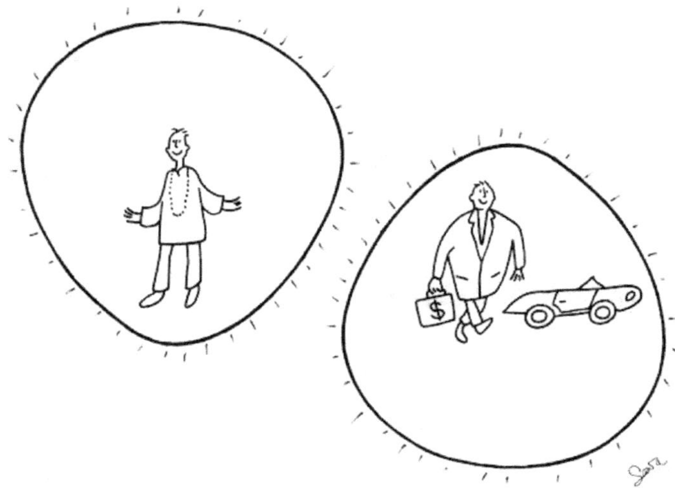

It would appear that we are here on Earth for good reason, even if we do not always understand it, and that life in the physical world is just as important as our Divine home, which is non-physical. Thus it is appropriate to honour both worlds and develop through all dimensions. The best idea is to have a balance, so that life on Earth can be infused with the heavenly energy that those with large upper etheric bodies know to be available.

When the etheric body is not balanced, there are bottlenecks in our inability to bring Divine energy and inspiration through from the inner world to the physical world of form. The aim is balance, even development, and the ability to ground our spirituality into our everyday physical lives.

Rips and tears

Rips and tears can be both seen and felt in the aura. They are caused by any of several factors, including drug use (getting ripped!), shock or severe trauma. The rips and tears can be healed, and when this is done the person feels very different. Energy from the soul is used to do this.

When someone takes psychedelic drugs, particularly if they do so regularly, holes can develop in the aura, which look to me as though someone has shot a cannonball through it. I see a big round gaping hole. These holes are variable; some people are not affected in this way. Others can be affected the first time they use it and, unfortunately, once the aura is ripped, any passing energy can get in and out of it. This includes non-physical life forms. These can enter through a hole and partially take control of the person, causing them to become seemingly schizophrenic.

Scanning the aura with the hands can detect these holes. They feel like a depression or absence of energy at certain points in the aura. They can be repaired. However, sometimes the affected area will still be weak and require quite a bit of inner self-care so that it stays healthy. Where drug use is concerned, there needs to be a decision not to use more drugs because if they do use them again, the problem is likely to recur.

Drug smoker has his ripped aura invaded Cords of attachment

When we look at the world from the perspective of our physical bodies, it is obvious that we are separate from each other. The concept of interconnectedness at this level is limited. When we move beyond the physical body into the realms of our etheric, astral and soul selves, it makes a lot more sense.

Connections exist between people who, on the surface, are not happy about being connected at all. Wherever there is conflict, there are connections of energy between people. These lines of connection become a source of irritation and cause energy to bounce back and forward between people in a way that escalates hostility. By cutting these lines and reclaiming our power, amazing things happen in terms of restoring peace into our lives.

When we interact with people, lines of energy form from our aura to theirs. When the interaction has a lot of energy, such as strong emotion attached to it, then big fat lines of energy form. These lines of energy keep us tied to the person at the other end of the line. This is okay if the person is warm, loving and kind to you, has your best interests at heart and is of a light vibration. Unfortunately, all of our interactions are not of this calibre. Think about your work colleagues, or your ex-boyfriend/ wife/ defacto/ mother-in-law, and you will see what I mean.

What would you think if a reliable source told you that your very energy was still totally connected to them? Most people I say this to are horrified. "Cut it!", they cry. So I do. (And show you how later.)

I just wish I could get him out of my head.

My client, Lachlan, was a warm, soft and beautiful young man who came to see me because he had uncontrollable fits of anger. In fact, he had just been expelled from school for hitting a teacher. I asked about the family dynamic and was told by his Dad, Frank, that he and his ex-partner, Julie, were in the middle of a bitter and drawn-out separation and divorce. Black lines of energy went from his body to both parents. Lachlan was like a large sponge, absorbing all the pain of the dispute.

I started to clear away the energetic debris and Lachlan felt his body start to tingle. I cut many of the lines of energy that kept him in his state of pain. Naturally, neither parent would knowingly have hurt their son, but as in every family, the children end up wearing lots of the family's dirty astral laundry and acting it out.

I asked if Frank would also have a healing. The black lines of energy to his former partner were immediately evident. We cleaned, cut, cleared and asked for Divine grace to replace all the hurt and pain. We asked for all of the energy Frank was carrying from Julie to go back to her, and all of the energy Julie was carrying for Frank to go back to him. Frank felt his body tingling, then felt himself move from whole body tension to relaxation, which a little later became a gentle bliss. Having been somewhat reluctant to sit in the chair for a healing, he was now reluctant to leave it.

As the energy cleared, the family dynamic also cleared. Lachlan was able to return to school, and Frank found it much easier to deal with his ex-partner. He met her for coffee and within one hour they had settled the family law matters, which had been unable to be resolved to that point.

Ian and Sally are another example of what can happen when we are able to cut lines of energy between people. They had been in a dysfunctional relationship for years, and after they had a child things went from bad to worse. Sally had a huge heart and was effectively used by Ian as a doormat. He would get angry, and in his mind his violence was always due to her provocation. Sally managed to get out of the house after years of domestic violence, but that was not the end of the matter. Despite court orders and police intervention, Ian continued to stalk her for six years. Wherever she moved, whichever change of phone number she made, he still somehow found her and followed her around in a menacing manner. She was terrified of him and believed that sooner or later he would kill her.

During a seminar we did an exercise that involved cutting the ties with people we no longer wanted to deal with in our lives. Sally did the exercise with gusto and, to her amazement, with great success. From that day forth, Sally never saw or heard of Ian again. After six years of stalking her, he just disappeared from her life. Thank God.

Whenever we have a line into another person, we can feel how they feel and get affected by their thoughts and moods. When we think of them, their astral body registers this. They get the impulse to think of us. Thankfully, few of us have the degree of dysfunctional connection that Sally faced. However, nearly everyone is hooked into a surprising number of people that they may not even remember. It is hard enough dealing with our own thoughts and feelings without dealing with everyone else's as well.

Even loving couples are encouraged to regularly disconnect from each other. This is because the energy which gathers in these lines of connection is frozen energy that holds us to the version of ourselves that we used to be. They stop us from feeling free to be who we are now. When we cut, we do not cut love, we cut our old expectations and limitations, our co-dependence and old issues.

Thus we remain free to stay and enjoy a wonderful partnership. For more on how to use the five dimensions of your being in relationships you can read my book Empowering Relationships and join into our Path of Ease and Grace relationship seminars; From Conflict to Connection,

Emotional Liberation and the Spirit and Soul of Relating. You can find these on www.pathofeaseandgrace.org and on www.shantimission.org.

When people 'cut' in our seminars, the feeling of freedom and lightness is very pronounced. The more refined and powerful the energy experienced when this takes place, the more successful the cutting will be. There is nothing like the energy generated by a group of well-intentioned people to help each other make this a very successful exercise.

The effect of thoughts

When we think, little energy packets stamped with the thought appear in our aura. Most of them are like air bubbles in water, they just bubble away and disappear. However, they build up a residue in the aura, which is like static on a TV picture, and create etheric debris. Negative thinking dirties the aura and creates blockages in the flow of energy. Taken in isolation, any given negative thought is rarely going to do much damage because it is only one thought. However, when you string together all the negative thinking we engage in over a period of time, the amount of etheric and astral debris created in the aura is pretty staggering.

Noise and debris in the aura

Clear out your aura

Repeated thoughts build up an image in the aura and can be read like a book by clairvoyants. Further, the things that are visible in our aura have a tendency to manifest in our lives sooner or later. What sorts of things do you think about? What is hanging around in your aura? What can you do to clean out your aura?

Exercise

Exercise has a cleansing effect on our auric fields. Ideally, we should do some exercise every day, we all know that. But there is another reason for doing it than simply physical health. When we get a sweat up and increase our rate of respiration, dirty energy is expelled from our bodies. This is the natural way to keep healthy etherically. However, because of our lifestyles these days, few people do sufficient exercise for this to work. Thus, we get into a situation where energy healing is needed.

Exercise is a simple practice through which we can clean our energy body. As we run along and our heart rate increases and we work up a sweat, isn't it nice to know that we are at the same time divesting ourselves of a whole heap of energetic issues.

After doing advanced practices, there is a tendency to become congested with spiritual energy, which makes us feel sleepy. This is similar to the way in which we become drowsy after being congested with food at the end of a rich meal. If we go for a walk, we can move the spiritual energy through faster and we are able to bring even more high vibrational energy into our bodies. Exercise really is good for us.

Salt water

Bathing in salt water or the sea also cleanses our energy anatomy. Those who swim regularly in the sea are helping to keep their energy clean and sparkling. For those of us who do not live by the beach, soaking in a bathtub filled with hot salty water can achieve the same effect. I do this after teaching a class, as the energy being cleared from students partially attaches to me. If no bath is available, I use handfuls of table salt as a scrub in the shower, which has the same, wonderful effect.

If you want to enhance the effect, throw in a couple of tablespoons of instant coffee. This is particularly good if you are feeling emotional, distraught, angry, out of sorts or depressed. After a good soak in salt and coffee, you will be amazed at how much better you feel. Of course, you will smell funny if you don't rinse off, and your housemates will look at you strangely if you start keeping coffee in the bathroom. Nevertheless, try it and see.

The salt, or salt and coffee, bath is also really good when you are feeling a virus or cold coming on. I have felt much better after using a salt bath or salt scrub in these circumstances. Why not try this yourself?

Size does matter

On average, people have auras of about two metres around their bodies. People who are successful in life, for example successful professional people, tend to have larger auras, perhaps three to five metres from the body. World figures have bigger auras again. Madonna, Bill Clinton, Elton John, Pavarotti: these people have huge auras when viewed clairvoyantly. They seem larger than life because energetically they actually are.

Their big auras give them an edge over their competitors, and allow them to achieve great success on a global level. When we work on ourselves and create big bright clear auras we become healthy, easily attain goals and find success relatively easy. People with small dull auras tend to lead small dull lives.

World spiritual leaders such as the Dalai Lama have huge auras which fill an entire city. It has been noted that crime rates fall when he is in town, such is the strength of the love energy that he carries.

Essentially, the bigger and stronger the aura, and the cleaner the energy body becomes, the healthier and more robust we become. We are more easily able to manifest that which we desire when we have more energy with which to do so.

The size and quality of your aura is unconsciously discerned by everyone you meet. You become more attractive to people as your energy bodies become stronger, cleaner, more magnetic and sweet.

You know when you meet someone with a really large aura because you can feel it. Start to notice the people in your life, their energy and its quality.

Perceiving the aura

Stand about one or two metres away from the person you want to scan. Raise your hands, palms outwards, and feel for a bubble around the person. When you contact it, you will feel heat, tingles or pressure on your hand. Sometimes you will feel as though you are being pushed back, because you are actually standing inside the person's aura. At other times you will feel that you are being pulled into it. Feel up high at head height, around the middle and down the bottom. Feel the left side and the right side, the front and the back.

Remember what I said earlier. Some auras are too yin and lean to the left. Others are too yang and lean to the right. Sometimes they are too far forward, reflecting future orientation, and sometimes they are too far back, indicating that the person lives in the past. Sometimes there are rips and tears. See if you can feel any of this.

You will be amazed at what you can discern from your first try.

Here is a checklist of things to find out about your own aura, or the aura of a friend.

- ☐ Aura leans to the left (too yin)
- ☐ Aura leans to the right (too yang)
- ☐ Aura leans to the front (too anxious about the future)
- ☐ Aura leans to the back (too wrapped up in the past)
- ☐ Aura is bigger at the top, like an ice cream cone (not grounded enough)
- ☐ Aura is bigger at the bottom, like a bell (too material, needs balance of spirituality)
- ☐ Rips and tears in the aura

DEVELOPING THE AURA: THE HOLY BREATH

This is a really great way to increase the size of your aura. This can be done as a regular quick meditation, or to centre you before an important event.

1. *breathe in, consciously breathing in Divine love, and affirm, "I breathe in the love of the Infinite".*

2. *hold the breath in and affirm, "I assimilate Divine love". Imagine that the breath (and love of God) flows through your whole body.*

3. *breathe out and affirm, "I expand Divine love". Imagine the love expanding out into your whole auric field.*

4. *hold the breath out and affirm, "I feel Divine love all around me".*

5. *breathe in, consciously breathing in Divine love, and affirm, "I breathe in Divine love".*

6. *hold the breath in and affirm, "I assimilate Divine love". Imagine that the breath (and love of God) flows through your whole body.*

7. *breathe out and affirm, "I project Divine love". this time imagine the love expanding out through your aura and throughout the whole world. If you like you can see it penetrating places on Earth that are turbulent, bringing love, joy, harmony and peace to these places.*

8. *hold the breath out and affirm, "I feel Divine love all around me".*

9. *Repeat seven times in a rhythmical fashion, ensuring that the out- breath and the in-breath are of equal length, and that the empty and full retention phases between the breaths are also of equal length.*

Chapter

6

Invest spiritually – great returns for this life... and the next

---

WHEN we die, our etheric anatomy does not die but is reabsorbed by our souls which are eternal. That etheric framework is placed into the next baby we become.

Over the years I have had occasion to treat many newborn babies for one thing or another. They have startlingly different auras and chakral configurations. If we were all born shiny and completely new, the energy bodies of all babies would be the same. They definitely are not. All babies are born with the strengths, weaknesses, karmic problems, talents and predispositions that flow from their previous lives.

An investment in developing our etheric bodies not only pays dividends this life; it is an investment that we can actually take with us when we eventually transit to another lifetime. Thus, as we learn to clean up and maintain, then build, our etheric selves, we develop a rich asset which will help us in this life and many more to come.

But I am not sure about this past life stuff

Neither was I. Raised Roman Catholic, it did not resonate with me. However, just because our dominant Western faith does not include reincarnation as a doctrine does not mean that it doesn't exist or was not known about by the early church fathers.

There is no doubt that alterations have been made to the Christian scriptures over the past 2,000 years. Whether this is intentional or not is a matter for speculation. The simple act of translating the scriptures from the original language of Jesus, Aramaic, into Greek, Latin and English, gives rise to many opportunities for meanings to change. Further, at various times, the usurping of spiritual teachings in an effort to exert power and control over the common man cannot be ignored. In this way, the spiritual teachings given by Jesus have most probably been diluted.

An example of the kind of mistranslation that can intentionally or unintentionally dilute the essence of the word of Jesus is the following account of what he said when on the cross. In the King James version of the Bible, translated from Greek, it says, "My God why hast thou forsaken me?", while in the Lamsa version translated from the Aramaic, it says, "My God for this I was spared". (For further discussion see *The Eye of the I* by David Hawkins.)

Another example is the assertion by Jesus that "I am the way, the truth and the life, and no one comes to the father except through me" (John 14.6). This has been used as the rationale for the assertion that

Christianity is the only true faith. In my view this is a mistranslation of 'I am'. See *Meditations on the Soul* by Master Choa Kok Sui for more information.

'I am' is the term for the Higher Self, which resides in everyone. No one can get to the heavenly Father/Mother except through their own 'I am' presence, which is within them. This then makes sense of the biblical quote "the kingdom of Heaven is within".

Ram Dass, author and spiritual teacher, and others claim that all references to reincarnation were removed from the biblical scriptures during the Council of Trent and the Council of Nicaea, very early in church history. One reference remains, where Jesus claims that John the Baptist was Elijah in a previous life. Elijah had demanded the beheading of many pagan priests. The law of karma is such that sooner or later Elijah would reincarnate and be beheaded, because what you give out you get back. John the Baptist, of course, was eventually beheaded.

Putting aside for the moment our prior learning about the finality of life upon death, it is useful to consider the accounts of credible people who claim to have witnessed past life memories, usually triggered through healing.

My own belief in reincarnation comes from years of practising as an Ignite Your Spirit Therapist. I have witnessed clients realize the past life cause of a physical or mental problem and deal with it so that the problem is no longer an issue in this life.

An example of its effectiveness is illustrated by a wonderful, spiritually minded professional man who came to me for healing in the area of relationships. He was in his forties and admitted to having had over eighty relationships with women. (No, he said this did not count one-night stands!) During the healing, he became aware that he and his wife from a past life had made a vow to never leave each other. (Note, wedding vows ought be made "until death us do part".)

This vow was strongly made by both of them, and neither recognized that never is a long, long time. When his wife died soon after the vow was made, she remained Earth bound and was unable to transit to where she was meant to be. She got stuck in his energy field. In this life, she had been pushing other women away by telepathically communicating to him the imperfections of each woman so that he was never able to get close to any of them. He thought it was just his own critical nature, because it *seemed* to be just his *thoughts*. During the healing, in a loving and emotional way, he was able to break the vow with his previous wife and release her, upon which there was a huge rush of energy and she was gone. Thereafter he had a two year relationship with a woman, which was more than four times the length of any previous relationship. The critical voice, where women were concerned, never returned.

For now, I ask that you have an open mind about the issue of reincarnation, and ask for higher guidance about it. Past lives are no big deal unless there is a problem that is not able to be resolved in this life. Then it is a logical place to look for answers. Apart from that, I am not interested in who I might have been, because over so many lifetimes, we have all been the good guy, the bad guy, kings, paupers and everything in between. I prefer to keep my focus on this lifetime.

Having said that, I derive great comfort from my belief in reincarnation as it helps me to make sense of many things I did not previously understand. Why else would terrible things happen to good people? Why else would children have terrible injuries or painful illnesses? They have not had a chance to develop significant negative karma in this life. However, if we take the many lives that they would have already lived, and if we consider that they may not always have been quite so sweet and innocent, we can more readily see the karmically fair genesis of their issues.

We reincarnate thousands of times to evolve and grow through a series of challenges. How we handle these challenges determines the skills and qualities of character we take forward with us, not only during this life but all of them. We keep growing, evolving and getting larger through all dimensions until, eventually, we once more reunite fully with the God force.

Can you prove a belief? No. Ultimately, a belief is always a matter of speculation based on subjective factual evidence. Nevertheless, we all have beliefs about all kinds of things. Often, we're not really aware of our beliefs. I now choose to believe something that nurtures me, rather than carry a belief that I hadn't given much thought to but simply adopted through my upbringing. Believing in reincarnation is very reassuring to me, and I've seen it proven to my own satisfaction during healings with hundreds of people.

PART

II

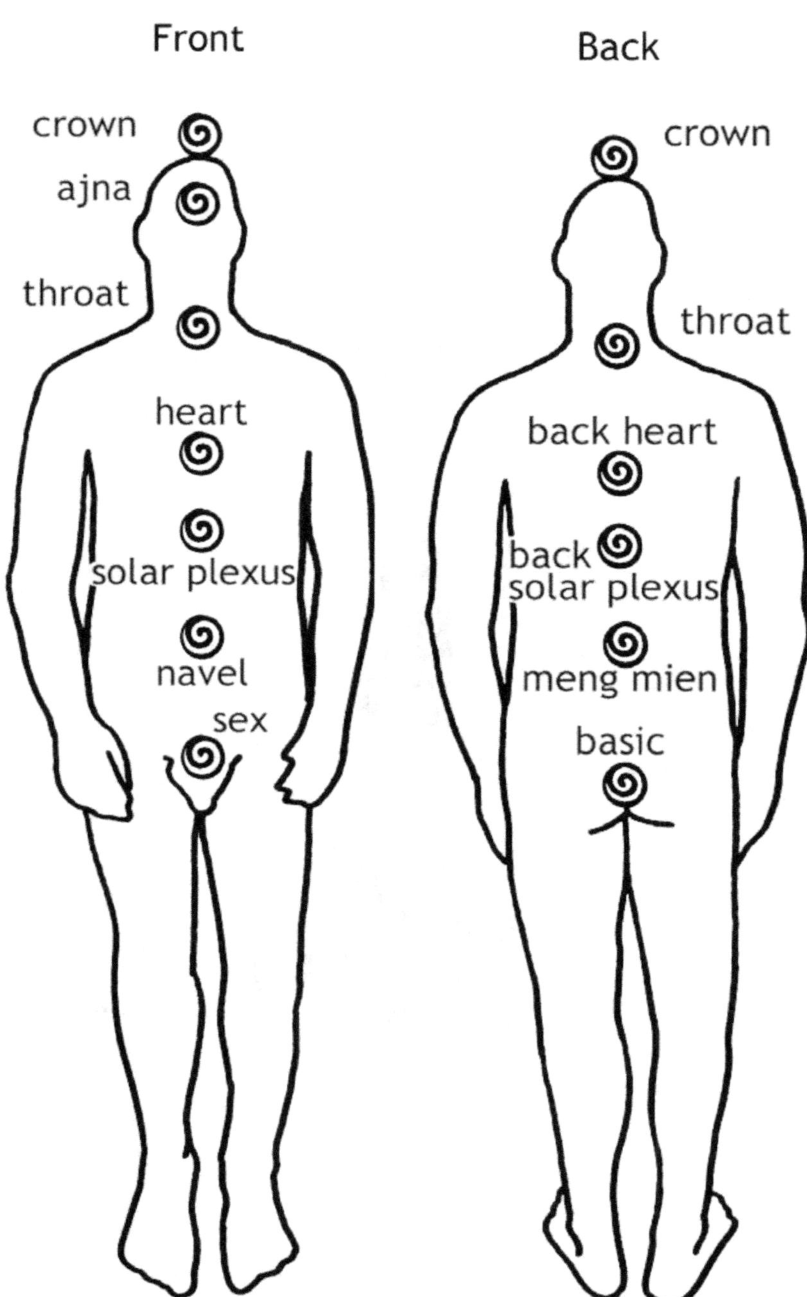

Major Chakras

Chapter

7

THE CHAKRAS

CHAKRAS, which are part of our etheric body, feed energy back and forth between our physical, mental, emotional and soul bodies. They also feed energy out to others, and from other people to us. Both the aura and chakras are containers within which our energy is kept; however, each chakra has its own set of functions and is more specific in nature than the aura. The aura is like a protective container within which we live. The chakras are very interactive with our environment, the people around us and other dimensions. They are the energy transfer units of the etheric body.

Chakras look like whirling vortices of energy and information that stick out the front and back of our body like old fashioned trumpets. When the chakras are active and robust, clean and bright, we are healthy and feel great.

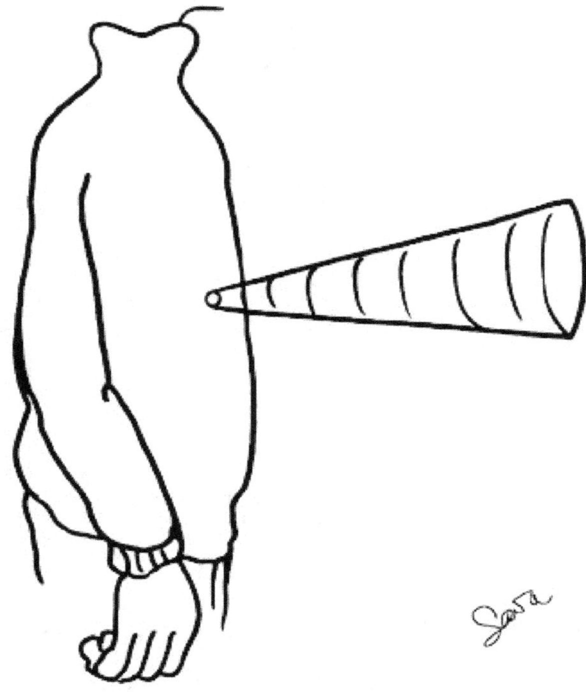

We have hundreds of chakras. Even more exist above our heads and below our feet. In yoga seven major chakras are referred to, as these seven have the greatest effect upon our consciousness. However there are hundreds of chakras; many have limited effect mainly to do with feeding energy into and out of specific organs or joints in the body. Seven invisible portals that affected our lives is already a lot right? On page 62 and below are diagrams showing the main chakras that we will be looking at in greater detail in the following chapters. These are the ones that, from my clinical practice, appear to have the biggest effect on our consciousness. Notice that as well as the solar plexus chakra we also look at the Navel minor chakra as it plays a significant role in certain ways that are set out below.

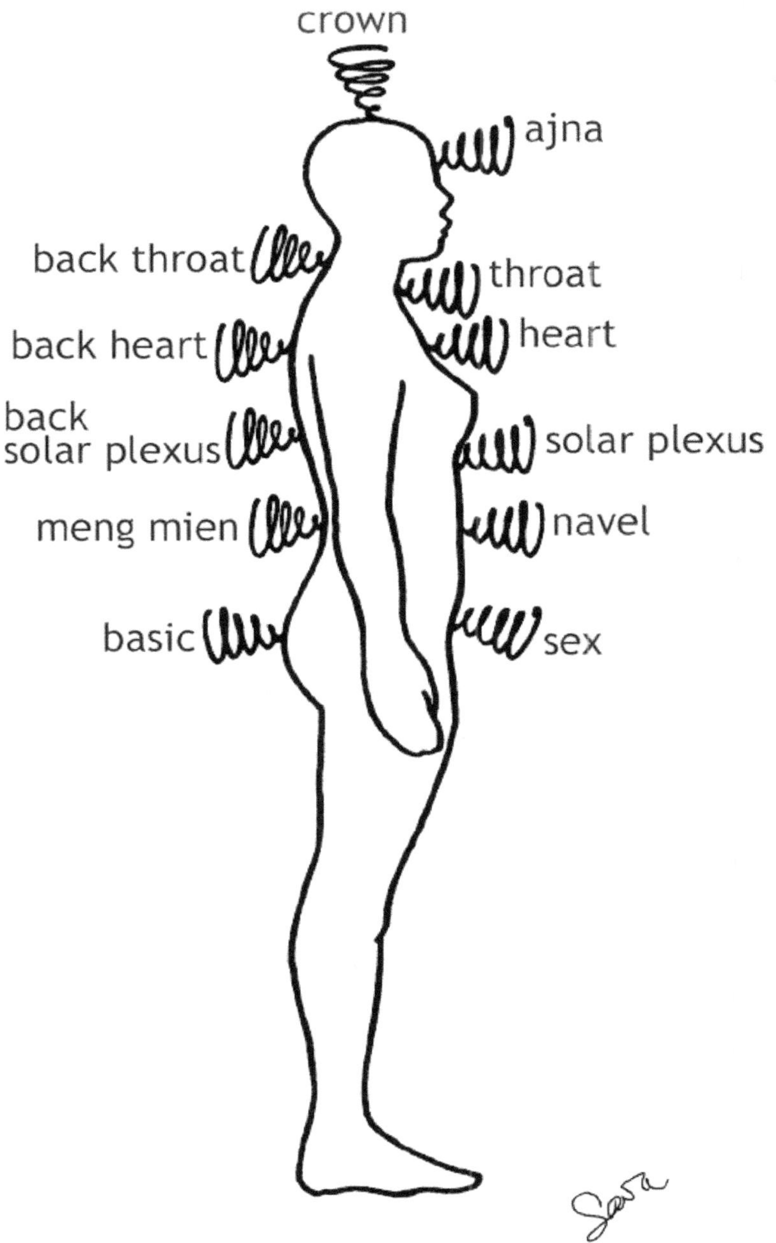

Chakras – Side View

How big is it?

Chakras vary greatly in size. Our major chakras are on average about 100 to 125mm (four to five inches) in diameter, and can extend anywhere from less than one metre to scores of metres in length. The major chakras, discussed below, are meant to be two or three times the size of the minor chakras.

The measurement of the chakras is important because it gives us a detailed understanding of how our own energy, and the energy of others, works.

When we talk about the size of chakras, what is important is the size of our own chakras relative to each other. Everyone is different. When we know how our chakras are shaping up, we can understand ourselves better. Our strengths and weaknesses are to some extent explained. We can then undertake specific exercises to strengthen the areas where we are energetically weaker, which in turn balances us up and helps us live more gracefully.

Having said that, when we compare one person's set of chakras with another person's, we can tell quite a lot about the development of one individual compared to another. Whether chakras are bigger or smaller on average is neither good nor bad; but it is like comparing a primary school student with a high school student. The more mature soul will usually have a larger etheric body. We bring our chakral development with us from our past incarnations. Big chakral development doesn't just happen, we make it happen, even if we are unaware of it.

Whatever the size and configuration of your chakras right now, you are able to make relatively rapid gains in development by following some pretty simple guidelines which we will explain to you as we go.

This information is intended to help you to develop, not give you a reason to beat yourself up. If your chakras are big, congratulations, you have done the inner work to develop them in this or some other lifetime. You can still make them bigger, clearer and stronger. If they are small, congratulations, you are coming to this work sooner than expected. You must have a lot of spiritual grace. Within the pages of this book you have at your fingertips some wonderful tools to assist you to develop rapidly, so you can hold more energy. This will become evident in all areas of your life, improving your ability to be healthy and successful, and to feel fulfilled.

Diameter

The diameter of a chakra tells us how developed the chakra is.

- Under 100mm (four inches) diameter is considered small.
- Between 100 and 150mm (four to six inches) is considered normal.
- Between 150 and 250mm (six to ten inches) is considered large.
- Over 250mm (ten inches) is considered very developed.

The chakra has a core, and what look like petals around that core which resemble a daisy open to the sun. We are not measuring the diameter of the petals, just the diameter of the core.

We can do exercises to increase the size of our chakras. This is like etheric weight lifting. As with physical weight lifting, we need to do it repetitively for there to be real development. Unfortunately, going to the gym once does not build a magnificent body. Chakral 'weight lifting' is the same.

People may have a chakra that is very large, 200 to 250mm (eight or ten inches) in diameter. This is pretty big, and would take sustained effort through a lot of lives to achieve. People who have most or all of their chakras at this size tend to be highly successful.

When a chakra is even larger than 250mm (ten inches), its ability to handle huge amounts of energy of various kinds is obvious. The person will have sufficient energy, development and oomph to be a leader, and to walk the world stage in whatever line of work they are engaged.

On the other end of the scale, chakras that are undersized may account for localized problems. People who are mentally slow tend to have chakras in the head area which are smaller than normal.

People with small sex chakras often have low libido, and so on.

Very large chakras give us a particular type of consciousness, depending on which one it is that is large. A big heart chakra and we will tend to think a lot about giving and things to do with compassion. A big base chakra and we will tend to think a lot about survival and making money. A big sex chakra, well, I guess we know what focus that gives a person.

By changing the relative size of the chakras we change the things we focus on.

Length

The length of a chakra, that is, how far it sticks out of our body, will also give us information about it. Irrespective of the size of the chakra (calculated by measuring its diameter), how long it is tells us how much energy is in it at the present moment. This is like asking, "Is your cup full, half full or empty?"

A chakra in which energy can be felt for about 1.8 metres (six feet) away from the body is a healthy average chakra. Sometimes when people are sick, or very depleted, the energy in the chakra is hard to feel. In fact, when scanning with the hand (which we will discuss in a minute) it can feel like the hand is being sucked into the person's body. This is a very depleted chakra. The person is probably very run-down, or if only one chakra is like that, there may be a health or emotional problem affecting that chakral centre.

A chakra that is bursting with energy will be three to six metres (ten or twenty feet) long. The bigger the diameter of the chakra, the more energy a chakra will be able to hold, because it is a bigger cup. On some people who have amazing development, chakras can be scanned from hundreds of metres away.

Clarity

We noted in the chapter on the aura that it can become congested with stuck emotions, negative energy, thoughts, contamination from other people, and so on. The same is true for the chakras. What is more, we can have some chakras that are very clear and others that are very messy.

The chakras that are the clearest will tend to be the ones that feed us energetically in the areas of our life that are easy and flow well. The chakras that are the most congested tend to be the ones that represent the areas in life where we are blocked and experience the biggest challenges.

Level of activation

Chakras work by spinning back and forward like a washing machine agitator. When they spin anti-clockwise they take energy out of our body and when they spin clockwise they put energy into our body.

clockwise spins energy in

anticlockwise spins energy out

Chakras sort our values and beliefs. After years of accessing and processing loads of information through education, listening to family and the media and interacting with others, our chakras are charged with energy and beliefs that reflect what we have fed them. Some of what we have fed them is good and wholesome, and this will make the chakra gather strength and flourish. Some of it is pretty toxic and harmful, and can make our chakras wither and slow down, eventually even stop. Stress and other forms of etheric debris can cause our energy centres to clog, which is why they slow down and partially stop working.

When a large amount of congestion occurs, the chakra will feel less energized, thus shorter than normal, and because it is not working it will slowly shrink. Chakras and muscles are similar in that you have to 'use them or lose them'. Essentially, what is happening is that the whirling motion has slowed or even stopped. If a chakra is very under-activated, it often only needs a cleanout to pop back into life again. Energy can flow back into it, and it will operate properly. Sometimes they need a bit more help. This is done by blessing the chakras. I will explain how to cleanse and bless the chakras in Part III.

The shape of things

Just as the shape of the aura gives us information about a person, the chakral configuration of a person also gives us information.

As a general rule of thumb, those with large lower chakras and small upper chakras are more attuned to the physical plane. They are interested in concrete things like assets, building a physical life and runs on the board. People with large lower chakras have receptors geared towards making and having money, and surviving in the physical world. In Western culture, more value is widely placed on this in daily life than on the attributes of the upper chakras.

People with much larger lower chakras do not have the etheric hardware in the upper body sufficiently developed to be able to perceive subtle stimuli, thus they are prone to proclaiming that it does not exist. To them it doesn't. Without development of the upper chakras, there will be little appreciation of the inner world.

Those with larger upper chakras have an easier time perceiving subtle energy and are more likely to be attuned to God and the world of emotions, angels and the like. They have bigger inner plane receptors (the upper chakras) so they are able to have real and meaningful spiritual contact. However, unless they also work at developing their lower chakras, they will struggle to flourish in the physical world. They frequently have financial challenges. They can be impractical, suffer from procrastination and lack direction.

Our thoughts, values, attitudes, and tendencies are held within our chakras and are brought to our conscious mind through the brain. When you change your chakras, you change the way you think. Not only that, you change your energy, your vibration, your resonance with people, places, and events, and therefore your life.

Chakral development

The Higher Self oversees the development of our consciousness and etheric body, including our chakra system, over hundreds of lifetimes.

If we are born in a country where survival is an issue, we are going to grow the parts of our energy anatomy which are important in regards to survival, most noticeably the base chakra.

When we need to exhibit a lot of self belief or inner strength over a long period of time, the chakra in charge of such things, the solar plexus chakra, builds up. When there is a lot of giving and service to others, the heart chakra builds up.

When done unconsciously the process is usually fairly slow, and growth will be very gradual and may take many lifetimes to achieve. Consciousness of the process speeds it up.

Over many lifetimes, the goal is to develop all of our chakras so that they become big and robust.

Chakras can be developed in specific ways to enhance various personal strengths, personality traits and characteristics, much like a weight lifter who focuses on certain muscle groups to build himself in a particular area. As we go through each chakra, I will explain the potential promise inherent to it and give easy exercises for its development. When we change the vibration and relative size of our chakras, we change our whole world.

Seeing chakral bodies

With development of the upper chakras comes an enhanced perception of reality. When they become sufficiently large and stimulated, certain chakras allow us to 'see' chakras.

In 1997 I attended a Pranic Healing seminar which was taught by a highly evolved spiritual Master. During that weekend we were taught about the importance of chakras and their development. We were given chakral activations, and at the end of the second day of the seminar a remarkable thing happened. I could see everyone's chakras. Not just hazy outlines, or a bit here and there; I could see all the chakras of everyone in the room. It was incredible.

At this stage I was still practising law full time as a barrister. My specialty was personal injury litigation; I helped those who had been injured, either in the course of their employment or in motor vehicle accidents. Thus, I spent a lot of time in crowded court rooms with people everywhere.

Returning to court on Monday after the pranic healing seminar, a fascinating vista presented itself. I could see the chakras of my opponent, the judge, the client, everyone. Some were big, some were small, some were blackened and on it went. The spiritual and emotional development of each person, or lack of it, was obvious. The effect of the stuck blocked energy was also evident, as was the correlation between that stuck energy and the painful health issues and injuries of the people at court.

I was so fascinated by this amazing revelation that I amused myself while I waited to present my cases by playing 'spot the injury'. I would look carefully at the energy anatomy of the injured people (legally represented by others) who were waiting to have their claims heard. I'd then hang around in court and listen to enough of their evidence to hear what the nature of their injuries were. The correlation between what I could see and what they said was very high.

After about six weeks this extraordinary, and seemingly permanent, altered state of consciousness resolved itself, and my sight went back to 'normal'. The chakral activation had placed so much energy in all my chakras that they all became large and super speedy. This gave me abilities I did not ordinarily have. Over time, I used up the energy of the chakral activation, and thus the chakras slowed down a bit and my perception became less acute. My consciousness expanded during the six week period of vision, and there was some permanent effect on my ability to see the nonphysical world. Thereafter, I was able to more effectively tune into people's energy bodies, particularly when I was doing healing, or after meditating. Other than that, everyone just looked normal, which was a huge relief after six weeks of having seen people's sex chakras waggling and their throat chakras constricting with negative emotions and intentions as they spoke. Too much information, let me tell you!

Being in the presence of developed spiritual teachers affects the chakras and the aura. The student is infused with the high vibrational energy of the teacher to the extent that the student is open to this experience. Not only does this expand the energy body as described, it speeds up events in the student's life. Blockages in relationships or projects are often 'miraculously' removed. This is really just the law of vibration in operation. However, the experience of this law is awe inspiring.

Chapter

8

FUNCTIONS OF THE CHAKRAS

AS we saw in the last chapter, chakras are multidimensional whirling vortices of energy and information. When they are working correctly, they spin clean energy into us and dirty energy out of us, like lungs in some respects. Below is a brief summary of the effects the chakras can have on us physically, mentally, emotionally and spiritually.

Physical function

A healthy chakra system is important to the wellbeing of our physical bodies. One of the primary jobs of the chakras is to bring to us energy from our surroundings. In this way, nourishment is provided to the internal organs, the endocrine system and the nervous system. This occurs through all of the chakras, major and minor. Most alternative healing modalities work on this level.

The major chakras feed energy into the smaller chakras of every organ and joint in our body. Thousands of meridians also carry energy around our bodies, as discussed in chapter 4. Often cleaning out the major chakras will cause all the others to come into balance. Sometimes it is more appropriate to work on the specific minor chakras of the body parts concerned. Master Choa Kok Sui's *Miracles Through Pranic Healing* is a wonderful book which covers major and minor chakras and describes an easy method by which healing of the physical body can be effected by working on the etheric body.

The way in which subtle energy and the chakras impact the physical body is similar to the way in which the regional electricity supply coming into your house affects the function of your electric heater or your fridge. A transformer converts current from thousands of voltage points to the voltage at which your appliances operate. Subtle energy is like electricity. There is lots of it, but if the transformer is broken and no electricity can get into your house, or too much energy comes in, then your heater and your fridge will not work. In fact, if there is too much energy, they are likely to blow up. Your body parts are a bit like the heater and the fridge, and the chakra is a bit like the transformer. Luckily, the problem is usually too little energy, rather than super charged chakras that cause body parts to blow up!

Every cell of our body and every atom of every cell contain energy. Through life events, this energy can become contaminated or congested with low vibrational etheric debris; for instance too much stress energy. This can be cleansed, and when the stale energy is removed, it gives people a wonderful feeling of lightness and wellbeing. This is done by infusing the chakras with energy, and intending that it flow into every cell of the body. This is possible because bodies are designed to receive energy through chakras, and because energy follows thought.

I once had a client who had a large cyst in her groin area. It was the size of a golf ball. She had suffered a cyst of the same nature before and had to have surgery to have it removed. I cleaned out all of the chakras in the area and removed the stuck energy inside the cyst. It shrank almost immediately, and over the course of ten days and three treatments, it completely vanished. This gives you an idea of the incredible physical impact that cleaning out stuck energy has on physical wellbeing. Master Choa Kok Sui, founder of Pranic Healing, has compiled some wonderful case studies that show how seemingly miraculous energy healing can be, and how you can do it yourself. See his book *Miracles Through Pranic Healing*. If you are specifically interested in healing the physical body I recommend you study Pranic Healing. What follows in this book has more to do with the emotional and spiritual effect of the chakras. I also point out some common physical consequences which flow from ignoring our mental, emotional and etheric bodies.

Emotional function

Chakras have a lot to do with how we function emotionally. Unhealthy, dirty and damaged chakras tell a story of unrelinquished emotional pain. I hasten to add that emotions per se are not the problem. Emotions are just energy, and when energy flows there is no problem. When we deny our emotions and resist the energy, they become frozen inside our chakras, and eventually this can flow into our physical body and cause disease.

Our thoughts and emotions form our consciousness of the world around us. When we are happy the whole world smiles with us. When we are unhappy everything seems bleak. Over a long period of time the effect of thinking thoughts and feeling emotions becomes cumulative, and the patterns of energy held in those thoughts and emotions lodge in our chakras. What is more, they lodge into specific chakras depending on the subject matter of the thought or emotion. If there is a particular issue that you often think about in a negative way, whether it be finances, relationships or self-esteem, then the chakras whose specialized job it is to look after that particular area of life are affected. When etheric and astral debris builds up in a particular chakra it can warp our perceptions and prevent our optimal energetic potential from manifesting. This means problems.

Thoughts, beliefs and memories

Chakras are a filing system for our thoughts, beliefs and memories. The things we think and believe template energy and bend it to the shape (energy pattern) of the thought. Thought forms are made out of energy encoded with thought, and these lodge in our chakras.

When I look at people clairvoyantly, I am able to see thought forms in their chakras. When they become dense enough they can lodge in the organs or other parts of the body. Usually by then there is some kind of disease affecting that part of the body.

For long term wellness, it is important to cleanse negative thoughts from our chakras. For clarity this is very important. In the end, we want to be thinking inspired thoughts from our souls. We cannot hear our inner voice if thoughts of yesterday are still clanging around inside us.

Where and what you think

You might think that you think in your head but that is just where you receive the thoughts in the thing called the mind. We need a good mind and it is a marvellous instrument of the soul. However, the mind is inherently subjective and at times self-deceptive; it will tell you what you want to hear or convince you of all kinds of nonsense. It also registers thought impressions from people and inner plane beings around you. This is a large subject to which we return in Yoga of the Mind. At times our mind is just regurgitating what the loud voice of the solar plexus chakra has to say. The 'insanity' of what we sometimes think is well described by Eckhart Tolle in his excellent book *The Power of Now.*

When we ignite our spirit, we strive to bring our consciousness

to the level of soul contact. To do this, a still mind is required. To achieve a still mind requires practice. The practice involves meditation. It also requires that we clean out all the old thoughts from our chakras, because the thoughts lodged in our chakras are part of what we register in our minds. The shape of our chakras, and their size relative to each other, determines the loudness of the thoughts resounding in our minds. A side effect of Igniting your Spirit is that meditation becomes easier and deeper and you really can access the consciousness that exists beyond the mind, which is accessed through inner stillness.

Instinct

Chakras are seats of instinct. Instincts with which we are familiar are those of survival, also the instincts to love, find a mate, reproduce and be safe. All these instincts are encoded in our energy matrix.

Instinct is developed in specific areas of life in which we acquire expertise. In martial arts, practitioners know what move is coming next and have instinctively responded to it before their brain has had time to register it. Police develop instincts about investigations. Mothers have instincts about their children. Good cross-examiners get instincts about witnesses telling porkies. Successful investors get instincts about the markets they invest in. This form of knowing without actually learning, enables us to attune to the energy of our specialty. It is a form of partial energy awareness, and where do we register it? In our chakras. When our chakras are robust, clean and activated, our instinctive 'knowing' is enhanced.

Attracting life experiences

By an almost magnetic resonance, we attract people to us who match the patterns of energy in our chakras. These patterns form as a result of past experiences, and the thoughts and emotions we hold about them.

For example, everyone who is interested in having a relationship would like it to be loving, nurturing and mutually supportive. However, what people want and what they end up getting are often two different things. Even though this is what most people want, if a woman has a pattern of energy in her chakras that says, "I believe that men are unfeeling and abusive", she will attract a man who has an unfeeling and abusive energy pattern. If the pattern of energy says, "I want to be in a loving relationship where there is a mutual flow of support, warmth and love", they will attract someone who has a matching energy pattern. Of course, these powerful patterns are subconscious.

Every chakra has its own set of records that beam out to everyone. You might have your money chakra beaming out, "I can get rich quick". If this is not your experience, then this is not what your base chakra is beaming out. It might be saying, "It's really hard to make money and when I do I tend to lose it again". You will know if this is what your base chakra is beaming out because it is what will be actually happening to you.

By increasing our awareness of what we are broadcasting, we can have a big effect on what we receive in life. When we change our vibration through cleaning and balancing the chakras, we will change our life experiences over a mere period of months. Like everything else, this is subject to the overall Divine plan, the plan of our soul for this incarnation (agreed to by us prior to our birth) and our karma. For more information about the plan of our soul for this incarnation see my books *Dimensions of Wealth* and *Yoga of the Mind,* and also Carolyn Myss' book *Sacred Contracts.*

Higher intelligence

As the vibrations of our aura and chakras become more refined and lighter through repeated healing and meditation, a wonderful inner and outer world presents itself.

Chakras are seats of psychic functions and faculties, including clairvoyance, clairaudience and clairsentience. Through the chakras we can access other dimensions and higher intelligences. Higher intelligences include our Higher Self, our spirit guides, angelic helpers, various ascended teachers, and great beings who work in service for the evolution of humanity such as real Gurus, Rishis and Saints.

When we develop our upper chakras, we develop the hardware through which we can attain ease of communication with these great beings. It is through the chakras, when they are sufficiently cleansed and developed, that we hear our Higher Self.

Hearing or perceiving higher guidance helps us with our direction in life and makes it flow much better. Part of our objective is to be able to contact this wealth of wisdom and loving support in all areas of our lives. We also aim to gain a clearer understanding of who we are and why we are here.

When we live in union with this form of consciousness, life is enriched and we move from thinking only in logical, linear terms to thinking conceptually, based on genuine intuitive guidance. Through this change in consciousness, we gain an understanding of universal principles and patterns, and we can do our part to move humanity forward on a developmental and vibrational scale.

Siddhis

Through extreme, intense and prolonged development of certain chakras, all human beings are capable of seemingly miraculous powers. These powers are called Siddhis in the Hindu tradition. Siddhis include such things as levitation. There is a school in America which teaches a meditation that builds up so much energy in the base of the spine that its practitioners rise up off the ground whilst they are doing it. I have observed a friend in this form of meditation. She was in total bliss, a big grin on her face, bouncing all over the place. The only problem is, it has to be done on a soft surface otherwise it can result in a few bruises.

Yogananda, in his book *Autobiography of a Yogi,* tells the story of a levitating yogi who used to meditate naked. This upset the locals who kept having him put in jail. He did not like meditating in jail, so he would levitate above the jail from the yard area, with no clothes on. Then he would float down to hover over the Ganges river. The police did not know what to do with him so they let him go. After that he used to meditate, stark naked, and cross-legged, a foot above the middle of the river where people would leave him alone. This was observed by everyone in the town, and he became a tourist attraction. A group of us visited the small shrine where he lived in Varanasi and the profound energy of his being-ness was still present even though our visit was years after his physical body had departed. Such astonishing stories of miraculous events seem to be quite commonplace in the remarkable country that is India.

Other yogis are able to suspend their breathing for long periods. Monks have demonstrated this by allowing themselves to be buried for hours at a time, clearly still alive when they are dug up.

When one particular chakra gets over-activated, the person concerned will develop super strength. Have you heard of situations where a mother has been able to physically lift a car off a child who has been trapped? This is an example of that kind of chakral activity. In that case, it occurs as an energetic response to an emergency. The mother would later be extremely tired and drained by the energetic experience, as well as in shock at having had a child in such peril.

With certain chakral development bilocation is possible. Bilocation is when a person can be in two places at once. Pretty useful skill, right? Unfortunately, learning to bilocate cannot be done with any conscious control until you are truly enlightened, a rare occurrence as yet on Earth. It is as though an energetic replica of the self can only go to people whom we care for, who care for us, or who have asked for help. There we can give comfort and assist those who are in need.

There is a very famous story of Padre Pio, a famous Franciscan (Catholic) monk, who was known for his extraordinary bilocation abilities. In World War II, while his physical body was asleep in his cell in the monastery, he appeared larger than life in the sky during an air battle. When the pilots saw his image in the sky, they knew it was a miracle and took it as a sign that they should just go home. Consequently, certain buildings of great historical and religious significance, not to mention many Italian civilians, were not bombed.

During the Bali bombing in 2002, one of my former spiritual teachers happened to be on the island. His physical body was asleep in bed. His staff saw him retire for the night, and one of them was doing computer work for most of that period in the lounge area. The Guru would have had to have passed right by to leave, which he did not. He never left the hotel building. However, many people reported having seen him ministering to the sick within the overcrowded hospital all night long.

Others with large and powerful chakras develop a photographic memory. This certainly has not happened to me, but I live in hope.

Certain chakral development gives the ability to bring fire from the hand. There is a Nan King practitioner in Java who has demonstrated this to his students many times.

Monks in Tibet have been buried in snow with no effect on their body temperature. They do not get cold because they are so highly developed that they can will their etheric bodies to create the heat they need to survive.

There are Indian saints who develop their etheric body such that they live for hundreds of years. They are known to 5 or more generations of the one family. Other Holy men are able to manifest objects or sacred ash. I visited the ashram of Sai Baba in the years 2002 and 2003 and witnessed manifestations of holy ash and other things. Sri Sakthi Amma in South India manifests sacred objects like pendants or small statues for devotees, something that I have witnessed.

To really develop any of these powers to a great degree, it is necessary to spend years of concentrated effort studying with someone who already knows how it is done. The people who can do these things are the Olympians of the etheric world.

It requires the same type of dedication to become an energy master as it does to become a great sporting hero. Similarly, some aptitude needs to be shown first. While most people are no more interested in becoming masters of energy than they are in becoming Olympic sports heroes, it is interesting to appreciate just what we are capable of if we are prepared to work on it.

How to work with the chakras

Chakras have been known about in various cultures for thousands of years. Christian images of saints and Jesus usually show a nimbus of light around the head. This is the crown chakra. Others have a halo all around them, which is a depiction of the aura. What is new is the way we can work directly with our chakral bodies to effect change in our lives and expand our conscious understanding of ourselves, the world and our place in it.

In the following chapters, we shall discuss each major chakra in turn, identifying its location, the promise it holds for us, the fears that need to be overcome to get there, and the consequences that can occur when we don't do this. After identifying the promises, fears and consequences, stories are told which illustrate the ways in which we can ignite the spirit in our chakras. Then at the end of each chapter you will see exercises that will develop the individual chakra, and affirmations to help. Before we begin let us clearly understand what is meant by the promises, the fears and the consequences.

The Promises

Each chakra will from time to time, or from lifetime to lifetime, demand your attention and be the focus of your development. The major chakras are a study in multidimensional potential.

When we learn to develop and master a chakra we get a bag of goodies to keep. This development is often hard won, having to be experienced, not just thought about. Like grist to the mill, the universe has an uncanny way of bringing us the circumstances that will unerringly give us the opportunities for balanced and rounded life mastery.

The Fears

When we live inside our comfort zones, mostly we are not challenged in any way that will have a large impact on our spiritual development. We just potter along.

Comfort zones are vexing things. They do not stay static. When we perpetually stay within our comfort zone, the whole zone shrinks. We become more isolated, constrained, habitual, smaller, deadened. Souls don't actually like doing the same thing all the time. Our spirit wants a bit of adventure, and 360 degree learning.

Life should not be a journey to the grave with the intention of arriving safely in a pretty and well preserved body, but rather to skid in broadside in a cloud of smoke, thoroughly used up, totally worn out, and loudly proclaiming "Wow! What a Ride!

Hunter S. Thompson, The Proud Highway: Saga of a Desperate Southern Gentleman, 1955-1967

As we dare to take even the smallest step outside of our comfort zone, the whole comfort zone expands. We get bigger, more uninhibited, more spirited, more alive.

When we overcome fears and release blame and attachment to the people, places, things, times and events that seemingly 'caused' us to feel that fear in the first place, we become free. We grow. Our soul is enriched. We find it impossible to be victimised any more. We have mastered it. We realize it was just a test that does not go away until we pass it. When we inevitably pass it (even if it takes years or lifetimes to do so) we are permanently enriched. It is forever encoded on our soul.

The creative part of this process, the growing of who we are, tends to take place in layers, like layers of sediment which create a rock.

The process of creation also has a destructive aspect, which is also healthy and necessary. This is the letting-go-of-the-past phase. Our negative experiences were no doubt necessary as part of our growth. Our soul would not have chosen them for us if we could not handle it. Any victim mentality needs to be released, recast, understood from a higher perspective, forgiven and let go.

What will happen to us if we move out of our secure (even if dysfunctional) comfort zone and patterns of behaviour? Will the sky fall in? Will we still be able to survive in the world? Will our feelings be so raw that we are unable to cope? Will we still have money? Will we still be loved?

Pushing through these barriers develops different kinds of strength. In the end, those who have ignited their spirits, despite the various ways they have done it, will invariably have developed the courage to be who they are, to speak their own truth and to form their own inexorable connection with the Divine.

The bigger we get, the bigger the challenges get. There would be no point presenting a kindergarten problem to a year eight student, would there? How would that develop the student? They would not even recognise that a challenge had been presented, despite the fact that they might have found it very challenging eight years ago.

In terms of spiritual development, by being granted various experiences to deal with we are able to move forward. The most educational experiences tend to be the ones that move us outside our comfort zone, challenge us and create tension. This tension might be physical, mental, emotional or spiritual in nature. The agenda is set by us, for us, before we incarnate and while we are still in the consciousness of our Higher Self. From the perspective of our Higher Self, winning or losing are not the issues. The issue is the journey: what we learn along the way.

The Consequences

The process of growth that I am describing cannot be ignored, skipped or avoided. Every one of us has to go through it. During different phases of our life, and during different lifetimes, various parts of our development are a focus.

If we do not rise to the challenge of bringing our fears to rest, they grow and attract physical and emotional experiences that illustrate what we need to work on; we notice resistance, difficult relationships, lack of flow, setback, ill health and other energetic blockages.

As you read the following chapters on the chakras, be attuned to what you identify with the most, for these might be your current growth areas.

When we break through our own personal barriers and deal with our fears, we find that we may alter course a little. When we get it wrong, we experience various unpleasant consequences.

This is not punishment, just confirmation that there is something amiss. When we get it right, we experience serendipitous circumstances. Helpful coincidences pop up all around us and we end up feeling more alive.

We find even in our darkest hour that there really is a path of ease and grace. When we find that, it is like landing on a ladder in the children's game, Snakes and Ladders. We zoom ahead.

Chapter

9

THE BASE CHAKRA

THE base chakra is situated at the base of the spine, extending out and back from our body. It is where we would have a tail, if we had one.

The Promises

- Strong survival instinct and skills. Physical security.
- Good tribal or family structures.
- Availability of physical resources.
- Healthy flow of money.
- Grounded approach.
- Practicality.
- Physical world focus.
- Strong physical body.
- Strong muscular and skeletal system.
- Strong vitality and healthy energy.
- Dynamism.

The Fears

- Letting go of something that may appear safe but is stultifying.
- Fear of physical injury to self or others.
- Fear of things such as spiders and heights.
- Not having a stable foundation.
- Fear of not being able to support oneself.
- Not being approved of.
- Financial insecurity.
- Rejection by family or other tribe.
- Fear of abandonment.
- Lack of physical security.
- Not belonging.
- Fear of living (related to suicidal feelings).

The Consequences

- Feeling the fears related to physical security, listed above.
- Back pain.
- No money.
- Insufficient resources.
- Anxiety based sleeping problems.
- Hyperactivity.
- Depression.
- Feelings of abandonment.
- Not being able to relate with family members.

Ignite The Base Chakra Spirit Groups and tribes

We all need some kind of societal support structure to keep us safe. The organization of family and community, and the structures that flow from them, are base chakra matters.

Emotionally, our most basic support structure is meant to be our parents, their parents and other blood relatives. If something goes wrong with these relationships, and this threatens our emotional sense of safety or challenges our ability to survive, we might need to develop our base chakras rather more quickly than other people. If we have a tricky family and we experience difficulties coping with this, we may develop problems in the base chakra.

The base chakra responds to the energy of the groups that we belong to. I have noticed that people's base chakra becomes quite destabilized after retirement, change of job, migration to another country or any other major life change. It becomes weak, and wobbles around all over the place until it is plugged back into another group or place. This creates feelings of ungroundedness, displacement, mild confusion, disorientation, anxiety and procrastination, all of which can range from very mild to quite pronounced.

Dr Christine Northrop, an intuitive healer and a medical practitioner in the United States, says that for true stability and lasting good health, we need to have our fingers in four or more 'pies'. We need at least four groups to which we belong and with which we have some identification. In this way, our base chakra can be plugged into numerous 'tribes' and forms of security. If things go bad in one or two pies, we still have a couple more. We do not become completely destabilized.

Most people have family and work associations. That's two pies. Many play a sport; that's a third. Dr Northrop also recommends being part of a spiritual community as one of the pies, and says that this is one of the important roles played by organized religion. If you are not the religious type, you can still find a group of like minded people to pray or meditate with, if you look.

Think for a moment, how do you derive feelings of security? If you do not have a firm foundation in several supportive groups, it might be time to attend to this. It doesn't really matter what type of group it is (so long as it is wholesome); it is more important that you feel a sense of identity and acceptance. I know a guy who is involved with a medieval society. Everyone comes along in full medieval dress, and great pains are taken to have a new costume for every event. They have sword fighting, drink copious quantities of mead and other medieval concoctions, and have a great time. For those who are involved, it is a large part of their lives; friendships form within the group and it is the backbone of their social community.

Approval

We have to meet our basic survival needs, and being approved of and accepted by the groups we belong to is crucial. As we grow and change, we might outgrow our group. This sometimes happens when people develop emotionally or spiritually. They find that the people who have been part of their life in the past now seem to be relatively negative and unsupportive. They no longer resonate with them and it is time to move on. Facing the fear of not being accepted by the group, and of finding new groups, is part of the process of development in the base chakra.

Jane came to see me with chronic back pain. She also reported lots of fears, such as fear of spiders, heights and getting sick. When I looked into her base chakra, I saw a television set. Weird, I thought, but asked her if television or television sets had been important in her life in any particular way. "No", she said. So I kept working, wondering about the possible symbolic meanings of seeing a television set in her base chakra. Then, Jane started wailing. After the wailing had died down, she told me she had experienced a memory of something she had not thought of for years.

Jane had been raised by two alcoholic parents who were both incapable of giving her any proper support, security or nurturing. She got only very rudimentary physical care. Every night, for as far back as she could remember, they used to go to the pub and leave her at home alone with a television set for company and support. The television was her babysitter and primary support! That's why it was in her base chakra.

We went through an energetic process of forgiveness with her parents and she came to see that, despite her unconventional childhood and downright neglect by her parents, she had developed a strong ability to be by herself, trust herself and provide for herself. She literally had to release the television energy from the base of her spine and reconnect with the reality of the physical Earth and the spiritual core of her being. Thereafter her back pain was greatly reduced, and she had more ability to function in the world and feel safe.

Money

One of the primary ways we survive in the world is by amassing enough of the energy which is valued by the community we live in. In our community, that energy takes the form of money.

During my career at the bar, I noticed that those who were earning huge money as busy and successful barristers had enormous base chakras. Often, they were ten or more metres in length and had large diameters. They literally had the capacity in their base chakras to anchor huge amounts of money.

Those with large base chakras have developed the consciousness and energy for manifesting security through money and resources. They resonate with the energy of money and therefore are able to attract money easily and in abundance.

We said earlier that our affirmations affect our chakras. Many people use affirmations about money which are not in keeping with the development of their base chakra. If you are on an income of $30,000 and you start using an affirmation that says you have an income of $300,000, chances are that your base chakra will not have enough energy at the present time to sustain it. If it did, you would be earning more already. Asking for a lot more than the base chakra can handle is a sure way to deplete it.

There are ways to test whether our base chakra can handle an income that is doubled. If the base chakra stays the same or gets bigger, you can handle it. If it shrinks, you are not yet ready for such a big increase in income. You will need to develop the base chakra before you are able to attract and hold the desired amount of wealth. The Dimensions of Wealth seminar and book discuss this in more detail, as well as other spiritual aspects of creating wealth.

Craig was an accountant, and he had always prided himself at being good at his job. Craig also had another aspect to his character. He was something of a philanthropist. He got a real kick out of helping others, and was on the board of many charitable institutions, including a group which looked after children of alcoholics.

For the past ten years, Craig had been in partnership in a country town accounting practice with an older, more conservative accountant, Henry. He had noticed that Henry had been becoming increasingly taciturn, but did not know why. In hindsight it became evident why. Henry's client base was dwindling while Craig was attracting more and more clients. So Henry decided to help himself by spreading some highly malicious information about Craig. He started to tell people that Craig was involved with the children of alcoholics because he himself had a drinking problem. This was untrue, and Craig was unaware of the allegation. He had no idea why people were leaving his practice in droves. Things got personally very unpleasant with Henry, and in the end Craig left the practice.

As all this was happening, Craig found that his energy levels were falling, and when he left the practice he went into depression. He felt that Henry was behind his failing practice but could never prove it, until eventually he was told of the scurrilous rumour Henry had put about the town.

Craig had been suffering depression for about eighteen months when he sought treatment from me. After the first treatment, which focused on the base chakra, his energy levels started to pick up. After the second treatment he was substantially improved and recommenced the business of building a new practice. He needed to come to terms with the malicious nature of Henry's actions, and it took a while for him to do so. Eventually he was able to forgive Henry and to understand that Henry was just a frightened old man. Hurting Craig's reputation had not really helped Henry, who was still as mediocre and taciturn as ever. When Craig decided that he was able to be secure and financially viable without Henry, who in a professional sense had been like a father to him (a base chakra relationship), his base chakra normalised and he returned to making a very healthy income.

Procrastinate, who me?

When the base chakra is weak there is a tendency to put off doing the physical things that one needs to do to function in the world. Dynamic people tend to have big base chakras. Procrastination tends to slow down the base chakra, and those who procrastinate a lot tend to weaken their base chakras. This is a chicken and egg problem. Procrastination over a long period has caused the base chakra to slow down. Because the base chakra is so slow, the person suffers from procrastination.

A spiritually developed healer can jump start the base chakra, setting the energetic parameter for the procrastination to be overcome. The person still has to actually do the physical things required to get things happening. This is much easier to do after a big clean-out and an infusion of higher vibrational energy, in the form of light or sound, into the base chakra.

Grounded and practical

People who are not properly in contact with the consciousness of the base chakra have trouble being grounded. As a result, they experience impracticality and an inability to look after themselves. People who have brains the size of planets but no common sense might be very developed elsewhere but have small base chakras. They tend to lose touch with physical reality, even though they are highly intelligent. When they grow their base chakra, they can combine intelligence with practicality. This will enable them to surge ahead in life.

Depression

Through the base chakra and our connection to the Earth we can experience a lot of joy. When this connection is not working very well, depression can result. When physical life is radically unpleasant our base chakras can pull up stumps and temporarily go on strike. It pulls out of the ground because it does not like what we are physically experiencing. When the base chakra does this, the result can be reactive depression.

During my career as a barrister I represented many teachers who had reactive depression due to highly stressful circumstances at work. As a result of the stress, they were not able to be present in an energetic sense, and their base chakras had shrunk. Of course, they did not know this and I was wearing a different hat so couldn't really tell them. (It could well have compounded their problems knowing that their barrister was peering at their chakras.)

I once treated a teacher who worked at a school for children who had been expelled from school because they were violent, or too difficult to deal with in the mainstream system. A security guard would accompany her to class and stand outside to ensure order was maintained. Here was a gentle, intelligent and articulate woman who had been a teacher for a long time, and a successful one. However, she was unprepared for the general level of brutality that the boys in this institution presented to her. On the first day one of the boys lunged at her glasses with two sharpened pencils and cracked her lenses. The security guard simply couldn't react fast enough to prevent it.

While events of this magnitude did not happen every day, the threat of damage to her body was real and present every day. She started to forget things, feel low and experience back pain. It was difficult for her to carry the boxes of books to class which had not previously been a burden. One day, as she was correcting a student, he grabbed her, physically lifted her up and hung her by her clothing on a coat hook on the wall. The other boys thought this was hilarious.

Can you imagine having to work in such circumstances? Is it any wonder her base chakra pulled up stumps and retreated? She experienced all of the classic signs of depression. No joy could get in through the base chakra. She felt low. She was tired all the time. Her motivation left her. She couldn't seem to get things done. She found it difficult to make normal everyday decisions, remember names or concentrate. She had back pain which seemed to be getting worse, although the doctors were not able to provide any explanation as to the physical cause of the problem. Energetically, of course, there was a huge causal connection between the base chakra and the symptoms with which she presented.

By letting go of the fears and forgiving her attackers, she was able to get some energy back into the base chakra. Then, it needed to be reactivated during several healing sessions for her to really move ahead. She fully recovered.

Survival

People with a strong sense of survival have healthy base chakras. People who have a precarious grip on life, or who wouldn't really care if they lived or died, have weak base chakras. As the base chakra becomes stronger, the survival instinct is also activated. Treating the base chakra is a helpful part of the recovery plan for those who have suicidal thoughts or intentions. Naturally, people who are very depressed are also advised to place themselves under the care of a reputable psychiatrist because energy healing and Western medicine work best when combined.

BASE CHAKRA EXERCISE

1. *To enhance the base chakra try the following grounding meditation.*

2. *Invoke. (See Part III)*

3. *Breathe in, and with the out-breath imagine that you can breathe energy straight down through your body, out the base of your spine and all the way down into the Earth.*

4. *Imagine that a big tap root is forming from the base of your spine, down into the Earth.*

5. *With the next in-breath, breathe in energy from the Earth, up into your base chakra.*

6. *Breathe out through the tap root into the Earth, and imagine that subsidiary roots are forming around the tap root, securely rooting you into the Earth.*

7. *Breathe up through the root system.*

8. *Repeat the breathing in and out through the root system for several minutes.*

When to do this

- As a daily meditation.
- Whenever you feel that the wheels are spinning really fast but you are not getting anywhere.
- Before challenging meetings such as job interviews and mediations.
- Before seeing difficult clients or colleagues.
- When you go to another country.
- Before you start anything new.

Base chakra affirmation

I am securely grounded and rooted to Mother Earth.

I am safe, strong, happy, supported, practical. I easily manifest money and all good things.

THE SEX CHAKRA

T HE sex chakra is located above the pubic bone.

The Promises

- Home of the seed of new life, primordial chi.
- Ability to reproduce.
- Divine union with your beloved.
- Ecstatic and long lasting orgasmic spiritual experiences through tantra or sacred sex.
- Healthy libido and sexual performance.
- Ability and desire to create.
- Birthing new projects in your world
- Magnetism, attractiveness to others.
- Youthfulness.
- Greater longevity.
- Healthy sex organs and bladder.
- Plenty of energy to feed the upper chakras.
- Healthy upper chakras, as primordial chi circulates naturally through the body from the sex chakra.

The Fears

- Letting go of a failed creative process.
- Releasing all stuck energies surrounding births, abortions, the deaths of children.
- Fear of not being good enough in terms of sexual performance.
- Fear of not being sexually attractive.
- Overcoming sexual abuse including incest and rape.
- Fear of physical injury to children.
- Lack of sexual security.

The Consequences

- Feeling lots of fears around the issues listed above.
- Libido problems.
- Infertility.
- Illnesses of the reproductive organs.
- Bladder problems.
- Lack of enjoyment of pleasures.
- Not being able to relate with sexual partners.
- Rapid ageing.
- Lack of charisma.
- Failing mental health.
- Creatively blocked.

Relationship To Other Chakras

The sex chakra has a strong relationship with the base chakra, and when the base is blocked often the sex chakra is also.

All the upper chakras are somewhat dependent upon the special primordial energy of the sex chakra circulating in a free and healthy way around the body. If this becomes blocked, then the upper chakras can become deficient. Certain mental conditions have been shown to be at least partially the result of not enough sex energy circulating to the brain. A study on Alzheimer's disease by pranic healers has shown that symptoms can be lessened by getting the sex energy flowing to the patient's brain again. This takes regular practice, but over a period of several months, real progress can be made.

Igniting The Sex Chakra Spirit Libido

Those with a large sex chakra tend to have a big sex drive. When the sex chakra is depleted and/or clogged up, loss of libido or creative energy can result.

Over the long term it can lead to a loss of the flow of energy into the sex organs or bladder, which can then become unwell.

Sexual union

When we have sex with someone, the sex chakra becomes highly activated, and it is not only the physical bodies which become joined. The chakras do also. In a fluid way, energy flows from one person to the other. If we look after ourselves and our energy bodies are clean and shiny, then our chakras will be clean, activated and bright. If your sexual partner has a different lifestyle to you, has had lots of affairs, done no personal development work, or smokes, drinks and eats garbage, you will end up wearing some of that energy cocktail. Naturally, the best thing to do is to give your partner a healing prior to sleeping with them, particularly new partners. If they don't run away, they will be glad you offered, as they will feel lighter and more vibrant, and everyone benefits.

Twisted sex

When the sex energy is perverted and expressed in a non loving way, dire consequences can result. This is because the sex energy is far more potent than any other form of human energy, so the consequences are bigger.

If a person is raped, quite often this has a freezing effect on the sex chakra, a bit like going into shock and becoming rigid. Women who have been raped have told me that they feel as though their body is no longer their own. They often have flashbacks to their attack, and/or they find that their sexual response is not like it was before the rape took place. If the energy of the sex chakra (or any chakra for that matter) becomes frozen, then health problems in the area of the body that it feeds are more likely.

Lucinda had been repeatedly raped by her first lover in her late teens. She had poor self-esteem and had come from an abusive home. Her father had been violent towards her, and to her sister and mother, though not in a sexual way. Still, Lucinda had some pretty negative experiences of men, and attracted a man who reflected her beliefs about relationships. She came to me about ten years after she had parted from her first lover, and had not thought about him or those experiences in years. She was suffering from ovarian cysts. This was interfering with her fertility, and she was not able to conceive.

When I looked into her sex chakra, it was full of red and black energy, and felt scary. Pictures of abuse surfaced, and we did IYS Energy Healing to release this stuck energy. She began to cry, and haltingly told me of her previous experiences. As she spoke, energy started to release through the sex chakra. After a while she decided to forgive her former partner, and as she repeated the words of forgiveness after me, the dark energy poured out of her. She rang me a few months later to tell me that the ovarian cysts were gone and that she was pregnant. She later gave birth to a healthy baby girl, and to date (four years later) there are no more cysts.

Divine union

Sexual energy is a form of Shakti or Divine energy. Mixed with prayer and meditation it can have a great effect on your life, physically, mentally, emotionally and spiritually. Ecstatic and long lasting states of bliss can be experienced through the practice of sacred sexuality.

If you meditate before having loving sex with a partner, then the upper chakras are stimulated relative to the lower ones. This means the upper chakras are spinning faster and have more energy in them. Divine energy can be brought in through the crown chakra and down to the sex chakra with the breath. Then with the out-breath, you breathe sex energy from the sex chakra up to the heart chakra and the crown chakra. This should not be done by people with heart conditions.

In other tantric practices the energy from the sex chakra is redistributed in various ways throughout the body. This is a super tonic for the upper chakras and the internal organs. If done regularly, this practice can delay the ageing process. People who look much older than they are generally have poor sex chakras. Those who have huge sex chakras and who transmute sex energy can look even decades younger than their chronological age.

In ancient times and in certain mystery schools, students are shown how to transmute the energy from the sex chakra to feed the higher chakras and regulate the sex drive. This is how monks were supposed to deal with sexual energy; it was thought that the energy, which is potent and precious, should not be wasted in the sexual act if procreation was not the desired result. Hence, in many traditions celibacy was prescribed for those who entered monastic life. It is not that sex is bad or immoral. How could that be the case when it is the means through which the continuity of the species is maintained? It is just that the energy can be used in other creative ways and to enhance conscious soul union.

Creative urges

This chakra has to do with the creation of new physical things. Having children is the ultimate creative process. All our other creative desires are fed from here also. Whenever your creativity is blocked, look at your sex chakra and get some healing.

Giving birth and aborting

How do we feel about birthing and our right to control our fertility? Any issues we have around these topics will lodge in the sex chakra. It does not seem to matter which side of the fence you are on, whether you are a pro-lifer or a free choicer, the nonacceptance of the opposing view will cause issues in this chakra. Such issues can have a more severe impact on the sex chakra than having an abortion can.

I have treated many women with fertility problems, or sexual health issues related to previous miscarriages or abortions. In some instances, the soul of the aborted foetus can still be attached to the woman, its astral body living in the woman's sex chakra. More interestingly, some women who have not lost or aborted babies in this life, still have babies that have died attached to them from previous incarnations. As such the energy body will not conceive now as it already considers itself pregnant.

Before we incarnate, we make soul agreements with other souls as to how the intertwined stories of our lives will be expressed. Part of the purpose of such agreements is to bring to us the necessary development that our soul is currently focused on. Another part of the purpose is to clear karma from the past. Through past life regression it can quite often become clear that the genesis of the issues causing the twisted lines of energy today resulted from previous complications between two souls.

When we lovingly release the unborn or aborted babies into the arms of the Divine Mother, a huge rush of warm blissful energy is usually experienced, as well as a teary farewell to someone our minds were not even conscious of prior to the healing. Many women who have this type of experience start to menstruate on the spot, so strong is the effect on their energy body. This happens whether they are due to bleed or not. Thereafter, many have gone on to enjoy good health and normal fertility.

Dead creative projects can be still attached to us through the sex chakra also. The process of letting go is the key to moving on and getting the creative energies to flow again.

Magnetism

The sex chakra is the centre of personal magnetism and charisma. Have you ever met someone you found physically unattractive, yet sexually desirable?

Such a person most likely has a large sex chakra, and while you haven't really noticed, their sex chakra is talking to your sex chakra, which is busy responding to all that energy.

SEX CHAKRA EXERCISE

To enhance and move sexual energy try the following exercise.

1. *Sit or stand comfortably. Close your eyes.*

2. *Invoke. (See Part III, Ignite Your Spirit, for more information.)*

3. *Be aware of the pillar of light, the column of energy which extends from above your head and moves down through your body and out through your feet. (Refer to chapter 4.)*

4. *Breathe in and down through this column to the level of the sex chakra at the top of the pubic bone.*

5. *Breathe out through the sex chakra, releasing all stuck energies.*

6. *Repeat this breath three times.*

7. *Raise your hands above your head, grab a handful of Divine energy, bring it down to your sex chakra and put it in. Breathe in as you do this. Then breathe out as you use your hands to move the sex chakra energy up to the heart chakra. Imagine that this energy is absorbed by the heart chakra. Do not do this if you have heart congestion.*

8. *Repeat three times.*

9. *Breathe in as you raise your hands above your head and grab another handful of Divine energy. Bring it down to your sex chakra and feed it in. Breathe out as you use your hands to lift the sex chakra energy up to the throat chakra. Repeat three times.*

10. *Do the same with the ajna (between the eyebrows) and the crown (on top of the head) chakras.*

11. *At the end of the exercise, the sex chakra and the other chakras involved in this process will be enhanced and strong.*

Sex chakra affirmation

I am creative, sexy, charismatic, full of life force.

I easily draw to me wonderful people, relationships and circumstances in my life.

Chapter

11

THE NAVEL CHAKRA

The navel chakra extends from the belly button, and the back end of the chakra can be found by drilling an imaginary hole through your belly button and out through your back. The back of the navel chakra is called the meng mein chakra.

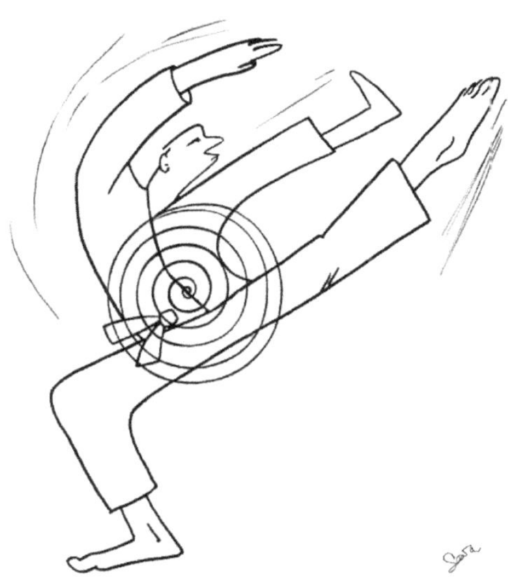

The Promises

- Good relationship with your own and other people's power.
- Storehouse of golden chi energy.
- Healthy, regular bowels. Fast reflexes.
- Easy birthing.
- Good boundaries.
- Ability to say no and mean it.

The Fears

- Lack of personal power.
- Fear of having power.
- Fear of misusing power.
- Fear of giving power away.
- Fear of controlling others.
- Fear of being controlled by others.
- Fear of being too slow.

The Consequences

NAVEL:

- Intestinal ailments.
- Constipation.
- Difficulty giving birth.
- Appendix problems.
- Relationship and personal boundary issues.

MENG MEIN:

- Back pain.
- Low energy levels.
- Kidney problems.
- High blood pressure when the chakra gets too big and full of garbage.
- A lot of unexpressed, pent-up anger.
- Difficulties in pregnancy, especially with blood pressure and kidneys.

Relationship to other chakras

If the navel chakra becomes blocked it can affect the proper functioning of the sex chakra. As I said earlier, the sex chakra has a special reservoir of primordial chi, and this life force energy is circulated throughout the body. If it is unable to rise because the navel chakra (right above it) is blocked, this blockage can adversely impact all the upper energy centres.

Igniting The Navel Chakra Spirit Personal power

The front and back of this chakra have slightly different jobs, but both have to do with power. I have noticed that people who do not have a comfortable relationship with their own personal power will develop problems in the navel chakra.

Often these people have had overbearing parents, or spouses who were very controlling. Finding the balance between power and vulnerability, between knowing when to be strong and when to give in, are issues that often have to be faced for the good health of this chakra.

Giving our power away can happen in the blink of an eye; half the time we do not even notice that we are doing it. We agree to things that, if we thought about it for a minute, we really wouldn't want to agree to at all. More and more requests are made of us to do this and that, until our time and energy are not our own. All our energy is spent fulfilling the agendas of others. We give our power away by agreeing to things we do not really want to do because we find it difficult to say no.

In the old days, I was so eager to please and felt I was such a strong person, I could say yes to heaps of things. Over time this became draining. I had to start learning to say no.

No one can take power from us. It is we who unintentionally give it away. With a bit of insight, we can start to notice when we are giving away our power. "Damn, just did it again!" How many times have I said that? It usually occurs in the small things, with those closest to us.

One of the strategies I have adopted is to say, "I will think about that", instead of agreeing automatically. This gives me time to decide in a non-pressured way whether or not I want to agree to the proposition that has been put to me.

Another good little trick is to imagine your best friend has just been asked to do whatever it is that has been asked of you and that they come to you for advice as to whether or not they should do it. When you can detach from the situation in this way, it becomes much clearer whether the request was a fair one or not. Often when I do this instead of agreeing automatically, my response is, "Are you crazy?" How could I possibly agree to type Peter's university assignment when I have two kids to look after, guests for dinner and am working for the next five days straight!

"Sorry, Peter. I can't help you", then leaves my mouth instead of, "Sure, no worries. I'll do it for you".

The navel chakra will suffer as a result of consistently giving away our power. In the example above, Peter asks you to type his assignment. If you really don't want to but you say yes anyway, you leak energy to Peter through your navel chakra. If you type the assignment because you want to, no energy leaks out. Same action, different consequence, because the energy is different.

Other interactions are more complex. You invite someone to your house to stay because they are teaching a seminar you want to go to. They hold it in your home and you get to do it for free. Then you find they have to come a couple of days earlier than planned. They expect you to feed them, and not only that. They want you to buy special food for them *and* cook it. You need two dozen red roses for the seminar centre piece; roses happen to be out of season and it sets you back $80. They are also incapable of cleaning up after themselves or making a cup of tea. What do you do? Do you become a doormat or do you apply the 'what-would-be-fair-for-my-best-friend-to-agree-to' test? When you are clear about what you are prepared to do and what goes beyond that, you can calmly say to the person that none of this was communicated to you and could they please contribute in whatever way you think is reasonable.

Taking back our energy is always a good thing to do, and when we do this we recapture our freedom and power to be who we want to be, not who others want us to be.

Lines of energy to others: who are we feeding?

Part of the process of reclaiming our power is to become aware of the people who are being fed from our energy. It is very common for people to build energy cords between each other through the navel chakra, and it is usually an uncomfortable situation. When the cords are cut, our energy flows better and the other person feels free also. We have more vitality and the dynamic between the people who were formerly attached shifts, often markedly. Later in Part III I show you how to cut energy ties.

Reflexes

The navel chakra has the fastest reflex response of any of our energy centres. It can respond to a situation faster than we can think. Good martial artists, racing car drivers, sword fighters and many other sports people require this level of reaction. It is as though the navel chakra knows what is going to happen without the need to think about it. Activities which require a quick response rely upon and develop the navel chakra.

I was doing a radio interview one day and the guest before me in the studio was the world yo-yo champion. He was able to do thirty-nine tricks in one minute with his yo-yo. Do you know how fast you have to be to do that? He gave us a demo in the station and I was amazed. The other thing that struck me about him was the size of his navel chakra. It was several times larger than his other chakras. He had undoubtedly been born with a large chakra and quick reflexes, and his obsession with the yo-yo and doing tricks at speed had honed them.

Digestion

When the navel chakra is strong, people have good digestive health. If the navel chakra malfunctions, the person has a tendency to suffer from constipation. I once saw a woman who had been constipated more or less for forty of her fifty years on the planet. Terrible! Her navel chakra was very sluggish and hardly moving. I energetically cleared it out and revved it up – rather a lot because she had been suffering for such a long time. Unfortunately, it was a bit much because the poor woman ended up with diarrhoea for two weeks, virtually non-stop. She rang me up absolutely delighted! This was a rare thing for her to experience and she had lost weight into the bargain. She was one happy customer.

Digestion of high vibrational energies

As well as physical forms of digestion, the navel and meng mein are able to digest refined types of prana.

The back of the navel, the meng mein, is a pumping station for energies arising from the base chakra. The more energy that floods into the base chakra, the more some of it will inevitably wind up in the meng mein centre. For this reason, it is always important to make sure that the client does not have high blood pressure, a sign of an already enlarged meng mein chakra, before putting copious quantities of energy into their base chakra.

Hanging off the front of the navel chakra are small secondary navel chakras, which are also relevant to the digestion of energy. They store it. When high vibrational states of consciousness are attained through meditation, some of the energy can be siphoned into the navel chakra then down into the secondary navel chakras, or dan tien. Instead of just dissipating, the energy is available for when you need it later.

Blood pressure

When the meng mein chakra is out of balance with the other chakras, blood pressure is affected. The meng mein chakra of a healthy person is usually between a third and a half of the size of the back heart and back solar plexus chakras.

When the back of the navel becomes bigger than that, the blood pressure goes up. When it is too small the blood pressure goes down. I have frequently used a blood pressure monitor in classes to demonstrate the effect of a quick healing on the meng mein chakra to reduce blood pressure. It really is quite astounding how quickly the physiology of the body reacts to subtle energy.

Super strength

When the solar plexus and meng mein become large, the person becomes emotionally excited and physically powerful. The person can be violent or have super strength. This sometimes happens with mentally ill patients who need several people to restrain them. It is also the kind of energy and excitement that can occur when there is an emergency. In such instances, people seem to develop strength they would not normally have, such as when a mother can lift a car that has run over her child. A huge surge of energy floods into the solar plexus and meng mein chakras, giving terrific strength for a short period.

As I have said before, if the meng mein centre is too big then hypertension or kidney problems commonly result. Thus it is not advisable to deliberately pump up this centre just to develop strength.

A little knowledge can occasionally be a dangerous thing. I knew a woman who had a daughter who was a champion athlete. The mum decided, having learnt a bit about the etheric body, that revving up the girl's meng mein chakra would help her performance by making her super strong. She did this several times per week over a period of months; the girl became very ill and no one could find a cause. Through Divine grace, the mother took the girl to a very experienced energy healer who immediately saw the problem with the swollen meng mein chakra. The healer began the process of rectification of the meng mein chakra and the girl got better.

NAVEL CHAKRA EXERCISES

To enhance the navel chakra try the following exercises:

1. *become involved in a sport or hobby that requires fast reflexes, like tennis, squash, ping pong or, if you are more daring, martial arts and other such sports.*

2. *At the end of your meditations, imagine that you can push all excess energy into your navel chakra. Imagine it filtering down into the holding sacks, the secondary navel chakras. Tell it to store there.*

Navel chakra affirmation

I am powerful, I easily digest life.

I take my power back from wherever I have invested it.

I call my spirit back now.

Chapter

12

THE SOLAR PLEXUS CHAKRA

The solar plexus chakra is located in the hollow where the two lower ribs meet at the front. It is quite close to, and directly underneath, the heart chakra. The back of the solar plexus chakra is directly behind the front, around the base of the shoulder blades.

The Promises

- Self love and acceptance.
- Courage.
- Inner strength.
- Daring.
- Healthy drive, desire to win.
- Perseverance.
- Tenacity.
- Assertiveness.
- Ability to be successful.
- Control over desires (being able to stick to a diet).
- Non-attachment to things.
- Healthy self interest: not being a door mat.
- Warrior energy (peaceful warrior).

The Fears

- Feeling of not being good enough.
- Poor self-esteem.
- Poor self image.
- Feeling of being unworthy.
- Lack of self love.
- Selfishness.
- Fear of failing (and of succeeding).
- Lack of courage.
- Addictions.
- Feelings of isolation.
- Fear of getting angry and acting inappropriately.
- Getting stuck in negative emotions and animosity.

- Fear of negative emotions.
- Resentment, rage and victim mentality.

The Consequences

- Experiencing the fears listed above.
- Door mat (please walk over me).
- Physical issues with the diaphragm, pancreas, liver, gall bladder, stomach and lungs.
- Diabetes, stomach ulcers, hepatitis and heart problems.

Relationship To Other Chakras

The solar plexus chakra is usually the most congested chakra in most people. It has a loud voice, and its concerns often sabotage us from making sound assessments of people, situations and opportunities. As the solar plexus chakra is cleansed, purified and strengthened, great benefits are noticed physically and emotionally. Self love and acceptance grow to replace many of the fears listed above.

Igniting The Solar Plexus Chakra Spirit 'Mine-ing' business

The solar plexus is the part of us that says, "I am going to do what I want to do. Hang what you want, and hang the consequences".

When we look at the world through the consciousness of the solar plexus chakra, we are looking at it from our own egocentric position. We are concerned about looking after ourselves. We want to know what is in it for us, and how we will personally benefit from any given interaction. There is no compassion, it is about being strong, courageous, daring, and persevering until you get what you want.

The solar plexus is the centre of consciousness through which we know ourselves to be individuals, living as separate beings in the physical world. Because we are separate from each other, we have a need to compete with each other for the seemingly scarce resources that we find on Earth. The motto of the solar plexus is: What is mine is mine, what is ours is mine and what is yours is mine, too.

The warrior

We have relied upon warriors as far back as human history extends. Warriors need to be focused on surviving (base chakra), having fast reflexes (navel chakra) and looking after themselves (solar plexus chakra). We don't really want them to be feeling their feelings and stopping to smell the roses, as they are going into battle. We want them to stop the rest of us from being pillaged, raped and plundered. Who cares if they have a big heart. Make sure they have a big solar plexus.

Today we still rely on our warriors to keep the peace, be they police, armed service people, spies or security guards. Warriors need a large strong solar plexus to be able to survive these occupations. Obviously, we do not want authoritarian bullies, which is why we want warriors to have a strong solar plexus chakra which is in balance with all of their other chakras, rather than having unregulated and dirty energy centres.

Whilst we want a strong and healthy solar plexus, it is undesirable to have a solar plexus chakra that is too much bigger than the other chakras, because excessive severity, selfishness and lack of compassion for others can result.

Competition

The competitive nature of our society is based on the solar plexus model of the world. If the heart were in charge, it would be a whole different story. A heart-centred society, as we will see below, would be one where cooperation and mutual benefit are emphasised, rather than the win/lose model that is so often presently experienced.

Dealing with fear. Yipes!

We all have different areas in which we experience fear. Some people are afraid of public speaking, others are afraid of spiders or being confined, others fear disease, and some fear commitment in relationships. People commonly experience fear for the safety of those whom they love. The more I have learnt to overcome fear, and been aware of others doing so, the more I am convinced that the main thing that we are fearful of is fear itself. When we stare our fears in the face, they mostly vanish.

I used to be scared of heights, which became a bit of a problem when I started snow skiing in my early twenties. It took tremendous courage for me to even get on a chairlift, and then I had a nasty tendency to scream unless someone had their arm around me. This was okay when I was skiing with my husband, but when he got sick of my slow pace (he is a very good skier), off he would go, and I would have to find a stranger to put their arm around me. It is amazing who will hug you when you calmly tell them that you will scream if they don't!

After a while I stopped being scared, and now I am able to take my kids on chairlifts without even thinking about it. Through facing my fear I developed a measure of courage that I did not previously possess.

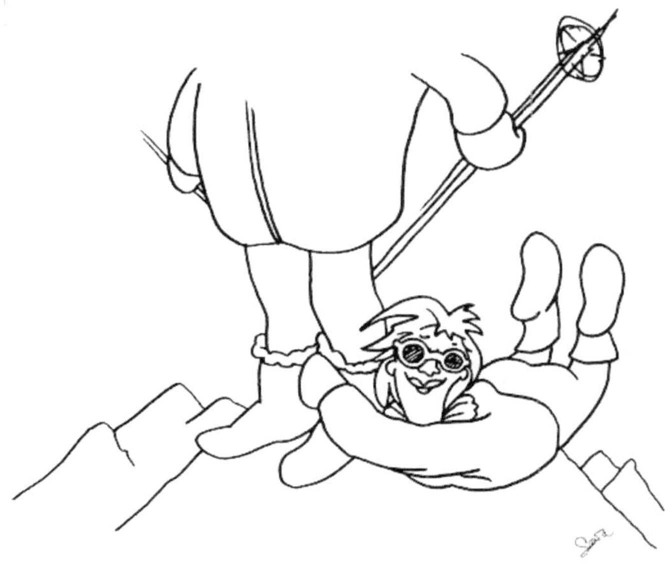

I feel safe

Heli-ski nut

One of my friends, Jason, was a very successful academic. He had a very large passion for skiing. Every year, he would finish his professional work around the end of November, spend December and January working as a ski instructor in Aspen and then spend February doing what he really loved, which was heli-skiing. This involved groups of people being flown in a helicopter to the top of an otherwise unskiable mountain, jumping out of the helicopter and skiing down slopes that no person in their right mind would even attempt.

I had occasion several times to have lunch with Jason and most of his conversation was about the risks, fears and dangers associated with his hobby. He would tell me about all the people he knew who had died heli-skiing since he started. Jason's lower chakras were all really big. His solar plexus, centre of courage, was huge. He was able to face more fear than I will ever do, and thus he was able to develop more courage than I will ever have.

Overcoming fear develops the solar plexus, and the inner strength of the individual.

Emotion soup

Just as fear and courage have a symbiotic, yet opposite, relationship to each other, so do many other emotions: happiness and sadness, jealousy and acceptance, derision and respect, anger and peacefulness. 'Opposite' emotions are not actually different from each other, they are just ends of the same spectrum. Thus, apparent opposites such as happy and sad are polarities of the same thing. The way to access the positive end of the polarity is to be able to deal with the negative end without judging it as unacceptable.

In Western society, we are often urged to rise above the so called 'negative' emotions. Well, if we were to rise above them, where do we go and where do they go? 'We' go into our minds, where we cannot feel anything. 'They' usually enter our solar plexus and over time worm their way into our vital organs. Then we get sick. It is much better to actually learn to deal with our emotions in a healthy way. Healthy ways to deal with our emotions involve radical acceptance, feeling the energy of the emotion and moving through it, getting stronger as you do so. For further information on how to deal with emotions as 'pairs' or 'opposites', read *Free To Be Me* by Barbara and Terry Tebo, and attend their seminar of the same name. I cannot recommend it highly enough. I present similar information in a different way in *Yoga of the Mind* and *Empowering Relationships* seminars.

Negative emotions per se do not make us sick. Suppressing them does. Dumping all over people is also not recommended, because people will dump back, and you could end up with a war on your hands. Dumping negative emotion, which is usually an anger based behaviour, will dirty and inflame the solar plexus. In time, it will cause the solar plexus to become much bigger than the other chakras. If the anger is suppressed, then some of the load commonly flows through to the meng mein chakra, and high blood pressure can result. Either way, excessive anger, whether vented or suppressed, causes imbalance which can result in a somewhat egocentric personality.

There are healthy ways to deal with anger, and I do not believe anger per se to be bad. It is the judgments about people, events and things that make us angry which need to be looked at. Anger is a very strong and powerful force of energy which, if properly understood, can be a wonderful evolutionary force. It becomes the fire in the belly of the Goddess, bringing needed change to our lives.

You have to love me because I don't

People with very depleted (no energy) and congested (dirty) solar plexus chakras often have very little self-esteem. The lack of self-esteem causes them to be very self critical and judgmental. People who need to go to great lengths to prove how good they are, suffer from an inherent feeling of lack of worth, which is a common characteristic of those with problems in the solar plexus.

Memories and experiences to do with self-esteem and self image are stored in the solar plexus. Many people who have bulimia and/ or anorexia have a very dirty solar plexus. They have terrible and unrealistic attitudes about themselves. The distortion in their solar plexus causes them to view themselves as unacceptable, fat, revolting. They starve themselves to become what they do not believe themselves to be: acceptable the way they are.

When we have little self love, it is like a proclamation to the world that we are not good enough. We tend to attract experiences and people who will confirm that we are right. The way to change this is to change the basic energy which is held in the solar plexus. I am good enough, and I deserve to love me. I love me, I am worth loving and, if you like, you can love me too.

Desires

Addictions are largely solar plexus issues. The back of the solar plexus chakra is especially affected. There are ways to help people deal with addictions by normalizing the solar plexus, which has usually become damaged. This damage, like ripping fine fabric, allows in energies which interfere with the usual operation of the individual's will. These energies get 'fed' by the energy released when the person engages in the addictive habit. The 'impulsing' from this diseased energy tends to bind sufferers to their addictive habit. ('Impulsing' is a non-verbal energetic cue to think, feel or do something. It can come from our Higher Self, other people or other kinds of beings.)

Every addiction has control over the person who is addicted. This control is maintained because engaging in the addictive activity changes the consciousness of the addict. For a few minutes, or sometimes hours, a better world appears, as a rush of good feeling accompanies the addictive activity. Afterwards, the old problems resurface and are compounded by the addiction.

The sufferer feels worse about themselves, and so indulges once more in the addictive behaviour to deaden the pain.

At the other end of the scale is asceticism. Mastery of the solar plexus is achieved by not getting caught in desires. Ascetics are people who have little or no desire for the usual pleasures in life, and many are like this because they have exerted control over the solar plexus through their higher chakras. They have replaced these desires with a blissful consciousness attained through oneness with their Higher Self. They have swapped one bag of goodies for another.

Others who seem to be without desires have really only buried them. They have not connected to Divine bliss and are just living in denial. This has a deadening effect on our energy and will lead to problems later.

Somewhere in the middle is the ability to understand that we are creatures of desire, but we do not have to be prisoners to it. As we develop and grow, the things we desire naturally change. The process can be quite graceful. Developing the higher centres, particularly the ajna (which holds the higher will, see chapter 15), provides great benefit for those who suffer from addictions and rampant desires.

Success

A big solar plexus chakra can manifest as a strong desire to win, and this often leads to success in the world. If it is tempered by an equally large heart, there will be compassion in the way this is done. If it is not matched by a big heart there is a tendency to harshness and severity. Results can be seen as paramount, and can justify unsavoury, even cruel, means.

The solar plexus in most people is the toughest and dirtiest of our chakras. To get off all the built-up garbage, it usually needs to be hosed out with the energetic equivalent of a fire hose. Nevertheless, when this is done, the solar plexus can become a pillar of strength, helping us to manage self care in a positive way.

SOLAR PLEXUS CHAKRA EXERCISES

PURIFICATION: ENERGY HEALING

The solar plexus responds well to energy healing. This can have a profound effect not only on our disposition; it can also help to release anger and other negative emotions. It is advisable to have a series of treatments with competent energy healers so as to facilitate a clean-out. Think of it as a 100,000 kilometre service!

CLEANSING MEDITATIONS

Certain meditations can rapidly remove toxic energy. The Archangelic Meditation, which was developed by Geoffrey Russell and myself, assists in the removal of energy garbage. This guided process asks you to anchor energy and repeat healing affirmations which, when combined with the breath, release garbage. After that, the mind is calmer, and heightened states of bliss are achievable because the blocking effect of the negative energy is removed.

SELF-DISCIPLINE

Self-discipline is simply the practice of doing what you say you are going to do, even when you really don't feel like it.

Rather than trying to leap mountains, start with something small as an exercise in self-discipline. This could be something physical, like going for a walk every day, or even watering the garden every day. The solar plexus benefits by overcoming the resistance which says, "Sod off, I'm not doing it" on those difficult days which I am sure even saints have. Doing what we said we would do, particularly when we don't want to, develops self-discipline and self-respect. It also develops the solar plexus chakra.

Solar plexus affirmation

I am confident, strong and courageous. I respect, accept and love all of me. I love me all the time.[5] *I am innately lovable and gorgeous.*

---

[5] This means even when I am fat, broke, angry, sad, addicted and fail

13

THE HEART CHAKRA

The heart chakra is located in the centre of the chest between the breasts, about level with the armpits. The back of the heart chakra is directly behind this, about mid shoulder blade level.

The Promises

- Feeling love and joy.
- Being able to give and receive ever increasing amounts of love.
- Access to development of the crown chakra, and higher energy centres.
- Doorway to soul consciousness.
- Sensitivity to feeling subtle energy.
- Receptivity to energy healing.
- Appreciation and gratitude.
- Contentment, happiness, peace and harmony.
- Personal freedom through forgiveness.
- Development of higher qualities such as compassion, mercy and kindness.
- Development of empathy.

The Fears

- Fear of giving or expressing love.
- Not able to forgive everyone who has ever hurt us or caused us pain.
- Unable to release grudges.
- Not accepting and releasing grief.
- Not accepting and releasing sadness.
- Fear of allowing people to get closer to us than they ever have before.
- Fear of losing love.
- Fear of being emotionally hurt.
- Fear of feeling the pain of others.

- Unable to overcome the fear that if we give up our fight or our grudge, we have failed and are nothing.

The Consequences

- Holding grudges, thus tying up our energy with other people and past situations.
- Inability to hold down long term relationships.
- Heart attack, heart disease and other heart problems.
- Lung problems.
- Issues with the circulatory system.
- Thymus problems.
- Repetitive strain type conditions in the arms.
- Not understanding where others are coming from.
- Emotional insensitivity.
- Inability to sense or perceive subtle energy.
- Lupus and other auto-immune diseases.

Relationship To Other Chakras

The heart chakra has two fascinating interrelationships with two other chakras, the crown chakra and the solar plexus chakra. The heart chakra is an exact replica of the inside core of the crown chakra, on top of the head. Thus, whatever is going on in the heart chakra is also going on in the crown chakra. The clearer the heart becomes, the clearer the crown chakra becomes, and the crown chakra is the front door to spiritual connection. Therefore, it is the heart that is the front door to that connection also.

The second important relationship is that between the heart and solar plexus chakras. The solar plexus chakra is about the 'separate' self, and the heart chakra is about connecting to others through love in such a way that there is only one self and 'we' are it. The solar plexus is about fears and the heart is about love. They are like opposites in some respects, and they have a strong influence on each other. When the solar plexus is bigger it overrides the voice of the heart, and when the heart chakra is bigger, it overrides the voice of the solar plexus. Our worldview becomes amazingly different when we make the evolutionary leap to develop a big heart chakra. Love becomes more important than it has been before, and we are on our way to learning to live in harmony and peace with ourselves and others.

Igniting The Heart Chakra Spirit Giving and receiving love

When we become attracted to someone and enjoy their company, our heart attunes to them and the heart chakra opens to a certain degree. Over the course of a relationship, this opening can continue. Usually this occurs incrementally, as trust is developed and it feels safe to 'open up'. If that trust is betrayed, there is a tendency to 'clam up'. What clams up is the heart chakra. I have seen people build energetic brick walls in front of their hearts to stop anyone ever hurting them emotionally again. The problem is, the brick wall stops love flowing in or out, and the person so afflicted feels isolated, lonely and often depressed. This happens when someone is unable to move through their fear of being emotionally hurt again on account of a past bad experience.

Through a process of spiritual awareness and chakral cleansing and healing, the brick walls can be taken down and gentle heart opening exercises can begin. As the heart opens, feelings of sweetness and happiness tend to emerge.

Even where there is no major trauma, the minutiae of daily life can have a clogging effect on the heart chakra. Small upsets which are part and parcel of everyday life can have a cumulative effect, clogging up the heart chakra and slowing it down. It is hard to feel loving and caring when the heart is feeling heavy and closed.

In successful relationships, there are often successive periods of heart opening and then stabilization, of coming together and then moving apart, before coming close again, even more so than before. Whilst this process continues, the relationship will grow. When one or both parties decide (unconsciously) that they will not open the heart any further, and not let the other any closer, relationships tend to stagnate. It takes courage to move closer in intimacy with a person. Here, the relationship of the heart to the solar plexus is important, as it is the solar plexus that holds the key to self-esteem and courage. Courage is needed to take the next step towards opening further to intimacy.

The health of the heart chakra has a direct bearing on the quality of our intimate relationships, and on all our different types of love relationships. With regular energy healing, we can improve the quality of our relationships.

Compassion and empathy

Compassion is being able to have awareness and concern for the distress or suffering of other people. Empathy is the ability to actually feel what the other person is feeling.

Many people are natural empaths. They are so attuned to emotional energy that they do not really know whether they are feeling their own feelings or someone else's. This is not as unusual as it might sound.

Emotions are not solid, rigid things. They flow like water, and emotional tides are flowing all the time. They flow from and through one person to another. Mass hysteria operates this way. People 'catch' how others are feeling, then they feel it too.

In our household, we are all empaths. When someone is feeling bad, we have a practice that allows us to simultaneously 'isolate the emotion' (see Part III, *Ignite Your Spirit* on how to do this), and the one who is left with it is the one who is reacting to a life event.

The rest of us suddenly stop feeling it.

The heart thrives on being of service to others, being compassionate, being kind to others, and feeling joy and peace. In many households such values are not displayed to children. Getting things done and coping with the day-to-day physical needs of the family can take up all the parents' energy and there is not much left over for kindness and compassion. Therefore some children do not learn by example from the home environment how to be compassionate and loving. You only need to listen to conversations that people have in public with their children to realize that tired, stressed adults produce tired, stressed kids. As a society we will need to address this shortfall sooner or later, and to develop strategies to help people to open their hearts as a normal part of their education.

Forgiveness

Grief is held in the heart, as are grudges. Whilst it is easy to find ourselves in situations where, following conflict, we are at odds with other people, the journey of life is about finding ways to forgive whatever has happened, allowing the heart to operate fully again so it can express love to everyone in our lives. If you really want to you can find a way to forgive anything. The forgiveness is for us, not for the other person.

We all have stories about people who have hurt us, done us wrong and invaded us. These stories range from disputes about where Christmas lunch will be this year, to being raped, battered, abused and conned.

When bad things happen it is natural to want to process it, to come to terms with it. Sometimes this is really difficult to do; we feel that we are victims to something over which we had no control.

Without wishing to underestimate the emotional pain that these types of events cause, we do in the end have a choice in how we deal with it.

If we identify with our history of hardship year in year out, then it lives continually in our consciousness, and everything is affected by it. The darkness stays with us. In this way, we can become very stuck. We can cut ourselves off from many of the pleasures and possibilities that life has to offer, because we cannot get over the event that hurt us, or the people who hurt us. Our identification is bound up in our position as a victim to the person or event in the past.

As a child I used to wonder how Infinite Intelligence could allow all the pain and injustices in the world to occur. It didn't seem fair. Having since discovered the concepts of reincarnation and karma, it all makes a lot more sense. Karma belongs to us, not to the Divine. Whatever we give out will come back to us either in this life or the next. It is our free will, it is always our choice how to respond to life. Karma is the spiritual law of cause and effect. Every action causes an equal reaction back to us. The reaction might not happen in the same lifetime.

My belief is that if something bad happens to me, then it is because I caused something bad to happen to another person in another lifetime. Thus I have to experience the consequences of my actions. Either the exact same thing will happen to me, or I will contract a disease or disability of the same energetic nature.

If a person is born with a terrible health challenge, then there are probably past life events which have karmically necessitated this type of affliction.

Many times during healing sessions, people have come face to face with perpetrators of violent and ugly incidents in this life. They have then travelled to another time and place and seen the rest of the story, how they themselves have treated the perpetrator in the past when the tables were turned and the perpetrator was the victim of the client. Having witnessed this, they are then guided through a forgiveness exercise, by which they can ask for forgiveness from all the people that they have hurt in this or any other lifetime. Then they are often able to make the decision to forgive those who have hurt them in this life.

The law of karma cannot be trifled with, but it can be affected by the operation of a higher law, which is the law of forgiveness. Jesus was the ultimate teacher of this law. He said that we should practise forgiveness, "turn the other cheek".

This is much harder to do than to feel rage, vengeance and intense emotional pain. Some people become defined by their tragedies and hang onto them as though there is no other alternative. Even suggesting that they might try forgiving the person who has hurt them causes an angry and accusatory reaction: "You wouldn't ask me that if you knew how bad it has been for me". Actually, I would.

For many years Angela was involved in very serious domestic violence. In the end, her husband broke her neck and she nearly died. I met her six years after her neck was broken. She had terrible neck problems and huge unresolved fears for her safety and that of her children. She feared not only her ex-husband but lots of things. She had been unable to even contemplate another relationship. She identified herself as a victim of domestic violence. Her speech was littered with references to "DV" (domestic violence).

Her energy body was very shut down. There were huge problems in her neck and heart centre. The key to it was the heart. This woman had courage, and was really over being tied to her past, but could not see any way to get free.

I helped her through a forgiveness process in the presence of strong soul energy. As she forgave her ex-husband, a huge black cloud of fear left her heart and disappeared. She underwent several treatments and attended all my seminars. Within twelve months her broken neck, which had been very disabling, was better and she was able to lead a normal life, which included playing tennis and lifting weights. When she thought of her ex-husband it was with compassion rather than fear.

Her two teenage boys had been badly affected by the domestic violence and had also been exhibiting signs of the same type of behaviour. As Angela healed, so did her children. They both calmed down, and started behaving better at school and helping her around the house.

Jenny is a highly intelligent clinical nurse specialist who was going through a nasty divorce. Her husband had stolen $30,000 from her bank account before taking off with a younger woman. He gambled the money and she had not been able to get it back. Bitter divorce proceedings ensued, and after two years the situation was grim. She came to me and we did some healing. Crucial to that healing was the exercise of forgiving him, and breaking the energetic ties that held her to him.

Within two hours of the healing, her ex-husband rang her, apologised for taking the money and offered to pay it back. They met in a café a week later, and true to his word he produced a cheque for $30,000. They sorted out their entire family law dispute and filed terms in court shortly thereafter.

For Angela and Jenny, and hundreds of other patients, the process of forgiveness is truly healing. Both these women cleared their energy, called back their spirits from the past and became free. Both experienced the return of their zest for life. Angela went on to help many others who had experienced domestic violence by sharing her story and her recovery with them.

Family history of heart attack

I have treated many people, particularly men, with congested heart chakras who have a strong family history of heart disease, and death through heart attacks. Upon close questioning, it is clear that the people concerned have emotional patterns whereby expressing how they feel is difficult, if not impossible. They are not really in touch with how they feel, and perceive other people to be "far more emotional than I am". In many cases, it also becomes apparent that the person being treated is very similar to their relatives in this respect. Often the style of parenting they experienced was somewhat harsh, in the 'spare-the-rod-and-spoil-the-child' pattern of upbringing, which responsible and caring parents adopted, thinking they were doing the right thing.

Even when clients said to themselves, "I will never be like my Dad!", they often realized that they were in fact much the same towards their own kids as their parents were towards them. Without conscious and sustained effort to change, the tendency is to become just like the people who raised us, including the parent or any other relative who might have offended us greatly when we were kids.

When changes are made in the patterns of how emotions are held, the patterns of disease which the person is likely to suffer from tend to change also. Thus, if you have a history of heart disease in your family, do not despair. Follow the guidelines for healthy heart maintenance, including a healthy diet, exercise and no smoking. In addition, however, it is really important to learn a new way of expressing emotions. For many people, it is necessary to start feeling emotions. It is also advisable to have energy healing on the heart chakra.

Spiritual development and higher consciousness

Almost always, the energy of terribly painful events that we have been unable to get over or forgive is held in the heart centre. This not only blocks our emotional life, it blocks our entry to the amazing spiritual world that can be accessed through a healthy and activated heart chakra.

In order to develop the higher centres and access the energies of love, it is necessary to deal with the sorts of issues that are set out above. In spiritual terms, the heart chakra is a gateway to higher consciousness. When the heart is open, purified and activated, a whole new world presents itself.

Receptivity to energy healing

The heart is a major centre of sensitivity to subtle energy. Those who have small or heavily congested heart chakras are less likely to be receptive to energy healing. They will decide in advance that it does not work, and if that is their decision, so be it. No healer should ever override the free will of a patient.

Clairsentience

Clairsentience is the ability to feel energy through our hands. People who complain that they are unable to feel energy through their hands will find a blocked heart chakra is often the culprit. When the blockages of the types referred to above are cleared, new sensitivity bursts into life.

Not everyone is naturally able to feel energy through the hands. Some people perceive energy differently. They might perceive it visually, or they might hear it.

When I first learnt energy healing, I could not feel the energy with my hands. The perception of energy is subtle, and clairvoyance when it starts is also pretty subtle. I did not realize for some time that I was actually seeing the energy. I thought it was just my usual thoughts or imagination, which would trot from one place to another without much control in the early days. After about a year of practising healing I was able to feel it through my hands as well as see it. Compared to my students, I was a very slow learner. In the Ignite Your Spirit seminars, our students have about a ninety per cent likelihood of feeling energy the first day they try. This high success rate is partially because we make it easy for them; but it is also because the whole human race is evolving and becoming more aware of subtle energy. This can be seen from the plethora of alternative healing modalities that have sprung up, and the widespread acceptance of energy healing by a sufficiently sizeable portion of the population.

Enjoyment of being of service: giving

Giving is a delicious experience. When it is done with an open heart, a great deal of satisfaction and joy is derived from it. Giving is an exercise which develops the heart chakra. Further, it is very beneficial for future karma. If you give to others, you can be sure that you have developed the karmic entitlement for others to give to you. What you give out you get back. Giving is a way of depositing grace in our spiritual bank accounts.

If we want to receive things, we have to give first. If you want more money, give money to worthy causes, spiritual teachers or local charities. If you want good service, give good service in what you do. If you want love, give it. If you want friendship, give it to others first. This principle applies to whatever you might want from life. If you want it, whatever 'it' is, try giving it to others and see what happens.

The heart-solar plexus relationship

We said earlier that the bearer of a large solar plexus was likely to be in the 'mine-ing game'; that is, what is mine is mine, what is ours is mine and what is yours is mine also. Those with very large solar plexus chakras which are out of balance with the other chakras often like to take rather than give.

Those with big hearts are the opposite, and tend to give everything, even to the point where they do not know when to stop. They may be creating fantastic and good future karma, but they might not stop to enjoy it when it comes. Living in a physical body means that physical needs have to be met, and the base and solar plexus chakras together create the consciousness to ensure this is attended to.

The heart is the centre of giving, but giving without receiving is very draining. Further, giving too much without receiving is often a symptom of deep feelings of unworthiness. The person derives a sense of self worth only from serving everyone around them. When people have big heart chakras and not much of a solar plexus chakra, they can risk becoming doormats for others to walk all over.

A strong and developed solar plexus chakra, founded on healthy self-esteem, is an invaluable asset when it energetically supports the strong and developed heart chakra. When a large, healthy, loving and giving heart chakra is supported by a healthy, self loving and worthy solar plexus, there is a balance in the energy field. Giving and receiving flow in a graceful, self-sustaining dance.

Somewhat paradoxically, once the heart chakra and those above it are fully activated and developed, manifestation of the things we need in life occurs differently and much faster. Ultimately, letting go of the voices of the lower chakras opens doorways into areas of life that are awesomely magnificent, whereby that which is desired comes almost instantly into manifestation. Great chakral development is required for this; but great chakral development is part of the eventual future for every single one of us.

HEART CHAKRA EXERCISES

THE ACT OF FORGIVENESS

1. Invoke. (See Part III)

2. Do pillar of light meditation (see chapter 4). Run energy up and down the pillar three times.

3. Think of a person you have had conflict with that you would now like to forgive.

4. Say, ***"I call on the spirit of [insert person's name]"***. Call three times.

5. Say, ***"Thank you for being here and clearing our energy today"***.

6. Say, ***"[Name], I now forgive you for everything that you have ever done to me that has hurt me in this or any other lifetime or plane of existence. I forgive you, I forgive you, I forgive you. Through the grace of God, so be it"***.

Breathe in, release.

7. Repeat step 6 three times.

8. Now attend to the other side of the equation: What you may have done to them.

9. ***"[Name], I now ask that you forgive me for everything that I have ever done that has hurt you consciously or unconsciously, in this or any other lifetime or plane of existence. Please forgive me, please forgive me, please forgive me. Through the grace of God, so be it."*** Breathe in, release.

10. Repeat three times.

11. Imagine lines of energy joining you to the other person.

12. Try to imagine where they are. Raise your hand and bring it down like an axe to chop the lines, and say, ***"I set myself free and reclaim my spirit now. I declare all karma between us ended by my sincere act of forgiveness. May you be free and may all good things happen for you. Through the grace of God, so be it"***. Breathe in, release and imagine all the lines of energy disappearing.

13. Do Archangelic Meditation (see my website www.shaktidurga.com for details) or a meditation that floods your energy field with light to replace the unwanted energy with love.

14. Give thanks.

GIVING

"Love all, serve all" is a primary spiritual teaching.

Any kind of giving or service work can be done to develop the heart chakra. As generosity becomes a way of life, the heart flowers, relationships are enhanced, compassion and empathy are developed, and warmth and love flow.

Heart chakra affirmation

I am loving, kind, compassionate, merciful, warm.

I forgive all who have ever hurt me in this or any other lifetime.

I am love, I am love, I am love.

Chapter

14

THE THROAT CHAKRA

The throat chakra is found at the base of the throat – in the hollow at the front and protruding from the back of the neck.

The Promises

- Speaking what is true for you.
- Having good communication skills.
- Knowing how to implement the ideas of the other chakras.
- Filing and categorizing skills.
- Good organizational and administrative skills.
- Ability to carry out detailed activities.
- Planning, making improvements
- Studying.
- Creativity which requires detail, such as painting and writing.
- Logical, ordered thoughts.
- Ability to act with appropriate timing in the physical world.
- Being orderly and neat.

The Fears

- Worry.
- Over meticulousness.
- Stubbornness.
- Fear of speaking your truth.
- Not being a good listener.

The Consequences

- Going deaf, or other hearing problems.
- Throat problems.
- Mouth, teeth and tongue issues.
- Being disorderly in your life.
- Having messy cupboards and drawers.

- Not being on time frequently.
- Speaking problems.
- Tonsillitis, laryngitis and asthma.
- Stubbornness.
- Neck stiffness or other problems.
- Inflexibility.

Relationship With Other Chakras

The throat chakra is very connected to the sex chakra. Both have to do with creativity. They operate as a team.

The throat is also the interface between the mind and the heart. A lot of pressure can be put on the throat when the heart and mind do not agree with each other, and when we do not speak that which is in our heart.

Igniting The Throat Chakra Spirit Speaking your truth

Have you felt a lump in your throat when you become emotional about something that you are talking about, or need to talk about? Have you ever felt your throat constrict when you are nervous or unsure of what you have to say? These sensations are a result of the chakra vibrating in response to the emotion in such a way that we can actually perceive it.

The movements of the chakras are not usually felt by people until they are pointed out. With practice I have become very aware of my chakras and how they respond to different people and situations. Much can be learnt through this awareness.

The more we practise gently speaking our truth the easier it gets. Not that it is always easy, even when we practise it. If we speak our truth when we are angry no one will ever hear it. All they will hear is an angry solar plexus. If we want to be heard, it is necessary to first let the anger pass through our bodies and then, when we are calm, speak as clearly as we can about what it is that is troubling us, beginning with "I feel...". No one can ever say we are wrong when we are only saying how we feel. It is much more effective than sentences that start with, "You are...", and your throat chakra will thank you.

If we want to express love to someone, we can tell them that we love them (throat chakra), but they will only believe it if the statement carries the energy of love (heart chakra).

Systems and neat drawers

People who have huge throat chakras can be perfectionists. They place great store in detail and are very detail oriented. You look in their wardrobe, and everything is in perfect order. The shirts are hung neatly in colour order on matching hangers. Their underwear is ironed, neatly folded and matching.

Whilst I envy this order, the downside is that these people often expect themselves and everyone else to be perfectly orderly all the time. This makes relating really difficult, because no one ever does things well enough for them. Perfectionists can be a pain in the neck (also controlled by the throat chakra) when they do not know when to accept things and people as they are.

I remember a wonderful aboriginal woman called Alice, who worked as a teacher's aide in a school for underprivileged indigenous children. Part of the function of the place was to feed the children, so that at least once per day they had a decent meal. Alice had a huge heart chakra and found herself unable to follow rules which dictated that children should be fed strictly according to the guidelines and not hugged. It was also not her way to be very interested in the detail of things.

Alice's colleagues, who were very detail focused, were angered by her "deliberate flouting of the rules", and continually criticized her for her 'lapses', which included slipping the children lollies or cake, and talking to them instead of doing her work as an aide. They thought that rules were there to be followed, that standards should be maintained, and that Alice should definitely fall into line. The children, needless to say, loved Alice and would do anything for her, including their school work. They confided in her, and she gave them a great deal of affection and support.

Had her throat chakra been the most developed chakra like her colleagues, Alice would have been naturally good at implementing neat systems. She would have been logical, and far more well-ordered, with better organizational, management and administrative skills. She would have naturally followed the rules, with a place for everything and everything in its place.

Instead of that, her heart was huge, and so it spoke with a louder voice. Alice loved giving to those kids. She thought rules were there to be bent when compassion or common sense required it. She lacked rigidity, and her colleagues saw this as weakness. They started to get on her case about doing this and not doing that. They insisted that she be more disciplined and do things by the book. To her this meant ignoring the obvious emotional needs of the children, which she found really hard to do. She ended up suffering from acute anxiety as a result of the relentless and irreconcilable pressure she felt herself to be under. She also ended up with a really sore neck and was unable to work. Doctors were unable to diagnose her problem, but it was all there plain as day in her throat chakra.

I represented Alice in her compensation claim. Luckily, she drew a judge whose heart chakra was almost as big as her own, and she was very successful in her claim. After the litigation was over, we discussed alternative healing, something she had not previously considered. I later heard on the grapevine that she had ended up having energy healing with a local healer in her area. She released all the stress energy, and healed her very battered throat chakra, after which her neck got better.

When we become, or when we are required to be over meticulous, as in the case of Alice, worry can accompany it. The throat chakra goes into overdrive and, depending on how we cope with it, we may develop issues in the parts of the body that the throat looks after, including the neck which can become stiff.

Lower conscious mind

The throat chakra controls the lower conscious mind, which is the part of our intelligence that computes things. It uses logic and is great for meticulous details, planning, studying, painting and higher creativity.

The throat chakra is no good at seeing the bigger picture and cannot fathom abstract thought. Also, it is not capable of factoring in loving kindness or compassion. Still, train timetables would not operate, libraries would not function, filing systems would not be possible if it were not for the fact that we have throat chakras. The throat chakra is important for carrying out the functions that our other chakras agree need to be achieved.

People with throat chakras which far exceed the development of their other chakras make wonderful followers of rules, and systems implementers. However, they should not be placed in positions where a broad overview is required, because this is not the function that they are energetically attuned to and they will not do it well. They can become highly critical and unable to see the woods for the trees. The ability to take a global view is more the province of the ajna chakra.

THROAT CHAKRA EXERCISES

LEARNING HOW TO SPEAK YOUR TRUTH

Some people use speaking their truth as an excuse to dump all over others. This is not what I mean. If you calmly and gently express how you feel regularly, then there will be no huge build up of stuck energy that will cause you to want to dump. Talking about how you feel in appropriate ways will strengthen your throat chakra and enhance your overall strength and development.

SINGING

If you use your voice to bring beauty into the world, then the throat chakra develops amazingly quickly. If you feel the throat chakras of most famous and successful singers, you will notice that they are very huge.

I like to sing chants. I can feel my throat chakra responding even if I think about singing chants. The more I chant, the less I suffer from sore throats or laryngitis, which plagued me earlier in my life.

DEVELOPING A ROUTINE

If you find that your life is a bit chaotic and that details do not get attended to, then it might be time to get some help to support your throat chakra. Getting systems in place for how you do things saves a lot of hassle, and this is assisted by being organised and orderly. This will then support the functions of the other chakras, and it will help you to operate in the physical world in a smoother way.

Throat chakra affirmation

I speak my truth.

I am true to my Higher Self and to my destiny.

I easily manage my life properly and thoroughly.

Chapter

15

THE AJNA CHAKRA

The ajna chakra is found between the eyebrows. Some people call it the third eye.

The Promises

- Alignment of your will with the will of your Higher Self and your Guru. The ability to exercise free will.
- Understanding abstract concepts and principles.
- Being able to take a broad view,
- Can understand and weave together many diverse issues.
- Quick overall grasp of situations.
- Alignment of all body systems.
- Deep nourishing sleep.
- The Master Chakra, which can align all chakras
- Developing objectivity and accurate perception.
- Development of wisdom from knowledge and intuition.

The Fears

- Difficulty in learning how to perceive higher guidance.
- Unable to discern, let alone trust higher guidance.
- Unable to let go of emotional fears long enough to allow the ajna to do its job.
- Fear of listening to higher consciousness
- Fear of aligning will with your higher soul

The Consequences

- Chaos
- Lacking a satisfying direction in life.
- Not being able to see the woods for the trees.
- Problems with the eyes, nose and sinuses.
- Pituitary and endocrine gland problems.
- Cancers.
- Allergies.
- Multi-system disorders within the body; that is, everything starts going wrong physically. Hormonal imbalances.
- Sleeping problems.

Relationship To Other Chakras

The ajna chakra can control all the other major chakras. It can light them all up in the proper sequence and to the proper degree. One can put energy into all parts of the etheric body through the ajna chakra.

Igniting The Ajna Chakra Spirit Will

Will is a soul faculty that is expressed within us through our chakras. The majority of people have a will that is dominated by the solar plexus. However, as we evolve and the upper chakras become bigger, the ajna plays a more important role in the exercise of will. The will expressed through the ajna chakra is to do with the will of our Higher Self, and is far more reliable in terms of an overall perception of the way forward than is the will of the solar plexus, which is driven by immediate desires.

When people have small ajna chakras, they are easily controlled by the will of others. As the ajna chakra grows and becomes strong, the experience of being out-willed by others diminishes.

Addictions

Addictions are dangerous because they remove our free will. No real addict has control over whether or not they gamble, take drugs, and so on. By increasing the size of the ajna chakra and dissolving the energy of the addiction, which is usually found in the solar plexus chakra, much can be done to diminish it. This in turn allows for an easier transition from addictive behaviours to 'normal' physical behaviours, which must accompany the energy treatment.

Abstract concepts

Through the ajna chakra humans have the capacity to understand abstract concepts and principles. Examples of this include philosophical questions, competing paradigms of thought, matters to do with belief, and understanding the nature of things from a global perspective rather than from the perspective of detail (throat chakra perspective).

Master plan

Someone with a well-developed ajna chakra can take an overview of a situation and delegate the things that need to be done, whilst maintaining the objective, and overall management. This type of skill is needed by managing directors of companies, project leaders, and so on.

Seeing things

When the ajna chakra is strong and developed, the person will have certain clairvoyant ability. This ability, however, is reasonably limited, as it is particular to the astral realm of thoughts and emotions. It is possible to see the thought forms of others through this centre, and also to see areas of darkness or disease in the physical body.

Higher forms of clairvoyance are not found within this centre. Higher forms of clairvoyance include visions of angels, ascended masters and the brilliant light of the inner world.

Chaos

When the ajna chakra is compromised or blocked, there is an inability to take an overview of our lives or situations in which we find ourselves. If the ajna chakra is blocked and this manifests in the physical dimension, it can cause major chaos throughout the systems of the body. People with serious medical conditions, particularly cancers, and conditions where everything seems to be going wrong, often have ajna chakra malfunctioning.

I once treated a wonderful man called Bill. He was seventy years old and had been a successful businessman all his life. Now he was retired and lived on his beautiful property with his beloved wife, deeply involved in his passion for painting.

Bill found out he had prostate cancer. He was told by doctors that the cancer had spread throughout his body and was inoperable. There were tumours on his lungs, leaning up against his spinal cord and in many other places. He was told he had three months to live.

I became Bill's practitioner, not because he had any faith in energy healing, but because he felt desperate. He told me so directly. I explained to him that there were no promises because a lot had to do with his karma. If he had developed sufficient good karma he would have the grace to recover, otherwise he would not. Either way I was confident that the healings would give him a better quality of life, no matter how long that life might be.

Bill entered the spirit of the healings with gusto. He was insatiable in his desire to learn about his energy body and how it related to his feelings, to others and to his physical body.

To treat his energy body I used pranic healing as well as IYS Energy Healing. After the first healing, Bill noticed feeling hugely tired, which was soon followed by a big surge of energy that remained until he saw me a week later.

During the second week of healing, we dealt with the urgent things, such as the growth of the metastases. Through a process of clairvoyant observation I was able to see many of the tumours and I used energy to dissolve them. He told me he had x-rays, which he brought with him on his next visit. I compared my clairvoyant observations to the x-rays and found that they were pretty close. Again we dissolved the tumours, and a few days later he had new x-rays taken. After seeing the new x-rays he rang me very excited, because many of the tumours had disappeared.

Bill continued having treatment more or less regularly for about six months. Much of it had to do with normalizing his ajna chakra, which had gone haywire. As well as the cancer, Bill had a heart condition, high blood pressure and a condition where there were not enough platelets in the blood. Bill's attitude was wonderful. He was a fabulous client because he took responsibility for his own healing.

In respect of the heart problem, we discussed his relationships with those he loved, and he had a big problem with one of his children, from whom he had become estranged. We went through a forgiveness process, which he did from the bottom of his heart, and several weeks later his son called him out of the blue. They had a reunion and Bill's heart centre picked up enormously. His heart pain diminished.

Bill had followed my advice and began meditation soon after his therapy started. During the healings, he found he could see colours with his eyes closed. At first they were greyish, brownish colours which he did not like. As he cleared, his colour palette expanded and he could see magnificent blues, greens, and yellows, much of which he ended up painting. His ajna chakra came back into alignment, and so did Bill's life. Some of the problems were not able to be completely eradicated, and he had to continue to take blood pressure medication and medication for his platelets. However, the quantity was reduced substantially and the conditions were much less severe. His heart became strong and the cancer disappeared altogether. He even got back his libido.

When the energy body starts to become congested or depleted, problems in one area flow over into other areas as well. None of the energy centres can really be looked at in isolation. The meridians are part of the reason for this, as the countless lines of energy within us keep all of our systems together and fuel our physical, emotional and mental selves.

AJNA CHAKRA EXERCISES

DEVELOPING THE AJNA

The eyes are connected to the ajna chakra and can be used to help develop it. This exercise is really simple, but really powerful. All you have to do is look up to the left then down to your left nipple, then up to the ajna chakra, down to the right nipple and up to the right. Thus the eyes have drawn a W. Then reverse it, starting at the top right and doing a backwards W, ending at the top left.

After that, sweep your eyes and breathe in and out three times through the ajna centre.

PROLONGED CONCENTRATION

Concentration on one thing for a prolonged period of time can develop the ajna chakra. Successful professional people tend to develop big ajna chakras, as they concentrate on the problem at hand, as well as big throat chakras, as they deal with the detail.

There are many meditations which encourage concentration on one thing only. These include focus on a flame, the breath or a single sentence or word (mantra). These meditations will all help to develop the ajna chakra.

Ajna chakra affirmation

I am in tune with the Divine will.

I exert my will lovingly and with respect.

I have free will and I honour the free will of others.

I am aligned with the Divine plan of love and light.

Chapter

16

THE CROWN CHAKRA

THE crown chakra is found on the top of the head. It is the front door for the entry of energy from the soul and higher dimensions, and the entry point for Divine energy.

The Promises

- Thinking in ways that are beyond logic, transcending what is known.
- Knowing through direct understanding without being taught.
- Entry point for spiritual energy.
- Centre of spiritual connectedness.
- Spiritual heart of Divine love.
- Understanding inner spiritual teachings.
- Understanding mythology and archetypes.
- Understanding continuous consciousness.
- Access to other lives, akashic records.

The Fears

- Fear of Divine union.
- Fear of being separated from God/Goddess.
- Fear of expanding into your full potential.
- Thinking you are going crazy.
- Not wanting to experience consciousness that is outside the rational mind.
- Not wanting to experience consciousness that is outside thought at all.

The Consequences

- Brain problems.
- Headaches (solar plexus is also often involved).
- Problems with the pineal gland.
- Inability to draw in high vibrational spiritual energy.

- Closed front door to Divine connection.
- Stress and anxiety.
- Inhibited spirituality.
- Insanity.

Relationship To Other Chakras

The central core of the crown chakra is, from clairvoyant observation, a direct replica of the heart chakra. As the heart chakra grows and develops, so does the centre of the crown chakra.

The crown chakra does not really start to operate fully until after the heart chakra has reached a certain level of clarity and development. This can take lifetimes. By developing the heart centre, and thus the crown chakra, many things that were previously not known become known. In turn, the development of the crown chakra eventually activates other chakras above our heads. This is when the magnificence of Divine connection can be experientially perceived by the individual. (I discuss the chakras that sit above our heads further in my book *Yoga of the Mind*.)

We said earlier that developing the heart chakra is achieved through loving service to others. Because the crown chakra is dependent for its development upon the development of the heart, loving service is essential for the growth of the crown chakra as well as for the growth of the heart chakra.

Igniting The Crown Chakra Spirit

Remembering our distant past

When the crown chakra is sufficiently large and clean, we attain vastly expanded perceptions, including memories of previous lifetimes. The records of every single thing that occurred in every lifetime that we have experienced are contained in the akashic records. Someone with a really big crown chakra can read these for you and give you clear information about all kinds of things, including why a conflict exists and how it can be extinguished.

In my healing practice, it is common for people with severe relationship problems to find themselves flashing back to another time space.

We have all been everything either in this life or previous lives: the good guy, the bad guy, rich and poor, royalty and beggars. Sometimes it is helpful to understand the root of a problem and to find where it originated, which may be several lifetimes ago. However, unless the past life has a direct therapeutic bearing on this life, I really am not all that interested. There are more than enough things to occupy me in the here and now.

Our souls are genderless, and incarnate as men or women depending on which will suit the purpose of the soul at the time. This makes sexual discrimination pretty silly, because if you are a man you have been a woman before, and vice versa. Racial discrimination is also ridiculous when you consider we incarnate all over the world in all kinds of cultures through our many lives.

When we die with unresolved big issues with other people, we tend to have to incarnate with the very same souls in our lives again to sort it out. Usually these are the people that you take an instant dislike to when you meet them. You experience an unconscious memory of what a pain in the butt this soul was last time round. Similarly, people we have an instant liking for are old friends from past lives.

The soul that might have been your brother in another life might be your mum in this life. If you severely upset him when he was your brother, don't expect to have a 'sweetness and light' relationship with your Mum now. So much pain can be explained and resolved through delving into the past like this. We've already seen in previous chapters the amazing results of healings where forgiveness is offered for the events of the originating conflict in past lives. I have had hundreds of people claim that they have been able to resolve conflict right after a healing that releases the energy from the dispute through all lifetimes.

I met a lovely woman, Judy, who went into a business partnership with a friend, John. Neither Judy nor John had a great deal of business experience, but both were very talented musicians. They decided to form a band and make a CD. Judy gave John the money to purchase the necessary computer equipment, including a sound studio, which he did. John moved from interstate to work with Judy, and then the unforeseen problems started.

The equipment broke down, and turned out to be faulty. It had been purchased second-hand with no warranty, and John and Judy, who had virtually no capital, were each blaming the other. John felt aggrieved because Judy spent so much time caring for her toddler instead of being with him writing music, and Judy felt upset because John had purchased equipment which, it turned out, was overpriced and unable to be used for the project. Tempers flared, and both said things that they later regretted.

John was so angry he could not even speak to Judy in the end. He came to me for a healing and almost immediately I saw the root of the problem. John and Judy had been brothers in a past incarnation, living in the East and involved with the spice trade. Their father was a wealthy merchant with ten children, of whom only three survived him. Those three were John, Judy and the man who had knowingly sold them the faulty computer equipment, Doug.

As brothers at the time, John and Judy were the responsible ones, and the father left the entirety of his sizeable estate to them. Doug did not picture in the bequests. John and Judy then ended up in a power struggle as to who was going to run the large family business; they were so busy fighting with each other that business was not actually attended to. In the end, Doug saw an opening and was able to shaft both John and Judy, whom he saw as having cheated him out of his share of the inheritance.

John proceeded to do a forgiveness exercise, forgiving both Judy and Doug in that lifetime, in this one and through all lifetimes. The energy that came out of him was amazing, and the change in his focus and consciousness was huge. By the end of the session he was able to feel compassion for Judy, and he and Judy were able to sort out their differences and move on.

Peace

If the solar plexus is the biggest chakra and is running the show, revenge will be more important to a person than achieving peace. If the heart and crown are running the show, peace will be more important than revenge. Developing the heart and crown chakras not only develops the sensibilities of the individual, it also develops a mass culture of people who are attuned to peace. Whether the conflict is between individuals or races of people, the events of past lives are as relevant as the events of this lifetime. When all of this can be cleared, the results are amazing. Let us hope for a future where direct spiritual assistance can be given to thousands of people at a time, on both sides of a conflict, so that peace can be restored in troubled areas.

When a sufficient number of people have made the transition from a solar plexus dominated energy body to a heart and crown chakra dominated energy body, world peace is likely to be permanent.

Oneness

When the crown chakra is really activated during advanced states of meditation, there is a sense of being larger than the body. The feeling is as though the physical body no longer exists, as though a vast sea of bliss surrounds and envelops us.

Sometimes brilliant light is visible. Sometimes angels are visible, or heavenly music can be heard. The feeling this brings is indescribably good. We feel oneness and love with all.

At times large concepts float into our brains, as do solutions to problems, and we completely understand them. This can lead to breakthroughs in any creative enterprise, or in the direction of our life.

With practice anyone can learn to access the inner light and bliss. Think of the windows on your personal computer. You might have half a dozen windows open at once, but only one at a time is usually in view. You have to minimize it to see the others. When you minimize it, it is still there, but you can see something else. If you keep minimizing and closing files, eventually you come back to the essence, the beginning. It was actually always there, but was shrouded by the other images.

All our chakras jostle for position in our consciousness. "Think me, think me", they say. The sex chakra is constantly feeding us with thoughts of sex, the base chakra says "think secure", the throat chakra says "think details", the solar plexus is busy arguing with people and wanting to be fed, and so on. They are like screens up and active on our desktop.

Our consciousness is like that which exists beneath the windows, and our chakras are like the windows we open to the world. When all of this is stilled, when the voice of all chakras are minimized, what is revealed is that which was in you all along: bliss, tranquillity, deep peace, happiness and love. If you couldn't see this before, you were simply not looking in the right place. You had to look underneath everything else inside of your own self.

It is helpful to have a teacher who can activate the crown to assist you with this self discovery, but this is not necessary if you practise sufficiently.

Cosmic consciousness

The crown is the centre of cosmic consciousness, of knowing through direct perception. This kind of knowing is beyond logic, which is only capable of saying, "If this, then this"; that is, linear thought, the way that a computer brain operates.

The consciousness of the crown chakra transcends what we usually call the mind. This part of our being is totally ignored in our education system. Crown chakra development allows us to obtain a super-fast overall grasp of a situation. The logical, or lower, mental faculty is really only meant to implement and apply the crown chakra realized information or solution, and materialize it.

Inventions occur because people tap into universal intelligence, where every idea already exists. They just resonate with it, and it pops in through the top of their heads. Even more amazing, when the time for a new idea has come, it is likely to fall into several heads in different parts of the world at the same time. Then there may be a dispute as to who actually came up with a certain idea or invention.

Inventions do not arise from logic, because logic needs a framework that is already known. They come from the Divine Void, the reservoir of wisdom and knowledge, and our crown chakra just plucks them out. Testing the invention and making sure it works are areas that need the assistance of both the ajna chakra and the throat chakra.

New concepts enter our consciousness the same way as inventions do, through the crown chakra. Sometimes we can become aware of 'new concepts' that are as clear as a bell (though they are not really new, only human awareness of them is new). The 'new' concepts grasped can be so amazing that it could take us months or even years to work out how to explain it in a way that people are going to understand, because the idea has not been on the planet before. To get it out to others, it has to drop down through all the chakras until it is grounded through the base chakra, and then it goes back up to the throat chakra so that we can creatively express it in the world. It needs to be understood and broken down into parts (which the ajna can oversee and the throat chakra can do) so that the throat chakra can comprehend the detail.

Crowning glory

When the crown chakra becomes very large and strong it clairvoyantly looks just like a golden crown on the head. In the old days, monarchs, high priests and cardinals would wear golden crowns or mitres on their heads, signifying large, developed crown chakras. They were referred to as 'we' (the royal 'we') because, through their very developed crown chakras, they were connected to their Higher Self, spiritual teachers and angelic guides. Thus, these rulers were literally divinely inspired. Their consciousness was well in excess of that of the ordinary person. They were revered as Gods because they had abilities and insights well beyond that of the ordinary person.

The golden crown placed on the head signified, to those who did not have the inner clairvoyant eyes to see, that the person wearing it had a golden crown chakra. The law as stated by these beings was considered to be divinely inspired, and thus worthy of being implemented and followed. This tradition of priest kings was evident amongst the many nations who regarded their emperors as Divine.

Whether or not our current monarchs and cardinals are really meant to be wearing golden crowns is something for the reader to ponder.

Mythology and archetypal energies

Every culture has its own myths about things that are of fundamental importance to it. These myths usually cover things such as how creation occurred, stories of gods and goddesses, miracles, and stories of heroic deeds and strong hearts. There are also archetypes, through which we can become identified with different aspects of being human. (Dr Carolyn Myss writes extensively and wonderfully about archetypes in her book *Sacred Contracts*. The late Carl Jung and Joseph Campbell are also authorities in the areas of archetypes and myth.)

Through the crown chakra, it is possible to grasp the inner significance of mythical stories, which may seem like children's fairytales if our consciousness is not illuminated by the crown chakra.

A simple example is the story of Sleeping Beauty. The sleeping woman is a metaphor for the sleeping kundalini fire which lives at the base of the spine, referred to in various traditions as Shakti or feminine Divine energy. The prince (male energy, Shiva or Holy Spirit) 'kisses her' (touches Shakti) and she awakens into full life. The awakening referred to is the full awakening of all chakras, which occurs when the Shakti and

Shiva energy become one, and the kundalini rises up the spine to the crown chakra.

Because of the dangers associated with kundalini activation, we do not recommend people do practices to raise the kundalini until they have done years of purification. We also recommend that you do this under the direction of a competent spiritual teacher who can control the kundalini force. Very few people can actually do this. The results of premature activation of kundalini can be messy.

CROWN CHAKRA EXERCISES

MEDITATION

Meditation will develop the crown chakra. Having said that, saying the word "meditation" is like saying "animal". Do I mean rhinoceros or kitten?

Meditation techniques range from simple relaxation exercises to complex breathing exercises. Using meditation, we can cleanse ourselves, grow our energy body, concentrate on certain parts of our energy body, create our futures and clean up our pasts. The possibilities are almost endless.

Two wonderful meditations that will develop the crown chakra quickly are Twin Hearts Meditation by Grand Master Choa Kok Sui, and the Archangelic Meditation by myself and Geoffrey Russell. Any pranic healing instructor should be able to provide you with a copy of the Twin Hearts Meditation. To obtain the Archangelic Meditation, and listen to sound samples from it, go to www.shantimission.com. I have seen people's lives blossom within a few months of regular practice of these meditations. Some people alternate them, which is also great.

PRAYER

Those who pray regularly are unconsciously creating a strong connection to their souls and the inner Divine world. Every time they pray, the crown chakra is activated. Over many lifetimes the person will develop a huge crown chakra, and be able to attain the states of bliss referred to above.

HEALING ANGER

When we get really angry, the solar plexus becomes huge instantly, and the crown chakra closes shut tight. That makes us feel even worse, but it stops unlimited amounts of spiritual power from pouring in through our crown chakra and fuelling the dispute. In fact, this is a safety device built into our energy anatomy.

To recover quickly from the upsetting effects of getting really angry, chakral rebalancing or meditation will help. It also allows us to gain some perspective over the situation.

If one has a tendency to have angry outbursts often, the solar plexus develops as though the person was pumping iron in that region. It gets huge and out of balance with the other centres. Cleaning out the built-up energy, and building up the other energy centres so that they are as big or bigger than the solar plexus, will help. The person will feel happier, calmer and less egocentric. They will become more aligned to living a rich life where people love and respect each other, and live with ease and grace.

Crown chakra affirmation

I am one with God.

I am one with my Higher Self.

I and my Higher Self are one.

I am one with bliss. I am one with all.

Chapter

17

MINOR CHAKRAS

THERE are numerous minor chakras in the body. Every organ and joint has chakras. If you want to become a specialist physical body healer, it is strongly recommended that you learn about these minor chakras in addition to the major ones already discussed.

My own practice as a healer has more to do with psychological and spiritual healing, conflict resolution and changing an individual's consciousness. During IYS Energy Healing, significant physical healing very often occurs as well, and patients have experienced rapid recovery from things as diverse as lupus, heart disease, high blood pressure, arthritic pain, burns, cancer, tumours and cysts. These remissions and recoveries occurred because the physical problems were the consequences of unresolved fears held deeply within the chakras. When we dealt with and released the fears, and any blockages around them, the chakras operated properly again. They were able to feed energy into the body once more and it could easily heal.

I do not propose to discuss all the minor chakras. However, there are certain minor chakras that appear to have greater significance in Ignite Your Spirit healing than others. These are briefly described below.

Hands

We all use our hands a lot, touching things and people in the course of everyday life. Because etheric hygiene is not widely practised, we are likely to pick up dirty energy, or etheric contamination, from our surroundings and other people. Healers, massage therapists, hairdressers, nurses and other health professionals who are touching people regularly, need to cleanse their hands regularly to stop themselves from picking up other people's debris. Otherwise they might find themselves becoming moody and chaotic. Washing the hands regularly in salt water and cleaning them with rubbing alcohol after each patient will help greatly. Cleansing the hands using the sweeping techniques in Part III will assist also.

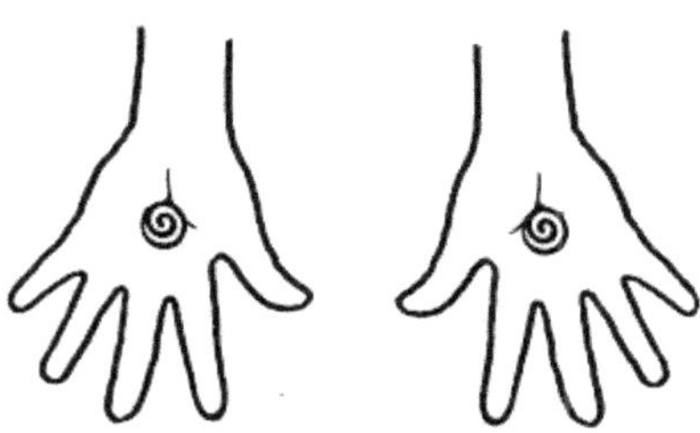

Forehead chakra

This is a small chakra located half way between the eyebrows and the hairline, in the middle of the forehead. It is usually about half the size of the other chakras. The higher realms can be perceived through this chakra. Such things as angels, fairies, inner plane teachers and masters are visible through this chakra when it is developed.

Whilst in most people this chakra is very small, this is not the case for everyone. Those with big forehead chakras have developed clairvoyance in other lifetimes, which is going to make it easy for them to activate this ability in this life.

When we say that someone has a very large forehead chakra this means it is large compared to the ajna chakra. These people have the natural hardware through which clairvoyance can easily be recognised.

Part of becoming clairvoyant is to have developed this chakra and the other upper chakras. The rest of clairvoyance has a lot to do with noticing and becoming acutely aware of subtle sensations that most people lack the stillness to observe.

This stillness is developed through meditation. The stillness to which we refer is like the difference between a choppy sea and a sea that is so calm and still that it looks like a piece of gleaming glass. In the former, not much is visible except waves. In the latter, many reflections can be seen just by looking.

The forehead has an important physical function in that it is the chakra that has the most effect on our nervous system. It also energetically feeds the pineal gland. When a person has any form of nervous complaint, including damaged nerves or multiple sclerosis, this is the main chakra to look at.

Paralysis and epilepsy can also be treated through this centre. I know a really powerful healer, Rev. George Dangel, who lives in Brisbane, Australia. I studied with George at one time and while I was with him, he was treating a man called Michael, who had been a paraplegic for six years. Michael had fallen from his motorbike in his twenties, just six weeks after his marriage. His arms and chest were powerful but beneath that his body was completely numb and his musculature was completely wasted from the torso down. His legs were like sticks.

I saw x-rays of Michael's spinal cord which clearly showed a broken neck, and the spinal cord severed. Over a period of about six weeks of regular treatment, George was able to induce sensation through Michael's body. Feeling gradually returned, first in his abdominal area, then in his sex organs and down through his legs, and when I saw him last, feeling was coming back into his toes. Further x-rays were taken which showed the bones had come back into alignment and the spinal cord had knitted back together. George had worked a miracle. Michael is now in intensive therapy, and is making the long journey back to being able to walk again by developing the musculature and the brain consciousness of walking, which had been wiped due to the severity of the injury.

George had treated the site of the break directly to regenerate nerve tissue, but he had also treated the forehead chakra to overcome the paralysis.

Perineum

The perineum chakra is located between the anus and the sex organs. It contracts when we squeeze muscles to stop the flow of urine. Because we sit on lots of seats, buses, ferries, public toilets, and so on, this chakra gets to be in contact with the energy of lots of other people, as energy lingers on surfaces after the people have moved on. We then sit on their energy, and some of it lands on our perineum chakra.

When the perineum chakra becomes blocked, prana is not able to flow from the Earth into the body properly, and from the base chakra down to the legs properly. Leg problems can sometimes be the result of blocked perineum chakras. When the perineum chakra is cleaned out, the base chakra is activated and energy can flow properly to the legs, alleviating or at least diminishing physical problems in the legs.

Minor Chakras

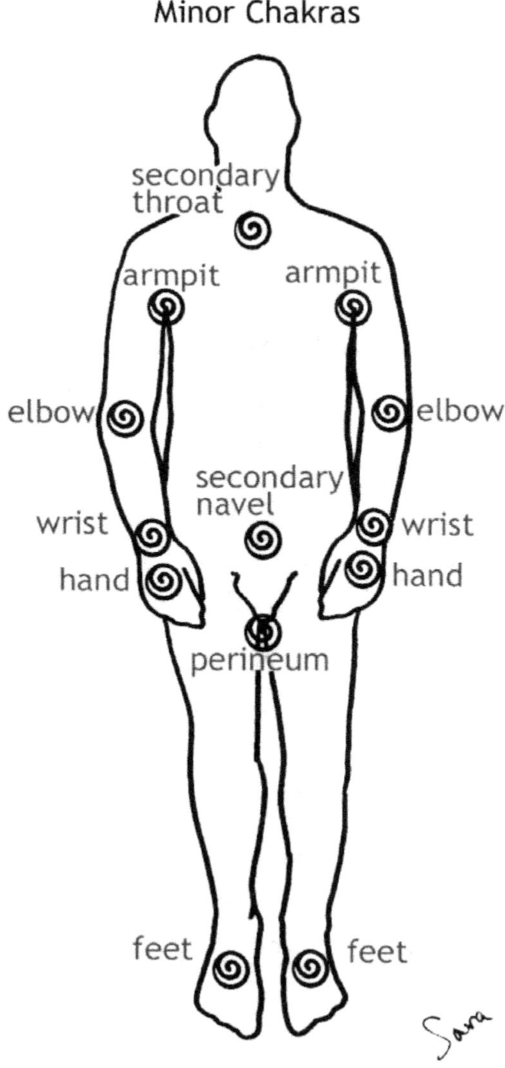

Feet

The feet chakras are important for grounding and stabilization in our life. In my experience, people with arthritic conditions often have very dirty energy in the feet; cleaning them out and soaking them in salt and coffee often relieves lots of aches and pains.

Sometimes I clairvoyantly see people's feet encased in concrete shoes, or other huge weights. These people want to move ahead in their lives but find they are unable to do so. Quite often the situation is freed up after they take off their concrete shoes in healing sessions.

In order to strengthen feet chakras, imagine big roots extending down from them into the Earth in a similar way to how this is done through the base chakra, as described in chapter 9. Imagine all dirty energy sliding out of your feet and into the Earth. Thank the unseen spiritual helpers whose job it is to clean up the mess that you release.

Spleen

Prana enters the body from sunlight through the spleen chakra. The spleen chakra then distributes the vibrations of the various colours of the sun to the chakras that require them. In this way each chakra is flooded with a different combination of colours, which gives them different properties and supports their various functions. You can find beautiful symbolic illustrations of the colours of the chakras in *The Chakras* by C.W. Leadbeater and *Miracles Through Pranic Healing* by Master Choa Kok Sui.

Physically speaking the spleen chakra feeds the spleen. When the spleen chakra is not healthy the person can experience a real slump in general wellbeing and vitality, and can even feel physically weak and depressed. It is a small chakra and very delicate, so treatment needs to be done slowly and gently. When too much energy is pumped through the spleen chakra people have a tendency to faint. It is safer to merely clean the chakra out, and allow it to regain function that way.

Armpits

People who have arm problems should clean out the armpit chakras. The lymph nodes in the armpits collect a heap of dirty energy and this stops the meridians that run down the arms from carrying the necessary amount of energy that the arms require.

By cleaning out the armpits, we also clean out the lymphatic system. Sluggish lymphatic systems, and fluid retention, can be assisted by cleaning these small chakras. In cases of fluid retention it is also advisable to drink more water and eat less salt.

Temple

The temple chakras have significance once we start to do advanced spiritual practices. They are doorways to expanded awareness, as are the back of the head, the forehead and the chakras in the tongue and roof of the mouth.

Head Minor Chakras

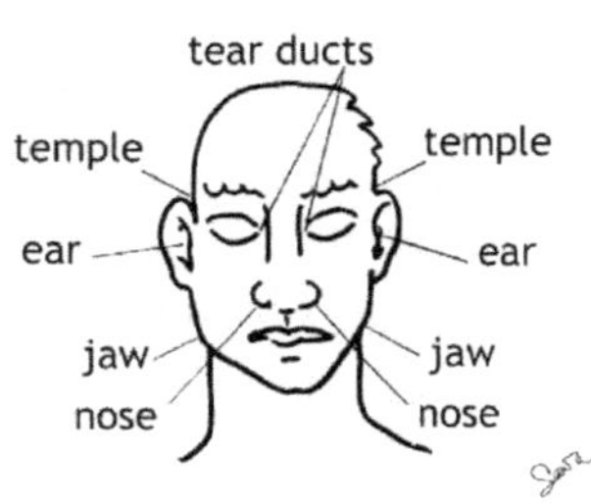

Chapter

18

PERCEIVING CHAKRAS

PERCEIVING chakras is somewhat easier to do than perceiving the aura as the energetic pushback from chakras is usually stronger, thus more recognizable.

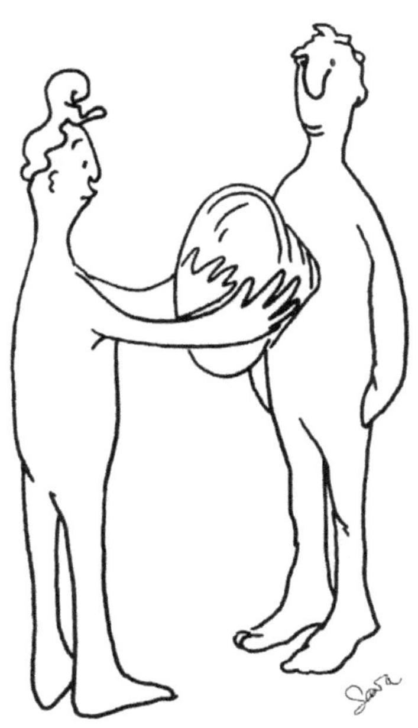

If you want to find out how big the chakra is, how much muscle it has, then place one hand on either side of it (see individual chapters for locations), gently pulsing back and forward until you can feel heat, pressure, tingling or a force field. Make a note of how far apart your hands are. This is the diameter of the chakra. The smaller it is the less power it will have. The bigger it is the more power it will have.

Measuring length

If you want to find out how much energy a chakra has in it at any given time, then place your hands about two to three metres from the body of the person and intend to perceive the energy of whichever chakra it is that you want information about.

If you have a feeling that your hand is being sucked in, then that chakra is depleted of energy. If you have a feeling that your hand is being pushed back, then it might be very bouncy and full of energy. If you have an uncomfortable feeling that your hand is in a dirty, crawly or prickly kind of substance, that means that the chakra is full of garbage and needs cleaning out. When it is cleaned out, it will automatically have a lot more energy in it, as the natural process of sucking energy in and out will occur when the blockages are removed.

Chakras full of garbage

Personal chakral profile

Use the following list to see the relative size of your chakras at the moment. Whether you are delighted or disappointed with what you find, remember that this is just the starting point. By following the exercises in the book you will be able to develop your chakras and the areas of your life that could do with some help.

If you do not get this first go, practise. Some people find it easier to practise on someone else's aura, and others find it easier to practise on their own aura, using the techniques set out above. Either is okay, just practise and you will be able to feel it. The feeling is very subtle at first, but nonetheless real. You might feel heat, tingling, a sense of pressure, cold, hollowness, or a sensation as though your hand is moving through very fine talcum powder. In our classes we assist people to strengthen their sensitivity, but this has to be done by direct contact, not through a book.

For ease of reference below you will find the figure displaying the location of the chakras. Remember meng mein ought to be half the size of the others.

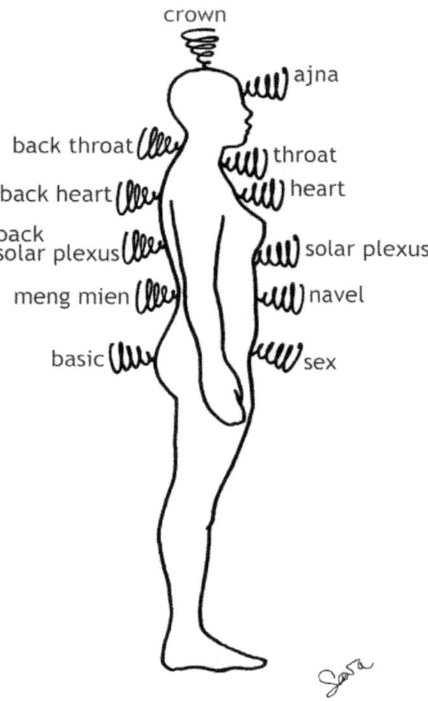

PERSONAL CHAKRA PROFILE

Chakra	Diameter	Length
Crown chakra		
Forehead chakra		
Ajna chakra		
Throat chakra		
Heart chakra		
Solar plexus chakra		
Navel chakra		
Sex chakra		
Base chakra		
Meng mein chakra*		

Note: Meng mein chakra should be no more than half the size of the others

Chapter

19

CHAKRAL DYNAMICS

THE chakras are storehouses of information and energy. Our perceptions of the world are coloured by the size and relative strength and clarity of our chakras. When we change our chakral configuration, our world changes because we are different. Expanded awareness is ours for the asking. Wellness, heightened understanding of our true natures and accurate perception are some of the gifts that come when we learn to change our chakral configurations.

Conflict and the chakras

It is interesting to look at conflict because it is something we all have to deal with. Most people have little or no training in how to handle it, and for most people, the way conflict is handled can be even more painful than the original matter in dispute.

Solar plexus

From the point of view of the solar plexus, you have done the wrong thing to me and I am angry. I am going to get you back. I might undermine you behind your back, or if I am really pushed beyond my limits, I might hit you. From the perspective of the solar plexus, you will deserve it, because you started it. The movie War of the Roses is a great example of this type of tit for tat escalating conflict, which usually ends badly.

If I subconsciously internalize the conflict in this chakra, I might suffer from diabetes, liver problems, stomach ailments or any of the other consequences listed in the chapter on the solar plexus chakra.

Meng mein

Often internalized pressure, stress, resentment or long term anger can travel to the meng mein chakra. Then, I will get kidney problems or high blood pressure, or I might get very tired a lot.

Heart

My heart chakra carries grief and sadness, and might become ill if it has to carry conflict for too long. If my heart chakra is developed, I will forgive the person with whom the conflict occurred and thereby free myself and all my other chakras, including the solar plexus, of the load that the conflict energetically places on me. My heart will transmute and diffuse the negative energy in the situation, no matter how huge it might be, and I will be free.

I will feel compassion for everyone involved, including you. I will even feel love for you. I want what is best for each person. My heart will be open to giving and receiving in a healthy way in order to appease the situation for the good of everyone concerned. If I look hard enough, there is always a way to find something in a deal for everyone. By just relying on my heart chakra, I might not be able to find the way immediately, but my heart's friend, my crown chakra, can.

Throat

My throat chakra stores up the details of what went wrong and talks to everyone who would listen about it to get sympathy and support. My throat chakra would be in cahoots with the solar plexus at this time, and would be coming from a 'poor me' perspective. Either that or it might suffer in silence and swallow down the rage that it wants to express. Then there are lots of throat diseases for me to unconsciously choose from, so that my rage can be expressed in my physical body instead of through words.

When my throat chakra evolves, grows and its vibration increases, it will listen more to my heart, provided my heart is big enough for its voice to be heard over the solar plexus, which is very noisy. Instead of storing all the details of the pain, my throat chakra will gather and store details of ways in which things could be fixed, and communicate them to my ajna chakra. It will speak to others only of solutions, and will not energize the problem by discussing it with all and sundry. It will help to keep my mind fixed on how to go about solving the dispute, instead of feeding it.

Ajna

My ajna chakra notices that my solar plexus chakra is angry and realizes that something in my physical life needs to be changed. Of course, my ajna chakra when highly evolved is conscious of more than just my physical life. My crown chakra will have told it about my distant past, and about the energy of the situation. Even before my ajna and crown chakras become this developed, my ajna is always able to take an overview of the physical situation, and it always does so without emotion. My ajna will chart a course, and so decide on a destination, what is to be done and how I am going to get there. When it speaks loudly, the other chakras fall into line, unless the solar plexus is really huge, in which case all we can do is wait until it calms down.

If the voice of my solar plexus remains very loud, and is dominant over my other centres, it may overpower the ajna and cause ajna to plot treachery. This brings darkness to me but solar plexus doesn't care. If the voice of my heart is very strong, ajna will hear it and will look at the situation from both sides and try to devise an overall solution which is fair. It will want love to be part of the overall equation for everyone. Then I can develop a plan that allows everyone to move forward and resolve the conflict.

If the ajna is unable to come up with a solution it turns to the crown chakra for inspiration. When the solar plexus is out of control and ruling the roost, my crown chakra is as silent as the grave. If my solar plexus is under the control of my heart and ajna, my crown has very effective, brilliant and divinely inspired strategies that will help everyone.

Crown

When my crown is sufficiently developed, inspiration will inevitably come. This may require me to develop patience and faith, for the perfect solution is in the mind of God/Goddess already, but may take some time to become physical. If the problem is offered to God, the solution will be given to me. Create a SFGTD box. This is a Something For God To Do box. In it put everything that is too hard to solve even with all chakras doing their best to sort it out. Meditate, pray, and do nothing about the conflict except imagine that it is all sorted out. Sooner or later, the solution will come into my crown chakra, which my ordinary human consciousness never would have thought of by itself.

Through the crown, inspiration is born. The ajna takes the big picture and understands it within my brain consciousness. The throat then understands what details need to be attended to and in what sequence. The heart feels light and beams happiness. The solar plexus, instead of feeling angry and resentful, feels strong and courageous.

You may ask, "What about the lower centres?" These become involved if their speciality enters the dispute, which is quite often the case.

Navel chakra

If the dispute involves trespass in the area of my own personal power, then my navel will support my solar plexus or my heart, whichever is the largest.

If my navel absorbs the energy of the conflict, it will feed it into the physical body that it controls, giving me tummy aches and other stomach problems.

Sex chakra

If the dispute involves sex, my sexual partner or threatens my position as a sexual partner, then my sex chakra will get involved and add all of its incredible energy to the dispute. If it decides to absorb the energy of the dispute rather than deal with it, then the dirty energy of the dispute is fed into my sex organs and bladder, and eventually, if I do this over many years, I will have health problems in these areas.

Where sexual relationships have been involved, disputes are often dirtier and more intense than will be the case in any other area. You only have to spend some time in the family law court to know that. This is because the energy of the sex chakra is so intense. Primordial chi is only found in the sex chakra, and there is no force like it on Earth. When it gets involved in a dispute, watch out. You better hope that your heart chakra is bigger than your solar plexus or the fur will fly!

Base

If the dispute involves money, threatens my security or my family, the base chakra will get involved. It will be impulsing me to be safe and have plenty of resources to support my physical life. It wants me to be secure.

If my base chakra decides to absorb the dirty energy of the dispute, then I might get back problems, money problems or depressed. If it is solid, strong and part of the harmonious chakral team, then I will have lots of vitality and a grounded approach to the implementation of the physical parts of the solution.

Positive teamwork

The aim of the game is to have all chakras developed, active and vibrant. When all chakras are activated and speaking from their own perspectives, the person is likely to be fairly balanced, with sufficient compassion and sufficient regard for the self and others. Things will be seen in an overall perspective. Communication will be flowing. Concepts will be easier to grasp. Inspiration and intuition will work effectively. We will be creative, spiritually aware, loving, deserving, sensual, sexy and responsible beings. Money will flow and we will be able to look after ourselves in the physical world.

Loving and living

As our chakras move into harmony and alignment, so do our relationships. If we have big clean balanced chakras, we will appeal to others who have big clean balanced chakras. Given that life is one big giant mirror, the way we really are is shown to us through how we experience others. If I am mean, I will find that everyone around me is mean. If I am generous, I will find that everyone around me is generous.

When we have a partner who has clean big bright beautiful chakras, they will glow, sparkle and glisten from within. If we see that in our partner, then it is happening inside of us, too!

Sometimes we think we are in love but aren't really. We are just in lust. If that happens, then clairvoyantly the only line of energy that can be seen between people joins them at the sex chakras. This will not be a long lasting or stable relationship.

When there is any kind of love between people, there is a connection through the heart centres. When two people are romantically involved and have a good solid relationship where love is present, they will meet through the heart and mind as well as through the sex chakra, and this can be seen clairvoyantly. This kind of relationship is a true treasure, and will be robust and satisfying. The resulting picture looks like this:

A more compassionate society

It is my view that to have a more compassionate and loving society we each have to become more compassionate and loving ourselves. Thus, we can all try as best as we can to develop the heart through giving and forgiving, service to others and financial support of those in need.

If you can find a way to give and forgive, I urge you to embrace it. It takes a little courage, a little faith and a healthy set of thoughts and beliefs, but you can do it. You will be enriched by the experience. Each little step taken in this direction brings humanity, as a whole, closer to the golden age of peace that we all want.

Energy healing for everyone

Now that we have an idea about energy anatomy, let us have a look at how we can clean, strengthen and balance it. Part III provides easy tools that both laypeople or trained healers can use to enhance their lives and grow their awareness. As a result, our bodies will work better, our minds will be calmer and stress can be removed as fast as we bring it on board.

PART

III

Chapter

20

IGNITING YOUR SPIRIT

What do we mean by healing?

Healing means to repair by natural processes (such as in the formation of a scar) to restore to health. There are many healing methods, many of which take years to study and provide detailed, specialist services which benefit mankind. Western medicine is excellent at alleviating the symptoms of many illnesses and accidents, providing drugs for when the body is not functioning properly, setting broken bones and surgery. Aren't we lucky to live in a time where such things are possible and relatively safe?

Ultimately, whilst western medical science provides a framework for healing, the body still has to heal itself. This is where energy healing becomes a great companion for medical science. Through energy healing we speed up the process of recovery. We can also work directly with the emotional and mental parts of ourselves.

It is strongly recommended that energy healing be used in conjunction with western medicine. Why not take the best from both approaches?

Below we describe a means of using Divine energy to assist in the regulation of our etheric body, and to dissolve emotional blockages. We refer to this method as IYS Energy Healing.

Why learn spiritual healing?

Of the people I teach, only about one third consider themselves healers. The rest are searching for something, just curious, or want to develop as people. They are quite surprised to learn that they have an ability to heal others as well as themselves. As they practise these techniques, they are delighted to find that their consciousness expands, and they become energetically stronger and more aware.

There are several good reasons to learn a form of spiritual healing. The main ones are discussed as follows.

Self Interest: Development of the etheric body

When we study challenging subjects that make our brains work, like maths or philosophy, our mental muscle strengthens. When we lift weights we build physical muscle. To become emotionally strong, we need to experience situations that challenge us emotionally. Performing spiritual healing helps us to develop a strong etheric body, and a stronger Divine connection. The bigger our etheric body, the more energy we will have to do whatever it is that we want to do.

If you do it right, performing spiritual healing will make your energy body bigger and stronger. I have seen students' energy bodies double in size in just twelve months by practising healing and using meditations that assist with balanced development.

Karma, baby!

When we build up a history of positive and loving action, it is like money in our karmic grace bank accounts. When we have healthy deposits in our grace bank accounts, we can withdraw it when required to help us through some really bad times. Healing is a wonderful way to develop good karma and a healthy grace bank account, which is essential if we want to live a life of ease and grace.

Develops multi-sensory awareness quickly

When we do spiritual healing, our multi-sensory awareness starts to operate. When I began doing healing work I was not clairvoyant. Within a short period I was able to perceive things when I was healing that I could not perceive at any other time, and the more I practised the stronger it became.

Feeling energy took a long time for me, but most people are able to do this very rapidly, either straightaway or within hours.

New career option

Some people are called to be healers as a career. Sometimes this can come as a surprise. No one was more surprised than me when I became a spiritual healer. For me it was a case of an interest becoming a hobby, then a passion, followed by a career. When we do things that we love, going to work ignites our spirits.

Helping loved ones

It is empowering to be able to help loved ones (and ourselves) if there is a crisis or chronic health problem. Instead of feeling helpless, we can do something. I have used healing on children who wake with high temperatures or stomach aches in the middle of the night. Cleaning their energy is usually enough to allow them to go back to sleep and get well. My son jammed his finger in the car door when he was three years old, and I was able to use icy cold blue energy on his finger to take away all the pain.

A friend I was skiing with fell and dislocated his thumb on an isolated mountain top. He was unable to get up from where he had fallen due to the extreme pain. I cleaned his hand and thumb and all the pain went. He was able to ski down the mountain. He then went to the doctor who reset his thumb.

I have relatives with arthritis and with IYS Energy Healing they are gradually making improvements in their degree of mobility. The pain is reducing and they enjoy increasing periods of pain-free time. It is a wonderful thing to be able to do this for those we love. The way I see it, basic healing knowledge is for everyone.

IYS Energy Healing is a form of Alchemy

Alchemy is just the transforming process by which one thing turns into another. Generally, several things get mixed together to form a new whole, as in cooking a cake. Raw ingredients are put through an alchemical process usually involving the element of fire (the oven) and out pops a cake. (Or, if you are me, something that may look like a cake but you could pave roads with it.)

During the Middle Ages, certain groups of spiritual seekers described themselves as alchemists. They told people that they were attempting to turn lead into gold. They were not doing this literally, but were engaged with processes to turn the lead within themselves into the golden light of Christ, love wisdom. Through purification, spiritual practices, meditation, prayer, right living and service to others, they were transforming themselves. Why make up the lead into gold story? Because they had to cover their tracks to ensure that the church officials of the day did not find out that they were pursuing their own form of spirituality. It may have been the end of them!

IYS Energy Healing has evolved through time and the influences of many spiritual teachers. The way we use it today results in rapid change in the lives of those who embrace it. Here we give you the building blocks of how it is done. For those who wish to become healers, or who want rapid transformation, we recommend the Path of Ease and Grace seminars. (Don't even think of doing these seminars if you want your life to stay the same.)

IYS Energy Healing: How it is done

First, grab yourself a plastic container and put some water and a couple of tablespoons of salt in it. Have it next to your patient so that you can flick energy garbage into it. Now you're ready to start. The steps that you will be learning are as follows:

1. Connect
2. Focus
3. Scan
4. Flow and Clean
5. Flow and Fill,
6. Scan – check your work
7. Seal and Save
8. Cut and Give thanks

STEP 1: Connect

Just as there are bugs in the physical world, similar types of things exist in astral and etheric form. Before we launch our consciousness out of the physical realm, it is wise to invoke for Divine assistance and protection. It is like putting on mosquito repellent before going outside at dusk in summer.

Invocation provides protection by surrounding you with high vibrational energy, which flows from the non-physical beings that you invoke.

If you are Christian you can call on Jesus, Mother Mary or any of the Christian angelic beings and saints.

If you are Buddhist you can call on Buddha or Quan Yin. If you are Hindu, call on Krishna, Shiva, Vishnu, Durga, Ganesha or any one of the hundreds of other deities.

If you are Muslim call on Allah, Celts can call on Brigit, and so on. If you have a spiritual teacher or Guru, call on him or her. I am Sagittarius and love a party. The way I see it, Buddha was a Hindu, not a Buddhist, Jesus was a Jew (as was his Mum), not a Christian. Quite frankly I don't think any of them could care less what religion we are, so long as we did our best to exercise loving kindness and non-injury. Thus, I call on many of them. The effect is amazing.

What is more, every time we invoke, we increase our own vibration and form stronger connections with these loving beings. When I invoke, I feel a tingling sensation on my crown chakra, like being out in the rain or under a waterfall, but it is not cold.

We also call on our own soul and Divine self, not because they are absent and need to be called in, but to place our awareness on that immense part of who we are and to strengthen our conscious connection there.

If you relate more to nature you can invoke the spirit of creation and the elements, or the Archangels and so on.

Here is a form of the invocation that I use, which you can add to as you feel is appropriate. Focus on the crown chakra and the meaning of the words as you say them.

I call on the Supreme God, Divine Father, Divine Mother

I call on my Soul and Divine Self

I call on my guides, teachers and friends in the Spiritual Hierarchy who love me unconditionally

I call on [name particular teachers, for example Jesus, Babaji,   Sri Sakthi Amma]

I call on the Healing Angels

Thank you for being here and sharing with me healing,   light, love, guidance and protection,

and may I be a clear channel for light, love, power and healing energy.

Through Divine grace, so be it.

If I am working on another person, I often add a safety clause to my invocation. I say at the end of it something like: *"I ask that if I make any mistakes during this healing that you fix it up. Thank you"*. For obvious reasons, I do this under my breath. Don't want to scare the clientele. However, it can be very important to add, as the following story might illustrate.

When I first learnt healing I treated a woman who had arthritic hips. She told me that she was suffering from osteophytes. This refers to bony growths in the joints, which cause pain when the joints are used. To expel the lumps I used a colour of energy that is like dynamite. As it entered her body I saw it change colour to an energy that is like cement. As this happened I realized that she was unaware of the accurate medical diagnosis of her condition.

"What did you say was wrong with your hips?" I asked her. "Osteophytes", she asserted confidently. "What does that mean?" I asked her. "It is when your bones go like Swiss cheese", she said.

She had meant to tell me that what she had was osteoporosis. Can you imagine what would have happened if I had put the dynamite energy into her hip instead of the cement energy? It might have shattered her weak and chalky bones and caused harm. Thank God I had asked for help from the healing angels before the healing. They just corrected the mistake and all was well.

To carry out effective healing for ourselves or others, we need to be strongly anchored into our soul self and so increasingly aware of this level of reality. The pillar of light meditation is one way to have our feet on the ground and our head in the world of spirit at the same time. It is easy and a good one to do daily. It only takes a couple of minutes. Please refer back to chapter 4 to refresh your memory on how to do this.

STEP 2: Focus

During IYS therapy you will be developing your capacity for focus. The focus can shift during the healing, but it is always there. Connect, focus and flow are the catch cry of the IYS therapist!

Having looked at what and why we are connecting with on the inner plane, we understand ourselves to be channels for healing energy of Divine origin. By focusing upon the Divine the energy will start to flow. This will in turn help you to develop stronger connection, and every healing you do will start to develop the inner corridors of light that are required for self-realisation over the course of a lifetime.

Focus upon the Divine and let the energy flow. Then, allow your focus to shift to your client as you sense what is required to help and serve them as a healer today. As you move your focus from the Divine to your client, you will be ready to sense their energy through step 3.

STEP 3: Scan

Some people are visual, some are auditory and some are tactile. The same is true of inner plane perception. Most people are able to perceive the inner world if they really want to, provided they are willing to practise.

We have already described how to perceive the aura and chakras in earlier parts of the book. The main focus ought be on perceiving the chakras, their relative size and state of congestion.

This step is not indispensable to the healing, so if trying to feel, see or hear energy is really frustrating you, don't worry about it. However, if you practise doing these things you will find over time that you can actually perceive things after all. It will help you to develop clairvoyance (seeing energy), clairaudience (hearing energy) and clairsentience (feeling energy with your hands and body). We sometimes use the generic term scanning to describe this step of the healing process.

In our IYS training program students are taught how to feel energy with their hands. The sensory perception for feeling energy deepens our intuition and helps us to be more sensitive to energy in many and varied situations.

Scanning will be a tool that gives more and more insight to you over time. It is often a key to finding the inner source of your client's disturbance or troubles. Working on the inner causative factors in their life will bear rich fruit and will eventually flow into the physical world as a shift in experience.

One of the unique factors of our training programs is that every person is receiving a current of energy from the beginning of the class to the end. Each time we teach scanning we offer every student a blessing on their hands, to help activate the palm chakras. This helps speed up the chakral activation in their hands, and makes learning around scanning more effective.

STEP 4 Flow and Clean ·

Flow is a beautiful experience of allowing yourself to be receptive or yin to Divine healing energy. Having connected with and focussed upon the Divine, you start to allow flow, and then focus upon your client and let the energy go out through your hands to empower whatever clearing or blessing you are engaging in at the time.

If you start to lose connection then focus again on the Divine and let the flow come into the top of your head, down through your arms and out through your hands.

You can allow the flow to go through one or both hands. When sweeping an aura, I have found it better to use both hands, with chakras it can be easier with your dominant hand. We will look more at chakras next week.

Important in practicing flow is to ensure that the energy that is going to your client is not coming from your own body, but from the Source and the inner plane connections that you have.

In order to make this simple, we intend that 80% of the energy we connect with and flow in through the crown chakra goes to the client, and 20% remains within our body mind and spirit. Thus, by the end of a day of healing our own energy field has grown, not shrunk. Getting this right is important for long term empowerment and success as a healer.

Imagine you are standing underneath a waterfall of pure light coming from the source of your connection

> Feel the energy flowing down through your body and into the Earth
> Draw the sacred energy in the Earth up through your body and offer it up to the source of your connection, becoming a pillar of light flowing up as well as flowing down from above.
> Bathe in this flow, repeating the up and down flow until you feel full and strong and like you are standing under a waterfall of light which is flowing into your body.
> Breathe in through the top of your head and feel that energy flowing out through your hands, just enough to move energy in

the cleansing phase of IYS healing. Keep a little flow coming out your hands throughout the cleansing phase, regardless of which method of cleansing you are using. Here are some methods of cleansing.

CLEANSING WITH YOUR HANDS: SWEEPING

You can pull dirty energy out of a person with your hands. Normally you can do this with a sweeping motion, as though you are dusting with a damp cloth and then shaking it out into the salt water.

Sweeping

Once we have connected, focussed and are flowing, we then use our hands to sweep out negative energy, negative thoughts, vibrations and emotions, and whatever is blocking the energy field of our client. We can sweep the aura, chakras, meridians and directly sweep cells, organs and systems of the physical body. During your training you will be shown how to be specific with sweeping and the kinds of energy you use to sweep with, all of which is wholesome and Divine.

Sweeping the Aura

When we sweep the aura, we are sweeping in a downwards direction, from above the crown to the ground, front and back, sides, and wherever we feel congestion. Avoid making swirling or upward motions as you want to encourage a smooth and consistent flow in the energy field of your client, so that energy can cascade easily in through their etheric body and down into the ground. We can enquire of our client, where do you feel discomfort in your body? And we can sweep the aura more intensively in that area. It is amazing how this can shift symptoms and allow energy to flow.

Sweeping the Chakras

This is a very exciting part of what we will learn, and will provide you with a life skill that can be used in countless applications.

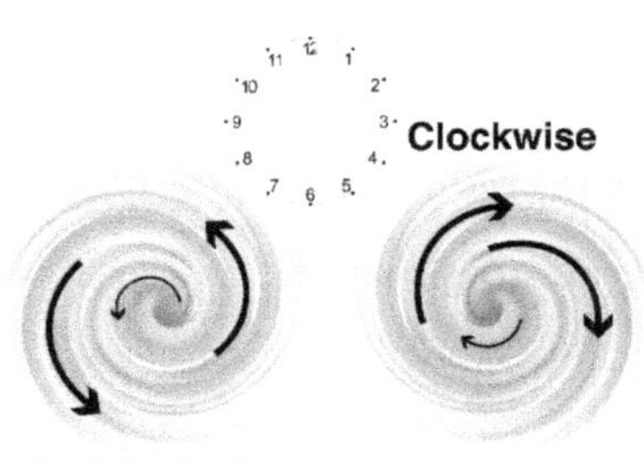

Chakras are swept anti clockwise to remove dirty energy. This is the most efficient way we have found to do it.

Sometimes energy blockages feel or look like ropes, strings, sticks, pieces of metal or other strange things. Pull the dirty energy out of the energy centres and the aura. Just pull them out. Make sure you do not allow the stuff to stay on your skin as it might sink in. Shake it off into a bucket of salty water. Clean it off your hands with rubbing alcohol, essential oils or soap and water. If it feels like it is crawling up your arm, tell it that it is not yours and that it must leave now. Breathe in, release through the hands. If it is very stubborn (unusual) hold onto an obsidian crystal ball and tell the crystal to pull the rubbish out of you.

Sweeping Story of Relief

If you have ever attended a Shakti Durga retreat you will be aware of the vital role sweeping plays in the care of the participants. It is common to start a day or a session with the instruction to buddy up and provide each other with "a sweep". Participants regularly report feeling significantly different after their sweep.

One of our volunteers, let's call her Celeste, arrived at a class early one morning to begin setting up for a sacred ceremony. She was rushing about and feeling agitated and unsettled. She'd tried talking to her inner child (on the run) and attempted to perceive the root of the unsettled feeling. She was aware that the ceremony setup was not employing the appropriate vibration so when a student arrived she asked her for a sweep. Just a simple sweep. After five minutes of sweeping the agitation had lifted. Calm, centred and heart aware service resulted.

The sweeping had helped to release the negative energy, that likely comprised thoughts, memories and possibly energy picked up from other people that resulted in distraction, impatience and mind-centric motivation.

Regularly sweeping and healing yourself, as well as receiving energy healing from a certified therapist, will equip you with examples of how sweeping has made a difference in your life. These examples will both equip you for introducing energy healing to people you meet and help you identify opportunities for helping as you address more varied situations in your own life.

Sweeping health rays in the aura

The aura is full of tiny microscopic hair like structures, which are known as health rays. Imagine that all over the body, tiny hairs are protruding and they are taking energy in and out of the body and its various systems, organs and cells. These can get knotted and tangled, blocked and unable to perform properly.

When we connect focus and flow, we then imagine that the energy is like hair conditioner and shampoo combined, gently sweeping, combing, and detangling these subtle structures, so that the aura is light and free, and the health rays are rehabilitated and able to bring energy into and out of the aura and body in an optimal way.

Why we clean before *Filling*

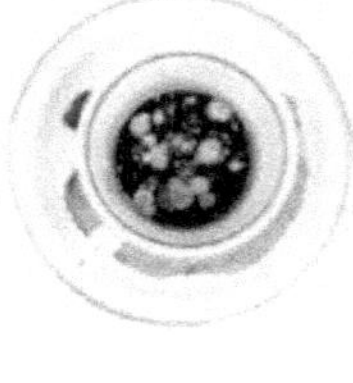

Imagine you only had one coffee cup, and your coffee from last week was still in it because you were in a rush and forgot to wash it.

To have a cup of coffee now you will need to use a lot of coffee pouring into that dirty cup to get a brew that doesn't make you sick!

Or, you can wash the cup first, then fill it up using just a cup of coffee.

That is what we are doing with healing. Flow and clean, then flow and fill.

When we have to remove dirt from something in the physical world we put a solvent on it to loosen it up and make cleaning easy. When we have dirt in the energy body we can't use soap, but we can use energy of the appropriate type to loosen it up so we can then sweep it away. To place energy in the body, we intend to do so, as the energy will follow the thought.

In IYS Energy Healing, we mainly use the light of the soul. For cleaning purposes we mainly use white energy, or we can use electric violet soul energy. This is also known as the violet flame. The electric violet flame is amazingly powerful and how you use it for healing is set out below. Should you need a gentler energy, such as when dealing with babies or the very elderly or people who are extremely ill, then just stick to white.

ADDING LIGHT: ELECTRIC VIOLET FLAME

1. Breathe in through your crown chakra as you do when practising the pillar of light meditation. Imagine that you are bringing light in from your Higher Self. Allow the energy in the breath to flow out your hands.

2. Visualize painting or spraying in turn each chakra of your client, starting at the top and working downwards, just as you would put stain remover on a dirty shirt collar.

3. If you are aware of any body parts that hurt or are malfunctioning, imagine painting them with light also.

4. Wait a minute, then proceed with next step, unless you would like to add some sound as well.

CLEANSING WITH SOUND

Harmonious and high vibrational sounds can be used to infiltrate the energy body and push out non-harmonious vibrations. Various mantras can be used, and a simple one is OM. This sound will clear people, places, businesses and homes. Simply sound OM and focus on each chakra in turn, intending that the sound remove the dirty energy that is within them. It works very quickly.

ADDING SOUND: OM

You can use sound instead of light for healing. I often use sound and light together. The easiest form of sound to use for astonishing healing effects is the chant OM. The symbol of OM is ॐ. OM into the chakras, aura and body of the patient. This is a very pleasant sensation for the client, and will move energy very quickly. You do not need a voice like Dame

Joan Sutherland, just let the sound come out naturally and strongly, with love and a desire to effect cleansing. Allow your voice to rise and fall naturally. Different chakras resonate to different notes, and you will automatically sing the right pitch and frequency to assist the person you are working on. If you doubt this, ask the person which notes they found most beneficial, the higher, middle or lower notes. Usually they are all good, as they each work on different energy centres.

When using the sacred sound OM, ensure that you impregnate it with your intention. Thus, keep clear in your mind that you are OMing garbage out of the person, and that it is being transmuted into love.

If you don't feel like a confident OM'er, then use a CD. The healing will be much stronger if accompanied by this sacred sound. Details of our OM CD are at the back of the book. You can visualize a brilliant OM spinning and dropping down through the crown chakra of the person, removing all fear energy as it goes. This is really powerful and will dissolve a lot of dirty energy quickly.

WORDS: ORDER OUT THE MESS

AS you are painting on energy during flow and clean, you can add spoken intention such as this.

"I command that all negative energy, negative thoughts, negative emotions, negative vibrations leave all my bodies now, through all time, space and lifetimes. Through Divine grace and my own will, so be it." Breathe in, release.

1. See the energy flowing into a suitable receptacle (see below 'What garbage receptacle?') so that it does not go everywhere.
2. Repeat the command and breath release three times.

3. Ask your client to be aware of their energy and their body, and to notice any energy movements such as tingling, heat or cold. Some don't feel anything, that is okay. Some might get upset, others might feel heavy or lopsided. These are all normal reactions.

4. Formulate a command that deals with the reaction that was elicited from the patient through the initial command above. Feel or perceive their energy as you do this.

5. Be aware of any parts of your body that feel heavy, or that become uncomfortable or painful. This will be related to the client. Tell the energy that it is not yours and command that it leave your body, with thanks for letting you know where to work next. Focus now on those parts of the patient, in turn if necessary, and adapt the command above so that it is specific to the problem. If, for instance, the right arm starts to feel heavy during the healing, get the patient to say:

6. *"I specifically command that all negative energy, negative thoughts, negative emotions, negative vibrations and all subtle bodies connected with it, through all time, space and lifetimes, leave my right arm NOW. Through Divine grace and my own will, so be it."* Breathe in, release.

See the energy flowing into the waste receptacle. Repeat the command and the breath release three times. By now the person is usually feeling lighter and quite calm.

CLEANSING WITH THE BREATH

If energy is really stuck somewhere, get the person to breathe in through the crown or the feet, and out through the affected part of the body or energy body. They are essentially pushing the blockage out with the out-breath.

STEP 5: Flow and Fill

When blessing people with energy, it is not supposed to be your own energy that you are using. If you use your own much needed vital energy you will soon get depleted and become sick yourself from giving it away.

To bless people, bring in some of the endless supply of Divine energy in a wonderful flow. Feel the energy coming down through your crown chakra from your soul. You may experience a tingling sensation, or expansion of your crown chakra, as you do this.

When you are filling, you will allow a greater flow than when you are cleansing, where a trickle is all you need.

When you are conscious of a lot of energy in the crown chakra, start to release some of it towards the patient. At the same time, ask that they be blessed. You can say something like:

"I ask that you be blessed with healing energy. May this be distributed thoroughly and completely throughout your body and energy body. Through Divine Grace, so be it."

Visualize energy entering the whole of their aura, and bringing balance to their chakras. Get them to breathe in and hold as long as possible. Ask that they breathe the blessing into the physical, mental, emotional and spiritual bodies, one breath at a time. If a specific part of the energy body was weak or damaged, focus energy there so as to strengthen that particular part. Remember that the meng mein and spleen chakras should only be half the size of the others, and unless you are an experienced healer you should not bless them directly as the energy will be too strong.

If, say, the sex chakra feels too small compared to the others, specifically direct a blessing towards it. For any chakras that need beefing up, you can simply direct energy into them, or for a stronger result you can energize them with a supporting affirmation. Choose from the affirmations at the end of each chapter on the major chakras to find ones that are suitable for your client, or devise one that suits. Make it positive and beneficial, bearing in mind the specific work that chakra does.

Warning

There are some parts of the energy field and body that we do not flow and fill, we just clean. You need to learn these five situation where flow and fill should not be used. These are:

1. **Eyes** – too delicate, put energy in through the ajna chakra
2. **Front heart chakra** – can lead to heart congestion. Add energy through palm chakras and or back heart chakra
3. **Spleen/spleen chakra** – the spleen is a delicate organ with its own chakras (all organs have chakras, see more in Physical Body modules. Spleen can be cleansed front and back but not energised.
4. **Belly of a pregnant woman** – the energy will be too strong for the baby. Be very gentle around pregnancy, sweeping is

always fine, but imagine an umbrella or shield in front of the baby and womb. Check with experienced healers if in doubt.

5. **Back Meng Mein and Base chakra** in the case of a person with high blood pressure

STEP 6 Scan

Check your work by perceiving the chakras with your hands. By now things should be starting to sparkle. Contaminated energy should be going or gone. Any prickly energy in the chakras should be gone, and it should feel light and clean, both to you and your client. Their pain, if they had any, should have diminished or disappeared. If not, repeat the healing commands and sequences again. Get them to breathe in light through the crown chakra and breathe it out through the pain as you pull it out as well with your hands.

If the energy body feels clean now, that is good. Note whether the chakras have come into balance; that is, they are all roughly the same size (with the exception of the meng mein which should be no more than half the size of the others). Also note any chakras that feel empty or diffuse, not easy to scan. These may need more energy and so you can just repeat steps 4 and 5, cleaning and filling.

STEP 7: Seal and Save

Working in someone's etheric body opens it up. This is safe to do because we have invoked for Divine protection and help. At the end of the healing we close it again and 'save' what we have done, like saving a document on your computer. This keeps all the new clean energy in, and potential dirty energy contamination out.

To do this, imagine painting the aura with brilliant light blue light, which envelops it like an egg shell.

As you create this seal, think or say:

"Stabilize, Seal the aura."

If a chakra is particularly weak at the beginning of the healing or needs a lot of healing, you can place the same type of seal on it, using the exact same method. Just intend that the energy be used to create the seal on the end of that particular chakra and it will happen.

STEP 8: Cut and Give Thanks

A. Cut

During healings, energy lines form between you and your client. If you do not cut them, any time the client thinks of you he or she can suck energy from you down this energy line. When you have a lot of clients and do healing for a long time, this is not an option for your continued good health. To avoid depletion, cut from those you have given healing.

Use your hand as though it were a sword to cut down the front of your body and say, "Cut".

Cutting can be done by every professional person after every consultation to minimize the amount of energy that a client draws out of you. It doesn't matter if you are an accountant, psychologist, doctor, nurse, lawyer or healer, you can practise cutting from your clients after they leave. You will be amazed what a difference this makes to your energy levels.

B. Give Thanks

At the beginning you asked for help, and help would have been given to you. It is appropriate to give thanks for the assistance that both you and your client have received. Gratitude is a healthy practice and strengthens the connection that you are building with the loving beings that are helping you. You can use your own words, and it can be quite short and simple. If you like you can use the following:

"I give thanks for the healing energy and ask that [name of person healed] be protected, and that the healing angels continue the healing for two weeks. With lots of gratitude and respect, thank you."

Cut and give thanks becomes an automatic way to complete your healing session. Make sure that you wash your hands thoroughly either with rubbing alcohol or soap and water to remove all etheric debris from your system.

Summary of Basic IYS Energy Healing

Doing this is actually easier than reading about it. Once you have done it a few times it will be child's play. There are just eight steps. See if you can remember what each one is for.

1. Connect
2. Focus
3. Scan
4. Flow and Clean
5. Flow and Fill,
6. Scan – check your work
7. Seal and Save
8. Cut and Give thanks

In our training seminars we go much deeper into methods of clearing and blessing and all kinds of amazing possibilities for healing are shared. For those who are interested in becoming healers we highly recommend that you come and learn, and we look forward to meeting you. Sessions are online and in person in various countries.

Guidelines for Self-Healing

1. Place two chairs facing each other
2. Imagine yourself sitting in the other chair
3. If it helps go sit in the chair and notice where your body is in relation to it
4. Return to your original chair
5. Do the whole healing as if a separate person – who happens to be you - is sitting opposite
6. Follow the steps of IYS Energy Healing

    a. Connect – who with, what am I asking?
    b. Focus – on your connection, then your energy field (in chair) and scan your chakras
    c. Flow – as you work, keep breathing in energy from above
    d. Flow and Clean – sweeping out any stuck stale energy particularly where you have issues
    e. Flow and Fill – ensuring your chakras are correctly balanced by blessing in energy to those that need it
    f. Seal and Save
    g. Cut to release energy and Give thanks

7. Make a note in your journal about your experience, what you noticed, how you are feeling.

Chapter

21

SPECIAL BLESSINGS

THERE are a number of simple but highly effective methods for specialized healing. They can be used in conjunction with the ten steps in chapter 20. All of these techniques can be inserted into the procedure at the relevant step. Below you will also find some safeguards to ensure your understanding of energy healing, and long term self care.

Grounding and energizing

If you want to strengthen and bless the base chakra, you can do this from the energy of the Earth. Instead of breathing in energy through the crown chakra, breathe it in through the base chakra. You do this by connecting to the Earth, as is done during the pillar of light meditation (chapter 4). Feel the energy build in your base chakra and then release sixty per cent of this into the base chakra of the person you are healing. The person may experience warmth, and this can spread through their whole body. They will feel grounded, energized and very secure.

Do not do this if the person has high blood pressure, because some of the energy will flow up to the meng mein chakra and make it bigger, thus forcing up the blood pressure even more. Instead, you can infuse Earth energy slowly into their feet chakras for a similar energizing effect.

Blessing the base chakra with energy from the Earth is really good for people who are not grounded, have been tired a lot, or who have weak physical bodies, arthritic conditions or other muscular-skeletal problems.

Blessing with sound

Sound has an incredible ability to strengthen our energy body. Singing chants or mantras into the energy body with the intention of healing and strengthening is really effective and fast.

Injecting cures and herbal remedies

If you find yourself in a situation where someone needs medication and it is not available, you can do this.

1. Ring an ambulance or other medical service provider, explain the problem and follow their instructions.
2. While you are waiting for the ambulance, you can connect, focus flow and clean the person as described above. If you know the medicine they need, invoke for the energy of that medication to be injected into the person in the correct dosage. Bless them with it. This can save lives. You will probably feel a huge rush of energy as you do this. I helped someone with an allergy to apples avoid anaphylactic shock by doing this whilst she waited for medical intervention.

Neutralizing toxins

If someone is bitten by a poisonous animal, such as a snake, spider or wasp, invoke and do normal first aid. Then, immediately start to sweep the toxin out of the body through the site of the bite and the nearest chakras. Imagine blue light flooding the whole area, invoke for the antivenene and say, *"Neutralize the toxin"*.

Get the person to say: *"This has no power over me. I now command that the toxin be neutralized"*.

Keep sweeping, tell the energy to disintegrate the toxin and command that it leave. Say: *"I command all negative energy from this bite to be extracted and expelled from your body, through all dimensions and through all of time and space, now"*.

Tell the person to breathe in and release through the site of the bite. Feel the energy flowing out.

You can also call on the deva (over-souling angelic intelligence) of the species that bit the person, and send love to them. You might have to say sorry for any unkind thoughts you have had about their species. Ask that God bless them, then respectfully ask their assistance in removing all of the energy of the bite. Afterwards, give thanks and cut from them.

As well as doing the energy work, get the person to medical treatment as soon as you can.

SPECIAL TECHNIQUES
FOR RAPID CLEANING

CUTTING LINES OF ATTACHMENT

When we associate with others, lines of energy form between us. These lines can become like anchors or chains, binding us to people we might not want to be bound to. This happens between family members and work colleagues, ex-partners, and so on. The more we think about people, the more these lines grow.

Many people going through disputes are shocked to find that they have fat lines of energy joining them to the other party they are in dispute with. By cutting the lines, which is simple to do, we can send back their energy and reclaim our own. Usually, when this occurs, there are significant breakthroughs in relationships. Do IYS Energy Healing steps 1 to 5 inclusive. Then say:

1. ***"I command that all lines of attachment to other people, places, things, times and events that are draining my energy now be broken. I call back my spirit and reclaim my energy, NOW."*** Breathe in, release.
2. ***"I now release all cords of energy that are binding us together. I ask Archangel Michael to help set me free. I cut from you, NOW."*** Breathe in, release.

Clean the body where the cords went in. They are often from the solar plexus and navel chakras, but can be anywhere on the body. Some people literally have hundreds of cords attached to different people hanging off them, and wonder why they always feel so tired! Do this a few times, and they will notice a difference. Finish the steps to complete IYS Energy Healing.

DEALING WITH YIN/YANG IMBALANCES

In chapter 5 we described how your aura can become unbalanced due to too much yin or yang energy. You can rake out the aura using your fingers and cupped hands. After adding energy as explained in step 4, start raking.

Get the client to imagine a point of light in the heart chakra. Tell them to breathe it out the front of the heart, around to the right and into the back heart chakra. Then out the front, around to the left and into the back heart chakra. As they do this ask them to intend that the figure eight pattern brings the energy into balance.

Have faith

The ability to affect our reality is largely determined by our faith in our ability to do it! The more faith the healer has, the stronger the treatment will be. The Divine assistance will be stronger and the result will be magnified. This is because many unseen helpers run around doing our will, and when we doubt, they all throw down their tools and wait for us to make up our minds about what we are going to do.

Imagine you are the boss in a busy factory. You say, "Okay everyone, we are doing this". "Right, we are doing this", say all the workers. They run around getting 'this' done. Then, in the middle of it all, before 'this' has been achieved, you say, "Actually, I don't know if we can do 'this', perhaps we should do 'that' instead". Everyone stops what they are doing. It is clear the boss has no idea what he wants to do. Eventually he says, "Okay, back to the original plan, let's do 'this'". The boss does not sound definite. The workers are uneasy and do not hurry about their business lest the orders change again. Then, he gets definite, and they realize he means business. "We are doing 'this'." They all get into it again, full steam ahead.

When we have faith, the inner plane workers work to bring our desires to fruition. We want someone healed, they help us. It is important to keep your focus, see the patient as healthy and full of life force. The inner world will rally around you. You might want to thank them. We live in a very interactive universe!

Medical intuition

Medical intuition develops fairly rapidly as we practise energy healing. If you get a passing thought whilst healing, do not dismiss it but ask your client about it. Chances are it will be a clue as to where to go next with them, and will lead you right into the heart of the matter. Annette Noontill and Louise L. Hay are fabulous medical intuitives, and I highly recommend their books to anyone who would like to develop further in this way.

Each intuitive develops their own language of intuition. Annie Besant and C.W. Leadbeater wrote a marvellous book in 1901 called Thought

Forms, which illustrates their particular language of intuition. With practice your own language will develop.

Avoid depleting yourself

When you are performing healing, make sure that you bring in more energy than you give out. Otherwise you can find yourself depleted of energy when you ought to be growing in energy during the healing process.

I once gave a talk at a spiritualist church, and before I started there was a healing demonstration by six spiritual healers. They came to the front of the church and each of them worked on a patient individually. As I watched clairvoyantly, five of the healers shrank. Their auras collapsed, although the aura of the patient grew.

One older woman was different to the others. When she gave energy to the patient, she did not deplete herself. She did not give them her own energy, she brought it in from above her and let a bit over half of it go through her hands to her patient. By the end of the exercise, not only was her patient glowing with energy, she was also. Her aura grew, as did the patient's aura. She could have continued healing for hours on end because she was recharging automatically as she was working. The other people were seriously depleting their energy as they worked. Over time this would have lead to ill health.

Many energy healers suffer from poor health because they are making a technical error; that is, they fail to keep some of the energy they bring in for themselves. Make sure you do it right!

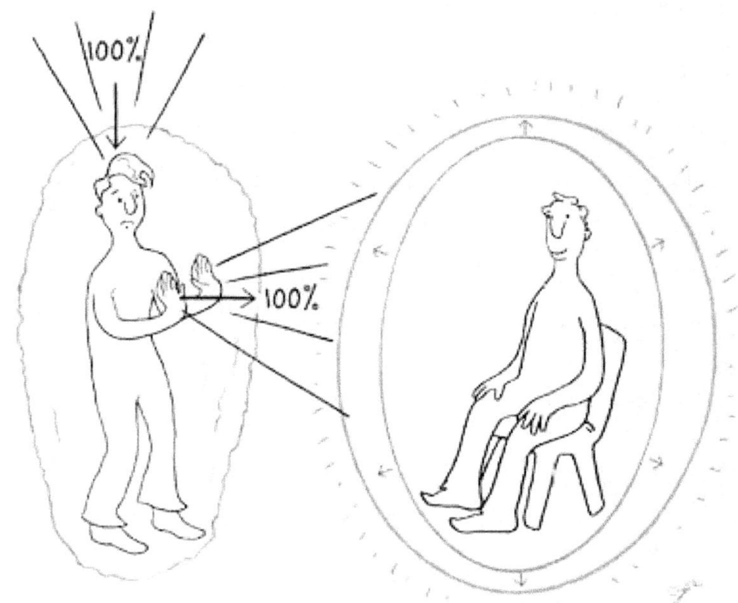

100% in, 100% out - healer is depleted

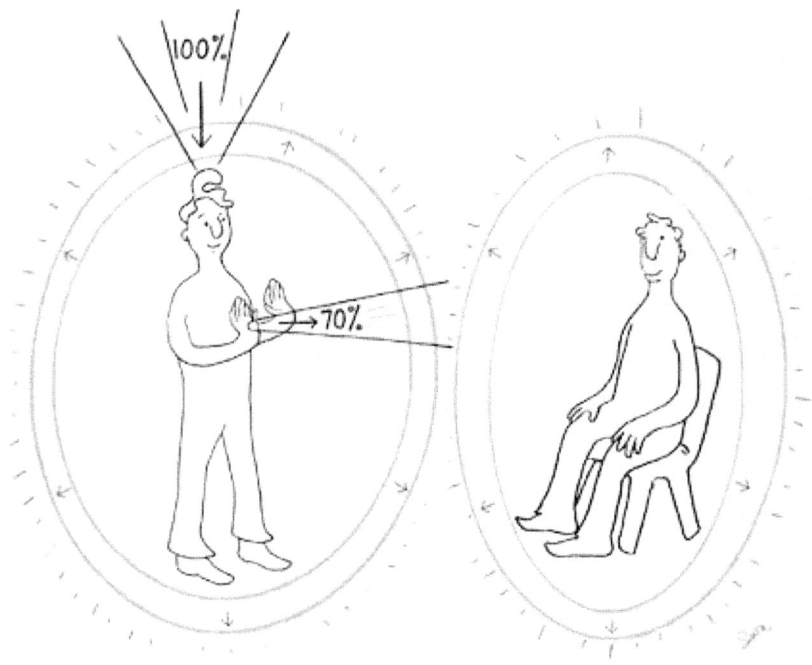

100% in, 70% out - healer is strengthened

Healers are individuals

The bigger your aura and chakras, and the stronger your connection to your Higher Self, the better the healer you will be. Thus, some healers are capable of astonishing, rapid healing that most are not yet able to do, and this is simply a matter of development. Nevertheless, the techniques described above will work for most people, and will work miraculously for those of you who are already very developed.

Self care for carers

When people are sick, they use up their own energy really quickly then start to use the energy of those who care for them. This is not conscious. However, you will notice that when you are around sick people all the time, you start to feel down yourself. You are! Your energy is being depleted, and you need to have a bit of time out: hug some trees, do self healing or go and see another healer or friend who knows about energy and get help. Otherwise you might be next on the sick list.

Performing self healing

The same ten steps that are set out above can be used to do self healing. Anyone can do self healing. The exception is if you are very sick and depleted, as you will not have the energy to do it yourself and would be better served going to another healer.

When I do healing, I prefer to sit the patient in a chair so that I can easily walk around them and get to the front and back of their body. Others prefer to use a massage table. It is fairly irrelevant. If you work with a patient in a chair, do that also for self healing.

Imagine yourself in the chair. If it helps, go and sit in the chair and notice where your body is in relation to it. Then get up, and imagine that you are still sitting down in front of you. Do the whole healing exactly as you would if a separate person were sitting there. You will be amazed at how effective this is.

Absentee healings

You can do a healing on anyone else the same way. It would still work even if they were on the other side of the world. Just be sure that you have permission before you go interfering in someone else's energy body, no matter how good your intentions are. Remember, if the great inner plane masters and teachers wait to be asked before they give help, so should you.

Beware of 'rescuer syndrome', and do not insist that people receive healing. Who knows what the plan is for them. They might have a bit more suffering to do before they reach the point of true receptivity through which real change will occur. Even Jesus, one of the best healers the world has ever seen, waited to be asked before he performed healing.

It doesn't always work

Just like any form of healing, energy healing does not always work. In medicine, chemical treatments do not work for all people, but they work for a statistically significant group, and thus they are said to be effective. Energy healing is the same.

If you have a patient who is not recovering as fast as you would like, don't think that you are not doing it right. If you follow these simple steps (as set out above) you will achieve significant gains for people in terms of their wellbeing and inner peace. If they do not recover, then there are usually two issues, either or both of which may be affecting them. These issues are lack of receptivity and bad karma.

Lack of receptivity

Some people do not want to be healed. They just deliberately block the energy, and that is that. So be it.

Some people think they want to be healed but deep down they do not. I once saw a woman called Belinda at the clinic. She had been off work for several years with severe body aches and allergies which had debilitated her to the extent that she could only walk short distances and needed a walking stick. She had chronic fatigue syndrome and many other medical complications which defied adequate diagnosis. Although she was only in her early thirties, she looked twenty years older.

Belinda only came to see me because a mutual friend gave her the session as a gift. After the first session she was able to walk without the stick and seemed really happy. She went home and saw our mutual friend Kirsty a few days later. Kirsty rang me, totally amazed. She told me that Belinda had heaps of energy and was not using her stick, but was blazing with anger towards me.

Despite Belinda's repeated assertions that she was dying, I had told her that I thought this not to be the case and that if we continued to work together she would make a complete recovery. Because she was a friend of a close friend, I offered to treat her for no fee. However, she was so irate that I thought she could recover that she refused to return for further healing and that was the last I saw of her.

This woman had an agenda. Her illness was her whole life. If we took it away, she unconsciously felt that she would be, and have, nothing. I heard that within a few weeks she was in more pain and discomfort than ever before. So be it.

Another memorable occasion was when I gave a demonstration of healing to a group of business men and women, many of whom had not been exposed to any form of alternative healing let alone something as 'out there' as IYS Energy Healing. In order to demonstrate what I do, I asked if anyone in the audience had pain. A large man near the front who had been sitting with his arms folded instantly put his hand up and started walking to the stage. Oh no, I thought. Look at his attitude. Then he told me defiantly that he had back pain which had been quite severe for eight years.

I started to project energy towards him and immediately saw it bounce straight out of him again. There was no way he was letting himself be 'duped' by this mumbo jumbo. Given that this was all taking place in front of eighty grinning spectators, this was bad news. I remembered my favourite mantra: "Don't panic". In a flash of inspiration, I told him that the sick energy centre responsible for his hurt back was the same centre that, if healed, would allow him to experience a greater flow of money into his life.

I struck pay dirt. The remote chance that energy healing might increase his cash flow was of considerable interest to him. Instantly his base chakra became receptive and in went the energy. I was able to remove a heap of blockages very quickly. His pain was significantly reduced in a matter of minutes, much to his amazement. As I never saw him again, I don't know what happened to his cash flow.

The point of these stories is that if people block the effects of healing they will not receive healing. This is their business and does not reflect on you. You can of course try to increase their receptivity by establishing a rapport with them, making them feel at ease and explaining what you are doing. They do not need to believe that it will work in order for it to do so, but deliberate blocking of the healing energy means it will not work. Tell them that you cannot help them and move on. What you want is openminded people, and most people are. I remember when I first had energy healing. I didn't think it would work but I was willing to give it a go. To my amazement, it did work. This is a common story.

Some people say that energy healing only works as a placebo effect and so is not worth having. I know that this is not the case, but even if it were true, if it takes away our pain and brings us into wellness, who cares? Placebo away, baby! I would rather be well and pain-free, than suffering whilst pontificating about the 'absurdity' of this work. Having said that, the number of miraculous healings that have occurred in my own healing practice and those of my students has been humbling and amazing.

Bad karma

As we said earlier, everyone has a debits and credits ledger which is presided over by angels of karma. Every thought, word, deed, intention, action and reaction that we ever have is recorded here and eventually we will experience the receiving end of it. This is why it is such a good idea to do our best to exercise loving kindness. Then, this is what will come back to us.

Some people incarnate with a need to clear a lot of negative karma. They may contract diseases which are not amenable to any form of treatment. They may suffer disabilities or paralysis, cancers or degenerative problems. It may be too late to alleviate their problems, but they can still be helped.

I have found that even with dying patients, energy healing can relieve pain, ease tension and illuminate their spiritual core. The death experience is transformed into a thing of peace and beauty. Bad karma can be alleviated by acts of kindness and generosity. By being of service to our fellow man, we generate good karma. This can offset the bad karma.

Another way to right the wheel of karma is to do what Jesus taught us to do. Forgive our enemies. The process of true forgiveness is entirely for our own benefit. The other person may not even be consciously aware that we bear a grudge against them, so letting it go will not affect them one way or another. It will however affect you.

When we forgive those who have hurt us, we should also ask that we be forgiven for any hurts we may have caused that person.

Usually conflict is a two way street. Be humble, and if forgiveness is done properly, a great deal of energy floods into and out of our bodies. Conflict is energy sucking, and detrimental to our wellbeing. The gift in it, however, is that it inevitably helps us to grow and evolve.

When forgiveness is done in a healing with a lot of energy present it is very powerful. It should be followed by the process of cutting cords of energy to that person as described above.

What garbage receptacle?

When you pull energy garbage out of a person, where do you put it? Don't put it on the floor, because it will give you sore feet. When I was taught this I did not really believe it so I ignored the instruction and just put the invisible garbage all over the place. Sure enough, after several weeks of doing this I noticed that my feet were aching a lot after healing people. Now I am careful to contain and transmute the garbage.

To do this, just use a container of water with a couple of tablespoons or a handful of salt in it. If water is not available, use fire. If no fire or water, then form an imaginary violet flame and put the stuff into that so it is transmuted into love.

Some energy healers in some cultures pull out the etheric debris and put it into eggs as a means of disposal. Some of them then eat the eggs! We will not be doing this my friends! Just give it back to nature through a salt water bucket, which eventually you can pour out into a drain, down a toilet or onto the Earth somewhere with a prayer to Mother Earth to transmute the energy into peace and love. Avoid putting the energy on animals or plants, and don't let your dogs or cats drink the salt water either.

Chapter

22

CRYSTALS FOR HEALING AMPLIFICATION

CRYSTALS are great tools to use in healing. Before use in healing, crystals ought to be cleansed thoroughly and blessed. Cleanse any type of quartz crystal, tourmaline or obsidian by washing them with soap and water, then soaking them in salty water for a few hours.

Perform IYS Energy Healing on the crystal, steps 1 to 10, until the energy of the crystal is clean, soft and full. You will be working on the aura and physical body of the crystal, taking out the dirty energy and putting clean energy in.

Whenever you use crystals on your body, ensure that you actually know the energetic effect that they are having. Just because it is pretty or you like it does not mean that it is beneficial. You need to scan your energy before you pick up the crystal, and scan again afterwards. If your energy expands while you are holding the crystal it is suitable for you. If, as is often the case, it shrinks your energy, give it away. It is weakening you. Crystals are too powerful to play with, get some guidance or learn how to do it yourself safely.

The crystals I use the most during healing are:

CLEAR QUARTZ

This amplifies energy, makes it stronger and more potent. Energy will flow towards the pointy end of the crystal (generator crystals have a point at one end). Hold one while you are doing healing and it will strengthen the energy you are using. Do not point laser crystals at delicate parts of the body, such as the head, heart or spleen, and do not point them at the belly of pregnant women. The energy is so strong that it can be damaging. I sometimes place a number of clear quartz crystals around the person during healing to increase the amount of energy available for the healing.

SMOKEY QUARTZ

I particularly like working with elestial crystals. These are funny skeletal-looking smoky quartz crystals which magnify and soften energy. They have a connection with the angelic realm and bring angelic energy into the healing. I place a number of these around the person when I am doing a healing and the effect is very strong. They seem to ground the higher vibrational energy into a matrix that is extremely beneficial in healing.

OBSIDIAN

Black obsidian balls or discs are the best extractors of physical pain and dirty energy that I have ever come across. Green obsidian is good too. Obsidian is a form of volcanic glass. Get the person to hold a black or green obsidian ball, or even a tumbled stone, in each hand and say:

"I command that all pain and dirty energy flow out of my body and into the crystal now!"

You will be amazed at what happens. Sometimes people feel like the crystals are large lead weights, so much energy is pulled out into them. Sometimes they get really hot. Even if the client cannot feel it, the crystal will be doing its work. People who have painful conditions are advised to sit with obsidian crystals on the site of the pain. Invoke, then breathe in through the crown chakra and out into the crystal for ten minutes or so. Intend that the pain (which is only energy) leave. Make sure you clean the crystals properly after every time they are used, by soaking them in salt water and performing IYS Energy Healing on them.

BLACK TOURMALINE

Black tourmaline is another stone that removes dirty energy very efficiently.

I once had an architect come to give me a quote on building a crystal healing studio at a property I owned. I suggested he might like to have a healing to see what it was like; it might help him to design an appropriate space. He eagerly agreed and we got to it.

Unbeknown to me, the man had a congenital heart problem and a shortened life expectancy as a result. I put black tourmaline on his heart for some reason, and many other stones all over him. I took him on a guided process, and he perceived many wonderful things about his former lifetimes as a sacred architect. At the end of the process, I began removing the stones from his body so he could sit up. When I touched the black tourmaline on his heart, I got quite a shock. Nearly half of the stone had turned to powder, and when I touched it, the thing just crumbled.

Tourmaline is not the kind of stone that usually just falls to sand in a couple of hours, at least not without the assistance of a ten-pound hammer wielded by a powerful man. The stone had absorbed the energy of the defective heart, and the strain of doing that destroyed the crystal's etheric body, causing its physical body to turn to dust. If I had not seen it with my own eyes I never would have believed it. The architect's eyes nearly fell out of his head when I showed him. He also knew that tourmaline would not normally crumble. He felt transformed.

ROSE QUARTZ

If someone is having trouble relaxing into the healing, get them to hold some rose quartz which will cause the heart chakra to expand. The person will become calm and feel nurtured. These are great to use with children also. While Rose quartz is known as the stone of love, in my experience its true value is to help us cultivate self love.

IYS Energy Healing is powerful

Early in my healing career, I attended a weekend seminar as the resident healer. A woman who was camping in the beautiful grounds of the remote convention centre where it was held was bitten in the middle of the night by something and she went into anaphylactic shock. This means, she broke out in hives, her body started to swell and the airways closed down. Without assistance she would have died. In fact, her consciousness had already left her body when we found her and she had stopped breathing. I invoked, started sweeping her and energetically 'injected' adrenaline and steroids into her blood stream, whereupon she returned to her body and started to breathe. I kept sweeping and injecting until the ambulance came an hour later. She remained conscious. Various other energy healers came and assisted.

By this time, it was 3 a.m., and we were pretty tired. We gratefully handed her over to the ambulance men and went to bed. I was unable to sleep. I felt I should have gone with her. My rational self told me not to be so silly, because she was in good medical hands

now. The next day we learnt that she had died as soon as she left our circle of light and had to be revived three times on the one hour journey to the hospital, and twice thereafter. She survived, but it was a terrible and nearly fatal lesson in the importance of following the voice of intuition. It also illustrated how powerful energy work can be.

Even when your regular healing efforts do not seem to be getting anywhere, watch and see what happens when you stop. Often the person will deteriorate. Regular healing will prevent a great deal of deterioration, even that which we expect comes with ageing. All kinds of miracles await us as we open to the potential of our spirit, and the inherent power within us to heal ourselves and our worlds.

Your spirit ignited

While it is sometimes complicated, and we get distracted and disheartened from time to time, the journey of self awareness and expansion of consciousness is the journey of our lives. Nothing is as satisfying as experiencing the lightness of being that flows from igniting your spirit.

Understanding the etheric body is just the beginning of the wonderful adventure of spiritual growth and wellbeing. I hope that you will discover for yourself an intensely wonderful inner world full of love, joy, harmony and peace.

May you be blessed and may all good things flow to you.

So be it.

TESTIMONIALS

PHYSICAL HEALING

ALLERGIES

Allergies cured in one session

I have been suffering from allergies since I was a young child which caused stomach issues, chronic sinus infections, headaches, and many other problems. As well, I was recently diagnosed with a histamine intolerance causing many symptoms such as rashes, an increase in asthma symptoms, insomnia, etc. When the histamine levels reach a certain level in my body, I'd have a major allergic reaction on one occasion requiring hospitalisation. Living like this was very scary; I never knew when this allergic response would occur.

In one healing session with Shakti Durga she identified the energetic cause in my body. She gave me tools to use each day to prevent symptoms and to heal my body. Since that day I have been free of all of the symptoms. The daily rashes are gone. I am sleeping better. My asthma has improved, my stomach feels better than it ever has and I am no longer living in fear that something I eat could send me to the hospital.

Stephanie, USA

Rash be gone!

I had a recurring rash that appeared over different parts of my torso over a few weeks. I consulted my doctor who advised it was likely an allergy. IYS Energy Healing addressed some deep-seated emotional issues around low self-esteem. The healing was very gentle, yet deep and transformational, and I have never had a recurrence of the rash in the years since that healing.

Trish, Marketing Coordinator NSW

Painfully itchy scalp and skin healed

I had painfully itchy scalp that for a month had prevented sleep and got in the way of focused work. This problem had occurred previously and I'd found help with using a steroid cream. This time I went for an IYS Energy Healing. After the healing my scalp and skin were completely back to normal, and so it has remained since then! Compassion and loving insight in this healing has shown me the miraculous at work.

Veronica, Teacher, NSW

BLOOD PRESSURE

High blood pressure

I was lying in the hospital with high blood pressure, due to sudden post partum pre-eclampsia and with the doctor's prognosis of not being released for many days yet. I received an IYS Energy Healing and my blood pressure came down low enough that I was discharged to recuperate at home the very next afternoon. Thank you!

Diana, Family & Kids Yoga Teacher NSW

Low blood pressure

After following Doctor's instructions for more than 4 weeks, there was no improvement in my energy levels, and my blood pressure was still at low to very low levels. Within three days of having an IYS Energy Healing I felt my energy levels improve and within a week they were back on track. This was confirmed by my next doctor's visit, where my blood pressure was tested and found to be back to a normal, healthy range.

Wendy, Operations Manager NSW

CANCER

Cancer prognosis

In February 2012 I was diagnosed with a 6cm lesion on my liver. Major surgery included a large L-shaped cut to my midriff and an expected fourteen days in hospital with a minimum of three days in intensive care. The prognosis was no cure, death without the surgery and a liver transplant within the next couple of years. In the six weeks leading up to the surgery I attended two Group Healing sessions and had weekly IYS Energy Healings. The outcome: the surgeon when making initial keyhole incisions to survey the situation, touched the tumour and to quote him, "It fell off, it was a bloody miracle". I was home in three days and fully recovered within two weeks. To date I have had no recurrence of cancer and continue to have regular healings as my only treatment. Having survived a less than positive prognosis, I have gained a sense of peace and purpose and now live a more fulfilling life to that pre IYS Energy Healing.

Julia, IYS Therapist NSW

Breast cancer

I was diagnosed with Breast Cancer and through IYS Energy Healing have found my strength. I have greater love and respect for myself now. I have learnt to live in the moment, see joy around me, cry if I need to. I have learnt life is a journey. Now I am learning to be myself, a powerful and feminine woman.

Jane, Retired Teacher NSW

CARDIAC

Atrial fibrillation, no longer part of my life

Following an Aortic Valve Replacement for a congenitally abnormal valve and also a Coronary Artery Bypass graft, I developed Paroxysmal Atrial Fibrillation. The Atrial Fibrillation always occurred at night, so I developed anxiety about nighttime. Following the IYS Energy Healing session, I instantly felt relief, as if a huge weight had been lifted from my shoulders. Three days later I woke up without even remembering that I'd had open heart surgery!! This was the first time, since being in the Intensive Care Unit. I felt very relaxed and comfortable. I don't think I will ever forget that feeling! Atrial Fibrillation is no longer part of my life and I now happily welcome the evenings and nights.

Anne, The Hill NSW

Cardiac problems resolved

I was rushed to hospital with serious chest pain and many symptoms of angina and other heart issues. I was given many tests that consistently showed a number of cardiac abnormalities. I combined traditional medicine and a series of IYS Energy Healing sessions and have recently had further checks. There are no symptoms or signs of any cardiac problems at all. The cardiologist said he did not need to see me until I am 80!

Mel, NSW

Recovery from cardiac operation

After the healing with Shakti Durga I felt a lot more relaxed and comfortable than I had felt since the surgery. I was more comfortable at Cardiac Rehab than I have felt before and I achieved new goals. My Cardiologist said my blood pressure was quite a bit lower than it had been, the echocardiogram results were good, the pressure through the valve had reduced from 80 to 8! My acupuncture therapist commented that he found my pulse to be very strong and very precise, and he was amazed that it had improved so much in a week! I was smiling to myself because I knew that my pulse had improved a lot because of the healing. He did comment to me at the end of the treatment that I always respond well to treatments because of the energy work that I do.

Anne, Retired NSW

DIGESTIVE/INTESTINAL

Clearing blockages

After having an IYS Energy Healing I felt relief from digestive issues, my heart felt more open and felt more empowered to express my truth in a healthy and wholesome way.

Linda, Retired, NSW

Long term digestive issue healed

I picked up giardia while travelling overseas resulting in long term gastric problems, pain and a very restricted no-wheat diet with no remedy apparently available. Thankfully I discovered IYS Energy Healing. I had four treatments over 12 months feeling an improvement each time until all the symptoms disappeared. It's so good to be able to eat pizza again. Thank you Shanti Mission!

Helen, Retired NSW

Healed intestinal inflammation & breast & lung abnormalities

I had contracted a very serious gut bacteria and lung parasite which became so debilitating that I physically could not function. Medical scans and tests diagnosed Heliobactor Pyloris and lung and breast abnormalities. Through weekly healings and sometimes daily healings I was able to recover. The healings relieved the pain and cleared the streaks in my lungs and the mass behind my breast tissue. This was confirmed after five months of intense healing work by follow-up scans and blood tests. The healings also helped with the depression caused through this debilitating illness.

Yvonne, Practitioner, Teacher ACT

Long term IBS

I have had a battle for nearly thirty years with parasites, causing irritable bowel syndrome and affecting my whole digestive system. I had every treatment possible, including drugs and hospitalisation but no cure. I then had a number of progressive IYS Energy Healings. I have now been free of all symptoms for six months. My life and health have greatly improved with these wonderful healings and I feel like a new man again.

Andrew, Gardener NSW

FERTILITY/NEO-NATAL

Fertility

Suffering severe anxiety after six miscarriages I was desperate to find help. I attended weekly meditation and had IYS Energy Healings and after just one month I fell pregnant again. Nine months later I gave birth to a beautiful and healthy baby boy. This healing modality has given me life's most precious gift.

Belinda, Public Service NSW

Neo-natal healing

My sister's baby was born after a complex C-section operation. After the birth, the baby was taken to intensive care due to severe jaundice. The doctors assessed his jaundice as requiring at least a week in hospital. With my sister's permission I organised for the baby to receive a distance healing. The next morning, I arrived at the hospital to find the baby had been discharged! The doctors said his blood tests showed levels in the safe zone and that my sister could take him home that day! It was a complete turnaround from the day before and literally a miracle.

Jacqueline, Filmmaker UK

More inner peace and a longed for baby

IYS Energy Healing has helped me in so many areas of my life. I feel more inner peace, self awareness, lightness and self love, and love for others, than I thought possible. After a long time trying to fall pregnant and several miscarriages, IYS Energy Healing helped me in a short space of time to become pregnant and have an easy, bliss filled delivery of our son. I am eternally grateful for this powerful healing modality.

Lindsey, Mum UK

INJURY

Healing of tingling and numbness

Before my first session I had altered sensation (tingling and numbness) in both hands, pain in the right side of my neck and right arm, causing difficulty in lifting the arm. This was the result of a work place injury and I was undergoing physiotherapy for treatment. After the session however, the sensations were reduced and I was able to lift my arm over my head. Over the course of seven sessions, there was continued improvement to the point that physio was no longer needed.

Perry, Warehouse Assistant NSW

Dislocated finger – no pain, full recovery

I had a fall on the pavement outside of a Shanti Mission Centre in Sydney and snapped the tendon at the back of my middle finger, which curled backwards and upwards. Two IYS Energy Healing therapists accompanied me to hospital. We waited about an hour to be attended to by a doctor, meanwhile my finger was continuously swept. Although the tendon had snapped there was remarkably very little bruising and swelling, and no pain. The doctors were amazed. I had a very quick recovery with full use of my finger.

Linda, Retired NSW

Walking Freely

After a serious motorcycle accident in which my foot detached from my leg, the surgeons at John Hunter hospital did a brilliant job reattaching it. They told me that if the ligaments and tendons mended it would be six months before I could walk properly. However, after six weeks of IYS Energy Healing my foot was strong enough to walk around Uluru and hike Kings Canyon; such an amazing complementary therapy.

Kain , NSW

PAIN RELIEF

IYS Energy Healing – a great gift of healing!

Through IYS Energy Healing, years of physical pain in my back and joints has cleared. Ten years of high blood pressure has ended! At sixty-two, I now feel healthier, brighter and stronger than I was at forty-two. IYS Energy Healing is a miraculous revelation, reconciliation, support and great fortune to receive!

Stephanie, NSW

Twisted ankle

A couple of hours after twisting my ankle I was in the most physical pain I had ever experienced... A few minutes after I started sweeping, the pain levels went from a 10/10 to a 4/10. Being able to sweep the pain out of my physical body, was an absolute life saver.

Kate, Shop Manager NSW

Pain relief

I knew how life changing IYS Energy Healing was on my emotions and thought patterns, bringing me much peace, confidence and joy in my life. However I am amazed at the effect this therapy could have on my physical body bringing relief from pain, clearing illness and strengthening my overall health. I am extremely grateful. Thank you, thank you, thank you.

Jennifer, Complementary Therapies/Teaching NSW

Pain, depression shifted

Being a nurse I was prone to a few back injuries. The levels of pain increased and was impairing my ability to perform, leading to frustration, depression and anxiety.

I had an IYS Energy Healing and when I was walking back home after the healing I realised I was no longer limping and was walking faster than I could before. Can't be grateful enough to all IYS Energy Healing therapists that have helped me. A true blessing in my life.

Denise, Nurse, London

Pain relief – back surgery prevented

For three years I had suffered from three slipped discs, a pinched sciatic nerve and couldn't sit down for more than fifteen minutes with back surgery now appearing to be my only option. I was in so much pain and had lost hope. After IYS Energy Healing my life changed from pain to peace. chaos to calm, from repression to freedom, and from apathy to vitality. With so much gratitude for this modality.

Angela, Care Worker NSW

Knee pain

Two years ago I was told my right knee needed to be replaced. During an IYS session work was done on both knees particularly the right. Immediately my knee felt like it had been braced, it felt stronger and less painful. I will certainly be seeking more work on my knees.

Cathy, Accounting NSW

Back pain healed

After suffering from a very painful lower back problem for several weeks, I experienced an IYS Energy Healing that completely removed the pain, the underlying emotional causes and left me pain free. It was such a relief to be able to move and to sit freely – it was miraculous.

Jacqueline, Spiritual Teacher NSW

To alleviate chronic pain

After the healing sessions I always feel clear headed, rested and peaceful. This also makes the arthritic pain that I experience (mainly in my feet) a lot better.

Margaret, Retired NSW

Pain eased

I had an IYS Energy Healing for pain and although the pain hasn't shifted completely, I feel a depth of insight into the cause.

Brenda, Sydney Fibromyalgia relief

IYS Energy Healing is a gentle healing technique using energy and breath to release negative energy and stuck emotions from the body. I received significant pain relief after one session of IYS Energy Healing for fibromyalgia by releasing pain from my muscles and joints.

Janelle, air traffic controller, Sydney

Chronic pain

I had long term pain. Through IYS Energy Healing sessions I now manage my pain so well. I am calmer and more in my body. My pain no longer controls me or my day. I have been given a great deal, I feel more grounded in myself.

jane, Retired Teacher NSW

Pain relief after operation, was able to sleep comfortably

I was diagnosed with a hernia in my groin. After an operation I found I could not sleep on my left side, it was painful and uncomfortable. I had one IYS Energy Healing and felt instant relief, the pain was gone and I could comfortably sleep on my left side.

Linda, Retired NSW

Resolve grief, resolve back pain

I had IYS Energy Healing for an old grief that surfaced unexpectedly. The bonus after the healings was that my recurring back pain of twenty years disappeared and has not returned.

Veronica, NSW

SPINAL/SKELETAL

I can walk again – a physical miracle

I was unable to stand or walk for more than five minutes due to L4-5 prolapse disc and severe canal stenosis. This caused acute nerve pain plus weakness and numbness in both feet with only about 20-30% sensation and a lack of balance. Shakti Durga did work on the L4-5 bulging disc and nerves. In the healing I could feel my spine strengthen and elongate. The next day I had 80-90% feeling back in my feet and I could stand and walk, with a huge reduction in pain. A real miracle took place in this healing. Endless gratitude to Shakti Durga and IYS Energy Healing.

Jeannette, NSW

Arthritis gone

Fifteen years ago I fractured a bone in my ankle that couldn't be healed. It would get very stiff if I ran or exercised for more than 30 minutes or sat still for long periods. The day after an IYS Energy Healing I woke up and the stiffness was gone. It is as if there is no arthritis there at all.

Natalie, Manager, Tourism NSW

Disc healed

I suffered for eighteen months with two herniated discs, experiencing excruciating pain and unable to do any exercise or even bend despite having weekly treatments of kinesiology, chiropractic, acupuncture and pain medication. I had one healing with Shakti Durga after which my back pain dissipated. I am back doing yoga and the pain has almost gone.

Helen, Spiritual Teacher NSW

Frozen shoulder healed

I had a shoulder injury which then developed into a frozen shoulder. The doctor wanted to give me cortisone injections but I preferred to try IYS Energy Healing first. In just two sessions I went from being in severe pain, hardly able to dress myself, to being completely healed with no more pain.

Linda, Retired NSW

SURGERY

Smooth sailing into surgery

I sought IYS Energy Healing to prepare my body, mind, and spirit for knee surgery. We also sent forth healing to the hospital: reception, pre- and post-op, the operating theatre and to the hospital team members who would look after me. I awoke from surgery) with a perma-grin. It was an ease and grace-filled experience.

Shelley, Natural Therapist NSW

Major abdominal surgery

I had IYS Energy Healing sessions prior to the surgery, assisting my mental and emotional wellbeing as well as energetically cleansing the hospital and medications and sending blessings to those involved in my surgery. I also had a healing immediately prior to the surgery and another the day after the surgery. The operation went well and my recovery was very straightforward. During the five days I was hospitalised, I felt a beautiful, loving energy was surrounding and supporting me.

Deborah, Teacher NSW

Operation avoided

I took myself to Gosford Hospital with a temp of 39.7, low blood pressure, nausea, gastroenteritis and an infection. I was very sick. The doctors wanted to remove my port-a-cath saying that the infection may have travelled and hidden itself there where the medicine wouldn't work due to the plastic nature of the port-a-cath. The only solution was to remove it and surgery was arranged for the next morning. The night before the operation a group of healers performed a distant IYS healing on all parts of my body. Next morning the doctors came around, checked my stats and told me I had improved so much there would be no operation and I would be discharged that day.

Kerrie, Unemployed NSW

OTHER

Hyperthyroidism

I could barely swallow anything, my heart was racing about 185 bpm, my ankles were swollen, I had night sweats and severe mood swings. The specialist suggested my thyroid would probably have to be partially removed. Three IYS Energy Healing sessions and I was able to stop medication and am eating normally again. It was so effective that I had to study and now I practise the therapy myself along with my body work.

Terence, IYS Therapist, Body Worker NSW

Swallow normally

I couldn't swallow normally for seven years and had pain in my joints. I had a healing. Forgiving was a powerful thing for me. I felt so relaxed afterwards! and I could swallow normally after seven years... And that after one healing... It makes me very happy!

Manon, Hairdresser Netherlands

Instantly well

A sore throat persisted then moved to my chest and I was exhausted for a week... I realised that I felt depressed. During the IYS Energy Healing session the congestion went away and I felt energised. The next day I felt joy and happiness again, all symptoms gone.

Laura, Self-Employed UK

Healed lump

A non-cancerous pigmented mark on my lower leg had been slowly getting larger, and had become raised over a period of three to four years. At my healing I asked if it could be removed. The healer did some work on it and within two months the lump and discolouration were barely visible. Six months on, there was no mark on my leg. I am very grateful and thankful.

Yvonne, Pharmacist/Yoga & Dance Teacher NSW

Insomnia cured after 20 years

I had insomnia that resulted in hyperactivity and exhaustion. I was unable to plan past a few days, had low energy and felt powerless to change. I was fed up and angry. Having tried sleeping tablets and counselling I started having IYS Energy Healing and now I sleep better, I can focus and am finding peace and joy again. I have hope for my future. I have my life back and a new career; it's the greatest gift.

Maureen, Bookkeeper NSW

Relief & acceptance to heal

Prior to my healing session today I was feeling frustrated about taking Warfarin, my previous unstable INR levels and the diet that I had been following. I felt that Warfarin had taken away my freedom. Now, after the session, I feel free and a lot happier. I feel a huge sense of relief. However, I do know that I will continue to work on the acceptance of Warfarin.

Anne, NSW

Healed tonsillitis

My throat was experiencing a lot of infections and tonsillitis. After receiving one healing I have never had to take antibiotics again and do not suffer from tonsillitis anymore.

Amanda, Disability Support Worker NSW

Chronic sinusitis healed

I had chronic sinusitis for a couple of years. A course of antibiotics and it would go away but come back after a few weeks, even a six week course of antibiotics didn't cure the problem. After an IYS Energy Healing session the problem has been under control now for over six weeks. There doesn't seem to be any of the regular pattern of it returning and that is such a relief.

Stuart, Manager NSW

Various physical healings

IYS Energy Healing has not only brought about deep physical and emotional healing for me, it has provided a bedrock for spiritual transformation.

I had my first IYS Energy Healing eighteen years ago, and from that first healing I noticed many differences. Just some of the healings I've experienced during that time include a twenty-year allergy to cats that was healed in one session; a miraculous healing of a badly sprained ankle, where the entire foot, which swelled immediately, lost all swelling and pain within minutes; headaches, toothaches, back aches- all dramatically reduced in rapid time; alleviation of blocked ears while flying... healing on bites, stings, scratches, bumps and bruises..

Sioux, Spiritual Teacher/Healer NSW

Urinary tract infection

When my sister died after a short illness, I was devastated and very run down emotionally and physically. I developed chronic urinary tract infections. When I treated the symptoms with antibiotics, the infection would clear only to return a couple of weeks later. This went on for months. When I went for healing on this issue the infection symptoms cleared that day and after a few more healings the infections stopped all together. I have been clear of this condition for nearly four years now.

Denise, Retired School Teacher NSW

Chronic psoriasis

Prior to IYS Energy Healing I was suffering with chronic psoriasis for thirty years. I had seen many top specialists, tried countless treatments (including chemotherapy drugs and three x my lifetime dosage of UV light). Prior to the series of IYS Energy Healing treatments I received, the psoriasis was the worst ever. Painful, burning, bleeding, covering most of my body. Following IYS Energy Healing the skin cleared, and I experienced huge transformations and freedom emotionally, physically and spiritually.

Justine, Dog Walker NSW

Body healing

Returning to Australia from overseas, I woke up in bed with my eyes open but unable to move my body. I could feel myself breathing but was unable to move. Eventually I was able to roll off the bed and crawl into the shower hoping the warm water would spark some life into my muscles. Eventually I got myself to hospital from where I phoned Shakti Durga and arranged an IYS Energy Healing session. The healing worked and the next day I was up playing a competitive game of football.

Kash, Manager NSW

Stroke

For seven months in 2016 I was the full time carer for my father-in-law. During this time he had pneumonia and two strokes. Following the first stroke he had lost function, movement and sight, down the left side of his body and was hospitalised for one month. Using IYS Energy Healing I was able to assist him back to full function. Following the second stroke

I was onto it immediately and he was only in hospital for five days with no serious symptoms.

Terrence, NSW

Recovered from UTI

I had a urinary tract infection (UTI) and went to the doctor as well as booking an IYS Energy Healing session. The infection and all discomfort cleared the day after the healing whilst halfway through the antibiotics. My doctor called me to discuss test results and informed me that the medicine prescribed was not the correct one for that particular infection. He was astounded by my complete recovery after further tests showed no infection.

Helen, VIC

STRESS, ANXIETY & DEPRESSION

Anxiety & depression

In 2011, I found myself not coping with life. My GP diagnosed me with severe anxiety and moderate to high depression; it led me to IYS Energy

Healing and I found hope for the future, my confidence improved and I was able to find employment.

Kate, Shop Manager NSW

Depression & pain

Having IYS Energy Healing helped me to feel myself again, to lift heaviness within myself and to feel more at peace. IYS Energy Healing also helped alleviate pain within my guts that was affecting my physical well-being.

Dorian, Unemployed NSW

From stress to peace and well being

I had my first IYS Energy Healing session because I was feeling stressed and generally dissatisfied with life. The healing was very pleasant, relaxing and I felt an extreme sense of peace and well being. Over the next few days I noticed I was feeling less anxious and judgemental and more peaceful and accepting of other people. I went on to have many healings over the past year and I now enjoy feeling very centred, happy and in control of my life.

Kelley, Fashion Designer NSW

Opened to the many wonders of happiness and healing

After many years of anxiety and lack of confidence IYS Energy Healing has opened my mind to the universe and provided me with hope and love. I am now open to so many fulfilling friendships and relationships as well as to many opportunities with work.

Ashley, Administrator NSW

Anxiety

I have had changes in my life from the very first IYS Energy Healing. I was a nervous person diagnosed with anxiety. I am no longer nervous or anxious and am very much at peace. My healing sessions have truly healed my anxiety and nervous system. With each healing I have, for the first time in my life, I am at ease and peace within myself, feeling free to find myself in every way.

Julie, Retired Nurse NSW

Depression

I had lived my life with severe depression, had lost my memory three times and also had been diagnosed with PTSD. I had experienced thoughts of self-harm, self-torture and suicidal ideation daily since childhood. After an IYS Energy Healing session the world as I had known it suddenly became calm. A follow-up healing helped me feel free. I am eternally grateful and have devoted my life to this miraculous therapy.

jo, Child & Family Health Nurse NSW

Lifting of depression

IYS Energy Healing has helped me enormously, with both acute distress situations and deep seated patterns addressed long term. I've grown into a strong, resilient person. I am a better leader, mother, sister and friend. I laugh a LOT. I've had so many amazing experiences arising out of IYS Energy Healing: pay rises, easy visits to the dentist, resolution of thorny family and work stuff, positive changes in relationships, more abundance. My therapists have been well trained and highly skilled. For me, IYS Energy Healing is a game changer and a life changer.

Alison, Manager NSW

Depression

My GP diagnosed depression and prescribed medication – I tried two different drugs (each for one week only) before discontinuing them due to unbearable side effects. I also saw a psychologist which was helpful. Soon after I was referred to IYS Energy Healing. Though a little sceptical initially I was open to it as my depression was not improving. From the second session I began to notice lightness in my body and less anxiety. As the sessions continued my mood improved, my self-confidence increased and I moved into a much more fulfilling job. Domestic life was challenging but I found that I could move through this and make right decisions. Sessions were conducted over Skype and this did not affect treatment efficacy. I have come through this whole process feeling happier, lighter and my depression is completely gone.

Arthur, NSW

Depression & anxiety

IYS Energy Healing sessions have been a huge blessing for me as it helped me to move through many challenges, including depression and high level anxiety, a lot quicker than I have previously. I have taken on new things and got my life back on track.

Anonymous, NSW

Stress therapy

IYS Energy Healing helped me get through some difficult situations when I was full of stress and anxiety and getting in my own way. It got to the root cause of the anxiety to release it for good. Now when situations occur that used to overwhelm me, I am able to look at them from a calmer place. Available on Skype, the sessions are convenient and just as powerful as in person.

Denise, USA

Severe depression, anxiety, emotional health issues

A domestic assault triggered PTSD; I felt 'broken' on so many levels. Over the next two years, I endured many losses and developed severe depression, anxiety and other emotional health issues. IYS Energy Healing prevented me from acting out suicidal ideations and to shift out of 'victim consciousness'. I am now depression free and eternally grateful to this healing modality.

Lisa, NSW

Depression no more

After several periods of reactive depression during my life, IYS Energy Healing has taught me that it is not the issues, but my thoughts about the issues in my life that make me spiral down into depression. I feel more positive, more empowered and I can say that I have never been happier in my life. I cannot recommend IYS Energy Healing highly enough.

Cathie, Semi-retired NSW

Changed life of depression

After my first weekend at Shanti Mission I felt like a huge dark shadow had lifted from my body and knew that I had found a modality of healing that was quite spectacular. That was the start of an incredible journey of healing that led me to becoming an IYS therapist and teacher. All my gratitude to Shakti Durga for bringing this therapy to the world.

Yvonne, IYS therapist & Teacher, ACT

Brought hope and love into my life

I had a mild depression for all of my life. It affected me enough to lose self-esteem in many areas, especially in relationships with my family and in my business. I didn't know how to love myself and others. I had IYS Energy Healings and the transformation was phenomenal. I could feel that my emotions were getting stable, even joyous and calm. Now I am a completely different person. I still get regular IYS Energy Healings and they help me to shift any negatives in my thoughts so quickly. My life is full of hope, love, joy, harmony and peace.

Christina, Architect NSW

Depression

I couldn't shake the feeling when my mother passed away that I had not done enough for her, even though everyone told me the opposite, and this led me into depression.

My first healing was incredible, I felt negative energy leaving me and these have completely changed my life for the better.

Kevin, Energy Healer NSW

Depression/anxiety reduced

IYS Energy Healing is one of the most dynamic and effective energy healing therapies I've experienced. I love that it's 'no touch' so I can really relax into the process without my physical body being jarred. I find the releases very helpful, they hit the nail on the head. This process has had long term effect on reducing my depression and anxiety to the point that when I feel these emotions today, I am able to turn to the tools I learnt during our sessions.

Faith, Student, Sydney NSW

Anxiety, post-traumatic stress, depression

I have experienced profound, positive, lasting changes in myself since receiving regular IYS Energy Healing. The modality has assisted me to identify and resolve high level anxiety, post-traumatic stress and depression. Lasting relief from the physical and mental "see-saw", my "normal", has enabled me to make some seriously life affirming decisions that support me achieving my goals. Ingrained instinctual behaviour that derailed me again and again was refined. Digging deep resulted in tangible changes in spontaneous instinctual behaviour. Reflecting upon my life experience today, I can confidently say IYS Energy Healing has changed my life.

Judy, Healer, NSW

Hope returned

My therapist was insightful and gave me guidance for my questions. She acknowledged similar experiences that gave me new hope. I felt held and nurtured in this sacred space to get on with my own healing and connect with the Divine. A blessing to have this place (Shanti Mission) for all to visit!

Amy, Nurse, NSW

Depression lifted, heart healed, hope installed

After a relationship separation I was left feeling depressed in mind, body and spirit. Life carried on without much sparkle or feeling of hope. It was after only two IYS Energy Healing sessions that the shift in my thoughts, feelings, self belief and gusto for life had lifted so much, and was so noticeable in my interactions and relationships, that many people commented on how well I was looking. IYS Energy Healing is an incredible modality and a game changer, somewhat in a league of its own. It is holistic, regenerating and profoundly diverse in its healing applications.

Brett, project delivery officer NSW

Fear of leaving home, anxiety and panic attacks healed

I had been suffering from anxiety and depression and for a long time was unable to leave my house at all. After IYS Energy Healings I am now driving and getting out and about more every day without fear and anxiety. This is truly a miracle for me.

Sylvia, NSW

Alleviation of fear and anxiety

My life has been transformed by IYS Energy Healings. Joy, love, empowerment, trust and creativity have replaced depression, anxiety and fear. Miraculous!

jenny, Artist/teacher NSW

A lifetime of anxiety gone

All my life I have suffered anxiety. In recent years I would wake up every morning in fear. Following four treatments, I no longer wake up to the dread of fear. My life is now full of peace and gratitude. My life is a miracle. Forever grateful.

Chris, Teacher NSW

No more anxiety!

My therapist helped me to let go of stress, anxiety and pain that was trapped inside me for so long. I had suffered from anxiety since childhood. After the healings people said I had a sparkle in my eye and a different presence. I felt taller, healthier and more at peace with myself and others. My life has changed permanently for the better. And my family have also benefitted greatly.

Paula, Teacher NSW

ADDICTION

Released from alcohol addiction

In addiction for over seventeen years, I was diagnosed with PTS and lived in a constant cloud of misery, doom and gloom, high stress, running from one place to another, being endlessly restless. After attending IYS Energy Healings: I stopped drinking alcohol, my PTS has eased, family relations have improved and I have my first committed relationship and feel 100% happier.

Jamie, Guest Services Officer NSW

Free of 35 years of substance abuse

Healing Clinics are a blessing. I attended these community offerings on a weekly basis, they helped me to gently release decades of suppressed emotions; process my pain with many kind and caring practitioners who unconditionally accepted me and supported my healing journey. By 2013 I had released all attachment to substance abuse and I am addiction free.

Lisa, TBD NSW

Drug, cigarette, alcohol addictions quashed

Through IYS Energy Healing, in conjunction with a 12-step recovery program, I lost the desire to use drugs, alcohol and cigarettes after struggling with these addictions for 28+ years. My life is completely transformed. I don't recognise myself or my life after almost two years clean and sober, and I am forever grateful to Shakti Durga and IYS Energy Healing for the freedom to live a conscious, purposeful, soulful life now.

Justine, NSW

EMOTIONAL

Nervous anxiety

After a fifteen minute IYS Energy Healing my butterflies and nervousness that have always been with me, were gone. I felt so relaxed and confident afterwards.

Vikki, Retired Nurse NSW

Deep and lasting emotional healing

As well as overwhelming physical healing results, I have experienced deep and lasting emotional healing of many old wounds, including grief, anger, shame and loss. Blockages to happiness have been resolved and my life is now joyous and filled with love.

Sioux, Spiritual Teacher/Healer NSW

Forgiveness

Separated from my husband, son and community, my self-esteem was really, really low and I was feeling bullied at work. Filled with confusion and rage I internalised it, an angry, bitter, resentful loop formed in my thinking, it haunted me for years. Now, after IYS Energy Healing, my life feels more joyful, peaceful and surrendered. When I awake each day, I feel grateful for my life and 'everyone' in it.

Rosemary, Account Executive NSW

Transformation

Several years ago I was introduced to Shanti Mission and it changed my life. When I first had IYS Energy Healing I was quite sceptical, but the changes I experienced in my emotional and physical body are transformational. IYS Energy Healing has become an important part of my life, it is my 'go to' every time I feel there is an issue to resolve.

Lia, Accountant NSW

Forgiveness freed me

My mum left my dad and my two brothers when I was nine. I believed I wasn't enough, always feeling separate, not able to fit in anywhere. I blamed her and was very angry, I had no idea that not being able to forgive her was hurting me, limiting me so much. IYS Energy Healing helped me to forgive, I am no longer a victim, I feel connected and my relationship with my mum is now strong and growing all the time.

Michelle, Artist/Teacher NSW

Emotional support through grief process

Having IYS Energy Healing as support when my sister was ill and when she died, helped me to manage my emotions and to grieve in a safe way. I felt held, supported, loved and nurtured through the experience. I was able to heal any relationship issues that we had and was able to come to a place of acceptance and surrender to the journey of her leaving her body at that time. I am so grateful to the presence of IYS Energy Healing in my life.

Denise, Retired School Teacher NSW

Saying goodbye to a dear family member

I had a healing to assist with processing grief around the death of my mother-in-law. We were very close and I felt a lot of pain both emotionally and physically. I was struggling. The healing began a process that helped me to resolve the many difficulties surrounding her death and the challenging circumstances leading up to it. I also gained the ability to connect with her essence in a very joyful and honouring way. Her parting gift - the grace to truly ignite my spirit.

Kylie, Hairdresser, NSW

Start anew

I had been through a lot and felt very congested. The healing helped me clear the congestion, and gain clarity. Forgiveness work was very helpful in helping me to be more confident and empowered.

Linda, Retired, NSW

Reclaimed joy

I would freeze whenever I felt threatened or overwhelmed. The IYS Energy Healing revealed the source of this fear and gave me the opportunity to release it. The result is that I feel a renewed sense of joy, playfulness and vitality.

Cheryl, Consultant USA

Forgiveness

I give great thanks for the IYS Energy Healings I have received assisting with my family's health. This has brought healing for not just me, it has helped our ability to communicate our true feelings to each other, without angry voices and blaming each other. I now hold gratitude because healing this has helped create who I am today and I now love myself.

Joanne, Mum NSW

Healing decades of old grief

I had an IYS Energy Healing to help deal with old feelings of grief for my mum's death over a decade before. I felt the grief I had been carrying for so long lift away like a physical weight from my body. I was profoundly healed that day. Thank you!

Jaqueline W, Film maker, UK

Grief after marriage break up

I received a weekly IYS Energy Healing session for about 10-12 weeks. I spent just a few sessions crying. I felt safe and loved. I learnt so much about myself, I became more loving to me, I began to nurture me, and cut attachments to my past. I began to be more "Jane" the real "Jane" in my body, grounded!!!

jane, Retired teacher, NSW

Deep healing

After a core issue, that I had done a lot of work on, suddenly re-emerged one day I took it into a healing. The therapist skilfully and gently guided me back to the time when the issue had begun and he masterfully helped me to reconcile it within my being. It was his sensitivity, attuned presence and skill as a healer that enabled this deep level of healing to occur.

Andrea, Therapist, NSW

Forgiveness

I have always carried an overwhelming guilt that I couldn't help my mum more, to not suffer as much, (both when I was young and she was an alcoholic, and when she passed away from cancer). It wasn't rational guilt however I didn't believe it was ever possible to forgive myself. Through IYS Energy Healing I was able to forgive myself wholeheartedly. I've felt so much freedom and joy since. I've had fifteen years of attending therapy and Al-Anon, however it was the healing that enabled me to access forgiveness completely.

Penny, Creative Facilitator NSW

Open to love

My healer perceived that past hurts were impacting on my self-esteem. Her soft, caring words flowed as she cleansed and released the past hurt and emotions. The healing helped me feel more whole, complete and worthy in all I say, do and be. This healing left me feeling beautiful, radiant, joyous and abundant. A special, graceful, empowering healing for which I am very grateful.

Linda, Retired NSW

Grief lifted

After a relationship break up and the recent death of a good friend, I was experiencing quite intense grief, like I had never felt before - and it was showing no signs of lifting... until I had IYS Energy Healing. During the healing I was able to release the deep source of the grief and the heavy sadness that had lingered for many months suddenly lifted. It was quite miraculous.

Andrea, Therapist, NSW

Stress release

The IYS Energy Healing was great and brought down my stress levels enormously and quickly. Thanks again!

Nicola, UK

Stress healed

Pregnant with my second child I felt stressed beyond manageable. I found myself turning to sources I never turned to before to keep me and my baby safe. I started having Skype IYS Energy Healings. These healings have changed my life in more ways than one - my inner self, my work life, my family life, my marriage and my life as a whole.

Nicole, USA

Empowerment & calm

IYS Energy Healings have led me to a deeper understanding of my inner self and empowered me to manage what life may bring. Each session leaves me with a sense of calm and hope.

Cathy, NSW

Profound physical and emotional healing

The grief I experienced after losing my sister suddenly had left me in a state of shock and disbelief and I was physically and emotionally exhausted. I booked an IYS Energy Healings. I was able to release long held beliefs that held me back from allowing support into my life. Harsh core beliefs around 'how I was meant to be coping' dissolved and flowed away. Within days I felt lighter and the exhaustion left me. Relationships

I had turned my back on healed and my overall health improved in all areas. My gratitude for this healing is with me still.

Carmel, OCV NSW

Healing of the past

The IYS Energy Healing enabled me to let go of old pain and suffering, which was coming up in my present life. I let go of tricky emotions (fear, anger...) and the feeling of being stuck. It really helped me to be more present in relationships and to nurture myself.

Penny, Teacher NSW

Marriage ending

After my breakup from a volatile relationship I was in a very fragile and vulnerable state. I had just left my career, I had no income, no home, I had massive debt and had to rely on friends and family to support me and my child. This situation was my biggest fear, and I felt like a complete failure in all areas of my life. This left me emotionally wrecked.

With regular IYS Energy Healing I began to gain strength again. I began to really heal my low self-worth. Within four months the whole separation was resolved, which was beyond belief. Although this was one of the hardest experiences of my life, I was able to face these fears and get through it with what I believe was the highest possible outcome for everyone with the highest integrity. I cannot be more grateful to the IYS Energy Healing I received during this time, it literally got me through.

Samantha, Forensic Scientist NSW

317

Joy is my birthright

My life was characterised by responsibility, dependability and hard work; even rich life experiences could not make me happy. In an IYS Energy Healing session the master therapist asked that I be blessed with the vast joy that she held. Some three years later, while trekking in Nepal, joy burst fully within and out of me. I know that session in 2010 rewired me for joy to be part of my reality.

Sharon, Therapist, Teacher NSW

Child 5yo sleeps in own room for the first time

My five year old granddaughter had never slept in her own bed in her own room alone. She always needed to be close to her mum or dad, often sleeping in their bed. She saw a master therapist who specialises in babies and children. Not long after this session she slept in her own bed, in her own room, on her own. After five years this is an amazing breakthrough.

Lynette, Teacher NSW

Green toad... self-esteem healing

During a healing the therapist said "I just perceived a green toad jump out of your crown chakra! Does that mean anything to you?" Yes, it did! In my childhood, a story had been read to me many times about a green toad who was full of self-admiration. It puffed him up so much that he burst! And that was the end of him. Unconsciously I had absorbed from this story that it wasn't OK to say nice or good things about myself. And without realising it I had so often felt uncomfortable when people talked about themselves with love. A clearing up of this made a big difference in my life. I could now accept a large part of myself that I'd rejected. The door was open to accepting love in others. All this from one childhood story and the perception of the healer!

Veronica, Healer, Teacher NSW

Feeling overwhelmed & fear of moving forward

During the healing session we worked on feeling overwhelmed and fear of staying in the game without faltering. The session was amazing and I felt energy shifted through me and I'm feeling great after it.

Jake, Entrepreneur NSW

RELATIONSHIPS

Emancipation

My relationships with others and myself were in disarray. Having regular IYS Energy Healing sessions and group meditations, the layers began to come away. It was a long process but finally I have relationships with kind, loving and powerful people and I live a life of purpose.

Ann, Kinesiologist, Singer/Songwriter NSW

Family history

I tapped into old family patterns of rivalry, bitterness and sadness. Receiving this healing allowed me to heal current relationships with my family members and to heal relationships between family members that were toxic before I was born. It broke the family habit of judgement, blame and shame between us. It gave me hope and support to awaken to more love.

Penny, Teacher NSW

319

Breakthrough healing of relationship

IYS Energy Healing is amazing. My relationships have blossomed and grown. I am free of old problems and patterns.

Susan, Cook, NSW

Resolution of family conflict

Relationships within my family were creating tremendous emotional strain. Through IYS Energy Healing I learnt to forgive, trust and surrender. Now many years later my family lives in harmony. My parents smile and laugh again, and I no longer fear phone calls.

Anon, Teacher, n NSW

Five minute healing – what a difference!

I attended a meditation after which they offered five minute IYS Energy Healings. The next day I was able to have an assertive conversation in which I needed to set boundaries and express my truth. I did all with relative ease and felt empowered to take the next step. I have no doubt that a huge part of this was my five minute healing the day before!

Julie, Educator NSW

Better relationships

After receiving an IYS Energy Healing session I had more clarity, was happier and I began to love and nurture myself more. Expressing myself clearly and communicating with others better, came with ease. I now have better relationships with work colleagues, friends and family. I am grateful for my life now and the abundance of love, joy and peace that surrounds me everyday. I have become more financially abundant and keep using my skills and healing sessions to expand that more.

Amanda C, Disability Support Worker, NSW

Closer to my soul self

I have two teenage children and recently became very aware of my self sabotaging nature. I was offered a healing and what happened was so uplifting and freeing. My challenges with the way my son was behaving seem to have disappeared. Priceless is the value I ascribe to that session.

Tania, Kinesiologist, NSW

Low self-esteem and family relationship issues

For over four and a half years I have received healings from trainee and trained therapists in the healing clinics on lots of things. Many healings on shame and blame helped with family relationships and slowed arguments right down making my house and myself more peaceful.

Vikki, Retired enrolled nurse, NSW

Taking my power back

One of my children, with partner and child, sold their house and wanted to move back home. I had them living with me a few years ago and it wasn't pretty. I went for IYS Energy Healing where we cut some cords and worked on taking my power back. I was able to stay in my power when I went to talk to them and I was able, for the first time, to say NO with LOVE.

Fiona, NSW

Isolation

In one healing with Shakti Durga I released long held blockages that had kept me feeling separated and always the outsider my whole life. I feel more easily able to relate to people and less fearful of challenging relationships. I have noticed a significant shift in the way I feel and how people respond to me. A most profound and noticeable change. I am now more able to engage with the world in a positive way.

Diane, Marketing & Communications Manager NSW

Irresistible

I had an IYS Energy Healing to help call in my Divine partner and have now attracted that partner into my life.

Amy, Director of Mental Health USA

Miraculous relationship renovation

My first IYS Energy Healing with Shakti Durga transformed a difficult relationship situation. Before the healing I was feeling emotionally drained, lost in the situation and without support or resources to make decisions about my next steps. In the healing I felt the confusion and mixed energy of the people involved lift from my body and mind. I felt like my lost self was rescued and lovingly restored and the energy draining me was returned. I felt lighter, and was able to think more clearly. I became emotionally calm and felt supported. This helped me to easily decide my next steps. I felt I was back to my old self again – only I was a better self.

Jacqueline, Spiritual Teacher, former Lawyer USA

Regular IYS

I have regular healings helping me to successfully transform how I see and deal with life and my relationships, especially the one with myself.

Helen, NSW

Healed relationship with mum

My relationship with my mother had always been filled with love but it was often tumultuous and seemed like there was something missing. I often felt that we were very closed off from each other. In my healing we did a lot of forgiveness work, especially around the past. I felt a lot of lightness flow into my relationship with mum. Since this healing our relationship has improved immensely and the void that was once there and unexplainable has dispersed. I'm forever grateful.

Arlene, Spiritual Teacher, IYS Therapist NSW

Like a miracle

My first healing was for me like a miracle. A lifetime of pain in my heart, due to a difficult relationship with my mother, was completely gone from my being and from my energy field. I felt lightness that I had never experienced before. I felt the absence of being bound in a very negative relationship. I was free.

Colleen, Teacher NSW

Relationship with business partners changed

For many years I was a director of a small business. I was always extremely stressed and my relationship with my business partners was challenging. I started having IYS Energy Healing, and my stress levels reduced, there were no more dramas at work and my business partners started being nice!

Tracey, Business Owner NSW

Changed my life

I was in a rut, feeling bored with life and discussing with my partner whether to end our fifteen year relationship when I went for my first IYS Energy Healing. During the next forty minutes I was transformed! I left feeling alive, energized and ready to face the world. Our relationship healed and continues to grow and change with us.

Helen, Retired VIC

Transformation

I had a lot going on in my life: separated from my third marriage, started a new relationship that wasn't going to my plan, and I felt emotional angst – I didn't know what to do. I had an IYS Energy Healing. The immediate transformation was incredible. I was still in the same situation but I felt differently about everything. My life has been transformed.

Debbie, Buyer NSW

PSYCHOLOGICAL WELL-BEING

Deep bliss

Thanks to IYS Energy Healings, painful and difficult emotions that felt normal, I now see can be healed and released. I can find new ways of being whole and at peace.

Graeme, Australia

Trauma healing

IYS Energy Healing is a powerful and profound experience for me. It has helped me deal with trauma, heightens my vitality and helps me release emotional ties to the past.

Danica, Exec Assistant/Singer/Dancer/Choreographer NSW

Healing of childhood trauma

I had IYS Energy Healing around a childhood trauma. After a number of sessions it was like the issue had never occurred, the pain no longer exists and I have not had any further issues. Previously I had had extensive counselling for this issue but was unable to release the pain. IYS Energy Healing was absolutely life-changing and I'm extremely grateful.

Melanie, Community Health NSW

Trauma

I had an IYS Energy Healing to help me overcome anger that I felt towards everyone and everything, a result of childhood abuse. I had tried other therapies with little success but after a 45 minute healing I was a completely different person. So many parts of my life changed as a result. I was able to feel happy, words are not enough to express my gratitude.

Kathryn, Healer NSW

Trauma release

I had suffered a few breakdowns and efforts to explain different planes of existence I was experiencing to psychiatrists were messy, so I learnt to say nothing and tried to hide even from myself. Through IYS Energy

Healing I now have understanding and clarity for all I see and sense beyond the physical and see the gift it brings. I am now so grateful for the dis-ease that brought me to IYS Energy Healing. I can wholeheartedly say I am in peace.

Janice, Artist UK

Stop self abuse

For several weeks I repeatedly 'accidentally' cut myself with the same small kitchen knife. In an IYS Energy Healing session I was helped see that the kitchen accidents were a symptom of the self-punishment I had been inflicting on myself since I was young. Acknowledging the pattern and forgiving myself for it stopped the pattern of unconscious self-harm. I'm now more aware, safer and kinder with myself.

Sharon, Administrator NSW

Trauma healed

During an IYS Energy Healing session I was held in a completely safe and supported environment to identify a past trauma, move through that experience and come to a place of love, gratitude and forgiveness. I felt empowered by the experience and able to come into more love than before.

Mel, Community Mental Health Worker, NSW

Cloud nine

My depression had returned. I felt enraged and sad at the world around me that I wanted to leave it. Guided to IYS Energy Healing, I left feeling foolish for spending the money but soon I was feeling scrumptious sunshine on my face, my feet lifting off the pavement; breathing the sweetness of the flowers and I felt myself smile. Surely this feeling was not because of a silly little healing... was it?

Lauren, Commercial Interior Designer NSW

Released family trauma

I had great difficulty letting people get close to me. The healing went straight to the core of the issue and transformed how I interacted with everyone, no longer fearful of allowing people to get close to me. A lifechanging experience.

Kerry, Spiritual Entrepreneur, NSW

Rapid shift in thoughts & feelings around past abuse

After years of therapy to deal with past abuse in my life, I found that the most profound healing happened for me when I had IYS Energy Healing sessions. I was able to fully release the deep emotions, beliefs and thoughts that were affecting so many areas of my life. IYS Energy Healing has been absolutely life changing for me! I am so grateful!

Lisa, Primary School Teacher NSW

Transformed traumatic childhood memories

When I was in high school I was bullied relentlessly. This memory has stayed with me into adulthood, and it has been very hard to let go of the anger and resentment. This was until I had an IYS Energy Healing session focused on this experience. My perception of the situation totally transformed. The anger lifted and I am now able to feel compassion, love and forgiveness for my childhood bullies.

Erik, Marketing NSW

SPIRITUAL

The way home

The journey to live from my Soul and from my Heart has been a long road.

I have had many healings; I am a qualified Ignite Your Spirit Therapist now and love the process. I have thirty-five years of practice as a counsellor / trauma therapist but nothing in the mainstream addresses the connection with the Soul. IYS Energy Healing opens doors to higher realms of consciousness, Love, Joy, Light and Peace and ultimately takes us Home to our own Soul... nothing else satisfies me. When I came to Shanti Mission I was in an unhappy state after a traumatic separation. Just recently I cleared and healed the core wound of abandonment and life is different now. IYS Energy Healing, satsangs, kirtan, blessings... it is my life now and constantly feeds the evolution of my Soul, as I grow in spiritual maturity... ever expanding.... into more bliss and readiness for service to humanity.

Deanne, Counsellor, Therapist, Healer NSW

Growing connection to universe and angels

Thank you for all the healings I have had with IYS Energy Healing over the past four years that has bought me to this present moment knowing I am enough. I am loved by the universe as I love me, and am grateful for my birth and all that I am. Thank you to the Angels of the Universe who unconditionally love and support my journey – may I continue to be in service to love, joy and peace with ease and grace.

j, NSW

Spiritual transformation – lift out of depression

Ever since I can remember, the deeper questions of 'why are we here?' and 'what am I supposed to be doing in this life?' have been in the forefront of my mind. The fundamentalist Christian upbringing I experienced left me angry at God, and I sought answers in more earth based spirituality. Despite being a 'spiritual seeker' all my life, I became depressed, suffered chronic fatigue, worried about the state of the world, focused on all the negatives, blamed others for everything, and felt powerless to make a difference in the world.

Through having ongoing IYS Energy Healings and using the tools taught at Shanti Mission, I have learnt to raise my own vibration towards love, peace and joy. The depression I used to live with is gone, my general health is vastly improved, I feel immense gratitude for everything in my life, I've made peace with the Divine, and I now know that I can make a positive difference in the world.

Ruth, musician/teacher NSW

Spiritual growth

IYS Energy Healings have been invaluable for my spiritual growth and general wellbeing. It's assisted me through some extremely challenging periods into higher states of consciousness, gaining new perspectives, learning and understanding what moves me into more peace, love and harmony in any area of my life.

Carmen, Australia

Healing clinic

The healing clinic so generously offers the community a loving and knowledgeable space where I can heal old wounds and clear stuck energy that holds me back. It provides insights into these matters and opens the way to let new, more loving, joyful energy into me and expanding this wonder and love-filled vibrancy to all with whom I have relationship. Thank you for re-igniting the spirit of Divinity within myself and to all beings in the world.

Kirsten, NSW

FINANCIAL ABUNDANCE

Able to enjoy abundance

I used to always be thinking about how to manage my money and was very concerned about my finances, even though I had a good full time job and worked hard. It seemed that I always did things 'on the cheap', worried a lot about spending money even on absolute necessities and would never 'treat myself' to anything slightly frivolous. IYS Energy Healings made me realize that I had been living with a poverty mentality all my life and this had significantly affected how I interacted with the world. Subsequent healings helped me develop trust in the process of life, security in myself rather than money, and to value and respect myself as worthwhile. I stopped thinking about money all the time. This was very freeing, and I was subsequently able to change my lifestyle so that I didn't have to work as hard or long, started to enjoy more of the pleasures in life, and allowed myself to do things that I would never have considered possible in the past, like travel overseas.

Ruth, Musician/Teacher, NSW

CAREER/VOCATION

Career boost

I had already spent quite a lot of time trying to finish my rehabilitation thesis but I couldn't complete it. I had IYS Energy Healings online and the result was that in a couple of months I concluded the writing, handed the work in and was promoted after finishing the report process with excellence. I was appointed as a professor in my field of research (the first at my university), a new faculty was built and my area was included in a newly established department for which I was elected the head. My personal life developed along the lines of my professional career, amazingly.

Barbara, Uni Professor, Head of Dept – Austria

Day job traded for dreams and visions

Even though I had played music all my life, and studied music at a tertiary level, I didn't consider myself good enough to be a 'musician'. I thought it was unrealistic and impossible that I could have a life as a musician so I contented myself with working as a nurse and teaching music 'on the side'. Through IYS Energy Healings and studying the Path of Ease and Grace at Shanti Mission, I came to understand that by addressing my low self-esteem, learning to respect and approve of myself, and calling on the Divine to work through me, I could accept that I really was a musician and had lots to offer as a performer as well as a teacher. I've been able to give up my 'day job' and have embraced a fulfilling and expansive lifestyle, following my dreams and visions as a musician.

Ruth, Musician/Teacher, NSW

Tripling my clients and income!

Business healing - I went to an IYS Energy Healing therapist for a healing on my business. I was finding it hard to get new clients and better income. We cleared up old beliefs around my value and old expectations.

The result was that I had six new clients book in within one day and my income that week was more than double that of the previous week. Amazing!

Lisa, Spiritual Teacher and Public Servant, ACT

Blocks to moving forward in my career cleared

After being made redundant in my early fifties I had high hopes of pursuing my healing practice and meditation classes. The reality of this began to falter as every self-sabotaging excuse I could find for not getting this plan underway arose. I had also experienced grief and loss of four family members in a short period during this time; I had lost the drive to move on. I booked an IYS Energy Healing session which unlocked doors that had been closed to me for a long time. Fear of failure was dissolved, freeing me up to start afresh. After the session I was able to set up my healing practice with enthusiasm and delight. Also allowing grief to be felt without judging myself assisted me in growing stronger and more empowered. I am so grateful for this modality – it provides an ease and grace way into living in peace.

Carmel, official community visitor, NSW

ANIMAL HEALING

Horse – founder and colic

I had a Shetland pony who foundered. Her feet were a terrible mess, she was in pain and the vet thought we may have to put her down. I gave her IYS Energy Healing every day for ten days, sometimes twice a day and her feet completely normalized. We had locked her into a small yard to stop her overeating the long green grass, the main cause of founder. Instead, she ate the sand and developed colic; often fatal. The prognosis was poor. I continued to give her healing. She made a full recovery. When I went to give her away several years later, the farrier who came to inspect her was told that she had foundered, but he saw no evidence of it at all.

Shakti Durga

Pet relieved from symptoms of bone cancer

My beautiful seven-year-old best mate Scrappy, was diagnosed with an aggressive bone cancer and given only thirty days before he would be in so much pain that I'd have to have him put to sleep. I took him to IYS Energy Healing animal clinic walking in with a very sick, lethargic and somewhat depressed dog. After the healing he was brighter, happier and full of energy. We then attended each month and Scrappy lived for 165 days and had a very good quality of life in that time. My vets were absolutely amazed at how well he was doing. My boy couldn't be saved, but the IYS Energy Healing managed to slow down the growth of the tumour and eliminate a great deal of the side effects of the medication while using less than recommended. In the end they prepared his soul and he was truly at peace.

Mandi, NSW

Puppy relieved of anxiety and medication reduced

I took a pup with special needs to an IYS Energy Healing animal clinic. Severe and savage abuse had given her a traumatic start to life and she suffered major anxiety and PTSD. She was on two different forms of anxiety medication. Within a very short space of time I was able to ween her off one of the medications. The evidence of how well the healing worked was more than apparent with every session we attended.

Mandi, NSW

Horse biting owner

A horse was biting his owner. After six months of being a good horse, he turned nasty. The IYS Energy Healing session revealed that he had an injury, the owner was unaware of it. As soon as this was realised, the horse started looking for hugs and connection. His disturbing behaviour stopped. He was then taken to a chiropractor and his injury was treated. A very happy horse and owner.

Vikki, Retired Nurse, NSW

Helped my dog Bindi

We adopted Bindi last year and found she must have been roughly treated and was suffering epilepsy. She has improved since receiving IYS Energy Healing.

Sue, Retired NSW

Trauma healed, lovingly re-homed

I first came across the Animal Healing Clinic in Cooranbong when I was a volunteer pet foster carer for a neurologically challenged puppy; Mia had been rejected by her mother. Healers offered insight to her health condition then went to work on her energetically. Over several healings, Mia was able to function more normally (not walking in circles so much) and her risk of death decreased dramatically. Mia was re-homed into a wonderful family that she loves very much.

Michelle, NSW

Distance healing bringing peace

The Animal Healing Clinic team have assisted me to re-home many hard to-rehome adult cats much quicker than usual. In particular, one very difficult cat named Lucy who I had in care for more than six months. Lucy was stalking other permanent and foster cats in my home causing grief and fear. She had a distance healing and the healer also cleared the way for the most perfect home for Lucy to arrive. Four days later Lucy was re-homed into a loving family where, months later, she resides happily.

Generally, I have witnessed energetic healings that offer cats and dogs inner peace and calmness. Energetic healing offers wonderful support to a rescue animal that has often been through difficult circumstances prior to coming into rescue. I have much gratitude for the assistance the healers provide me in my work as a foster carer.

Michelle, NSW

Angry cat healed

An angry cat was attacking his new family. Having moved four times, he was full of constant fear and insecurity. He received an IYS Energy Healing session after which he quickly recovered from his torment. His owners were finally able to play with him and even hug him. He was a new cat, walking around after his human family, looking for affection.

Vikki, Retired Nurse, NSW

Support for end of life

Thank you for the Animal Healing Clinic for its support and healing through a difficult transition for both myself and my dog Rajah. Rajah, who has now passed on, was a fourteen and a half-year old German Shepherd, who in the end could hardly walk or pass motions. He was/ is a valued family member. A special thank you to the healing clinic facilitators, through their love and support we were both able to move forward and let go.

Ron, NSW

Healing of anaemia in new kittens

In February 2015 my cat had three kittens. At four weeks old one of the kittens became very sick unexpectedly, dying at the vet that night. Tests indicated anaemia, very few red cells left.

The two other kittens were also found to be anaemic, one being even worse than the first, both not expected to survive. The vet suggested a blood transfusion, followed by antibiotics. it is rare for such small kittens to survive a transfusion and they were already very sick and weak.

Energy healing commenced straight away, I also contacted the animal healing clinic. With ongoing energetic support they lived through the transfusion and further treatment. On day five the vet called and asked if we could collect the kittens as they were too lively to keep in the hospital. They became healthy and happy and moved to their new homes at three months of age.

Anonymous

IYS on animals

My horses have had many healings helping them heal much more quickly from injuries. I've helped many horses with behaviour issues and used healings during the breaking-in process. In fact, I use this work in all areas of my life; it makes everything easier.

Vicki , NSW

PLANT HEALINGS

My new fruit trees loved IYS Energy Healing too!

Using IYS Energy Healing on my new fruit trees when I first planted them has really made a difference. My white nectarine tree is less than a year in the ground and happily bearing fruit already. I've not lived there now for three months but she's still okay. I love IYS Energy Healing!!!!

June, Volunteer, NSW

GENERAL

Better life

Every time I use IYS Energy Healing I'm always struck with how much I get from it. Mentally – understanding self and guidance. Emotionally – getting more self-mastery. Physically and spiritually – feeling of satisfaction in my soul. IYS Energy Healing is very practical, it helps all aspects of life; health, relationships, self-esteem and addictions.

Yevgeniy, NSW

Expanding consciousness

IYS Energy Healing ignites everything – my mind, body, emotions, energy, understanding, ideas, enthusiasm, motivation, will and spirit too. Encourages me to turn over rocks that I've been determinedly keeping in place, the stubbornness dissolves and allows me to see what I've been hiding from and bring it to the light for healing, leaving me seeing things from a higher perspective.

Patricia, NSW

Shifts the 'tricky stuff"

IYS Energy Healing sessions are deep, transformative and powerful; intuition and energetic skill shift the 'tricky stuff'. My connection to the divine has strengthened and this awakening of Self has led me to having more fulfilling relationships with the people in my life, with more fun and joy.

Aimee, UK

Transformation

I have experienced a transformation in my life where my default setting is now joy and self-worth. I could never have anticipated that this journey could be so much fun!

Janice, Healer, Scotland

Transformation

IYS Energy Healings are powerful and transformational.

Deb, Native Sharman Healer NSW

Life-Changing

I have felt safe enough to explore the depths, to drop down into my core in our IYS Energy Healing sessions.

Andrea, Newcastle NSW

I left a changed person

I came in with the hope of learning a little more about the blockages in my life. I left understanding the reasons for those blockages and an acceptance that I could change. I left a changed person.

Stacy, Tamworth

Healing clinic

I spent a beautiful morning at the healing clinic for meditation and healing. What a wonderful place! I leave feeling much lighter, with more peace in my heart.

Gwen, NSW

A healthier version of myself

I always leave the IYS Energy Healing feeling light, happy and confident that I am making progress towards a healthier version of myself. I have made tremendous progress with my career and personal life. I feel much healthier and balanced than ever before. I highly recommend IYS Energy Healing for all people in need of healing. I am confident that through my therapist's help and support, I am able to heal my mind, body and soul.

Loren, Actor, NSW

Rejuvenation from IYS Energy Healing

I was feeling very tired and floundering with my life's path. I always feel more relaxed and connected after an IYS Energy Healing. I recommend these IYS Energy Healings to anyone.

Nell, Retired/carer, NSW

Healing the past

I was feeling generally well and healthy but chose to seek an IYS Energy Healing for a general etheric polish. I was amazed by the intuitive perception of the therapist. She identified a period of challenge that occurred when I was twenty-one years old, over twenty years ago. She gently brought this to my attention and we were able to heal this past event. My self-awareness was widened as I reflected on this event with an expanded consciousness.

Richard, army officer, NSW

Core issues healed

I felt so heavy, drained and stuck. The IYS Energy Healing allowed me to let go of past hurts and to forgive. A truly remarkable breakthrough. I am now ready to start afresh.

Linda, Retired, NSW

Regret

I found that IYS Energy Healing heals the big things, but much of its beauty lies in healing the subtle things. For me nuances of regret for what I didn't do or say in past situations revisited me. Even though I knew I did the best I could at the time, these regrets were like fish hooks tugging at my heart. My healer assisted me to release these from my energy body and free my heart to experience deeper self-love.

Colleen, Teacher, NSW

Life much improved

My husband and I had poor health and low vitality. Our family and work life needed a lot of attention. Through IYS Energy Healing we have learned how to love, honour and respect ourselves. I now experience abundant energy and vitality. My working life is filled with laughter and very loving relationships with colleagues. We greet each other with love now. Another family member has moved from the depth of despair to increasing health and happiness.

Catherine, Aged Care, NSW

Life direction

I was confused about where my life was going. My therapist helped me to lift the confusion and to see clearly. I could now move forward to where my heart and soul were calling me. My strength and courage returned and helped me to make the right choices for my continued spiritual and educational growth. This allowed me to let go, to move forward and to take steps towards a brighter future where my authentic self could prosper. As well, a very old physical injury was healed.

jenny, Teacher, NSW

Healing clinic

I find the healing clinic friendly, comfortable and safe. Recommend it to anyone.

Mark, Chiropractor, NSW

More time in my heart

It was wonderful to receive tools that are so gentle to use, easy to use, creative and that fitted me exactly. I use them to expel a complaining inner voice. They help me to be in my heart and to be generous towards myself and others. What a gift!

Veronica, Teacher, NSW

IGNITE YOUR SPIRIT THERAPISTS

Certification as an Ignite Your Spirit Therapist involves awakening your innate capacity to heal as well as your intuitive awareness. Growing in compassion and love, we help our clients to heal from a place of non-judgment and open new doors of opportunity for those who seek our help. Therapists learn specific applications of energetic healing to realign the systems of the body with good health. Training also involves spiritual counselling, communication and listening skills, ethics, self-care to prevent compassion fatigue, and advanced spiritual healing techniques. Assessment and feedback throughout the training, as well as continued Professional Development after certification, ensure a very high level of ability, professionalism and support is offered by each and every one of our therapists to you, our valued clients.

If you want to train as an energy healer go to www.igniteyourspirit.com for core training curriculum and healing electives.

To Find a qualified registered therapist near you go to:

https://www.IgniteYourSpirit.com

Our Australian charity The Well Being Initiative raises money to provide energy healing to those who cannot afford it. You can enquire about sponsored or free healing, or donate to help others, on our website https://www.igniteyourspirit.com

Two pilot studies into Ignite Your Spirit healing are able to be accessed via our website along with other scientific evidence supporting energy healing efficiency. We hope that more studies will be done in this important emerging area of health.

BIBLIOGRAPHY AND SUGGESTED READING

Bailey, A.A.	*Esoteric Healing*, Lucas Trust, New York, 1953
Besant, Annie & Leadbeater, C.W.	*Thought Forms*, Quest Books, Theosophical Publishing House Adyar, India, 1999 (first published circa 1930)
Brennan, Barbara Ann	*Light Emerging*, Bantam Books, USA 1993
Capra, Fritzof	*The Tao of Physics*, Shambhala Publications, Boston USA 1975
Choa Kok Sui, Master	*Miracles Through Pranic Healing*, Institute of Inner Studies, Manila
Choa Kok Sui, Master	*Advanced Pranic Healing*, Institute of Inner Studies, Manila
Choa Kok Sui, Master	*Meditations for Soul Realization*, Institute of Inner Studies, Manila
Co, Master Stephen & Robins, Eric B. MD	*Your Hands Can Heal You*, Free Press, Simon & Schuster, New York, 2002
Hay, Louise	*You Can Heal Your Life*, Hay House, USA, 1982
Hawkins, David R.	*The Eye of the I*, Veritas Publishing, Arizona, 2001
Leadbeater, C.W.	*The Chakras*, Theosophical Publishing House, Madras India, 1927
Myss, Dr Carolyn	*Anatomy of the Spirit*, Bantam Books Australia, 1996
Myss, Dr Carolyn	*Sacred Contracts*, Random House Australia, 2001
Noontill, Annette	*The Body is the Barometer of your Soul*, Gemcraft Books, Australia, 1994

Northrop, Dr C & Schultz, Dr Mona Lisa	*Awakening Intuition,* cassette set, Hay House, USA 1999
Powell, A.E.	*The Etheric Double,* Quest Books, Theosophical Publishing House Adyar, India, 1925
Wolf, Fred Alan	*Taking the Quantum Leap,* Harper and Row, New York, 1989
Zukav, Gary	*The Dancing Wu Li Masters,* Rider, London, 1979

OTHER PRODUCTS
BY THE AUTHOR

EMPOWERING RELATIONSHIPS

Relationships are a vessel within which we can discover ourselves as well as work towards enlightenment. In this book Shakti Durga shares her multi-dimensional philosophy about relationships, and how to be an empowered peacemaker.

This easy to read book contains a lifetime of tools and techniques that Shakti Durga uses and

teaches to become inspired, respected, happy and fulfilled within relationships. Even bad relationships can become good, and good ones truly Divine, as we move deeply and skilfully into the vast potential inside of us.

This book is also the text for three inspiring seminars awakening you to Empowerment through Relationships.

CHILD OF GOD

Shakti Durga's second book focuses on how we can master our thoughts and the mysterious Astral dimension to unblock our potential in breathtaking ways. We are multidimensional. There are 5 main dimensions in which we humans live. By learning about

these dimensions we learn about ourselves. We can enhance our lives, solve stress, find our hearts and souls, live in Divine splendour and achieve our highest destiny. This book is also the text for the seminar Yoga of the Mind.

SPIRITUAL MASTERY

Spiritual Masters exist in every religious and mystical tradition, and their job is to guide us home, each one taking us a little further on our evolutionary journey. Mere knowledge or theory is only helpful when we actually embody it in our day to day existence.

Spiritual Mastery entails the capacity to generate

inner peace, personal power and prosperity in whatever range of circumstances are presented to us.

This book covers the many tools and life changing ideals that have helped thousands to find peace, power and prosperity on the Path of Ease and Grace©. Witty and sparkling, practical and easy to read, it will help you to recognize the spiritual laws, hallmarks, pitfalls and practices that bring us closer to Spiritual Mastery. This book is also the text for the seminars Spiritual Mastery Laws of the Soul and Spiritual Mastery Hallmarks of Awakening.

DIMENSIONS OF WEALTH

Have you ever used affirmations until you are blue in the face, yet some areas of your life stubbornly stay the same? Have you worked at the Law of Attraction but still experience the same old problems? Chances are you have done part of the work needed to change your life, but the  most powerful part of your wealth anatomy, your soul, may still remain a mystery.

Beyond anything you have read before, *Dimensions of Wealth* takes us on a spiritual journey of discovery into how to attract wealth and opportunity. Natural manifesting is a spiritual science and art, creating powerful life change. It requires energy as well as thought, stillness as well as action, soul as well as mind. Affirmations can set the scene, but our powerful soul must be in really good shape for natural manifesting to succeed in anchoring the Kingdom of Heaven on Earth, for ourselves and for others. Discover the five Dimensions of Wealth and the 12 Mansions of the Soul. Come on an amazing journey of the spirit as the means to attract miracles is revealed.

CHANT, MEDITATION AND SEMINAR, LIVE CDS

A large range of live recordings, including audio files of seminars and presentations made by Shakti Durga over the past 20 years are available from Shanti Mission centres and online www. shaktidurga.com and www.shantishop.org

STRENGTH OF THE SOUL CARDS –

TRANSFORM YOUR CAPACITY AND POTENCY OF THE SOUL

Shakti Durga has created this set of 54 cards, designed to assist you to attune with the amazing power of your soul as a means to transform your life, facilitate healing and blaze through the obstacles in your life.

MORE STRENGTH OF THE SOUL CARDS –

TRANSFORM YOUR CAPACITY AND POTENCY OF THE SOUL

Accessing the power of your soul is an incredible gift that is available to everyone. Shakti Durga has created this second set of 54 cards, designed to assist you to attune with the amazing power of your soul as a means to transform your life, facilitate healing and

blaze through the obstacles in your life. This stand alone deck is a companion to Shakti Durga's first Strength of the Soul deck. They are designed to be used together or independently.

WEALTH WISDOM CARDS –

NATURAL MANIFESTING WITH EASE AND GRACE

Wealth Wisdom is a multidimensional approach to leading an abundant life. Shakti Durga has created a series of cards based on her teachings to assist everyone to gain clear soul guidance on a daily basis. Card decks are

available to buy from Shanti Mission Centres and online www.shaktidurga.com. Beyond affirmations, learn to align with the strength of your soul and the Archangels to enter the flow and anchor real goodness in your life. There are 72 beautifully designed cards in this deck.

Seminars by the Author

❏ *The Path of Ease and Grace*©

Shanti Mission offers a path of awakening, healing, illumination and self-discovery designed to help you to Ignite Your Spirit and get more out of life. The Path of Ease and Grace© interactive courses are taught in easy-to-understand steps that allow you to learn at your own pace through a series of inspiring seminars, designed for everyone. Be supported on your journey through optional one-on-one IYS Energy Healing sessions with a registered, qualified IYS Therapist. A range of books and CDs and a friendly, welcoming and open community comprise a treasury of resources available to support your personal progress. We know that there is an endless potential for increased self-fulfilment, love, joy and peace, as well as a wealth of opportunity sitting untapped right under your nose. Our job is to help you find it.

The Path of Ease and Grace© shows you how to connect to a deeper level of your own consciousness, so you can take the next step towards a happier, healthier, wealthier and more fulfilled life.

Seminars include:

❏ *Ignite Your Spirit - Energy Healing Made Easy*

Learn about your own energy body and how it is affecting your life every day. Learn simple energy healing techniques to help you manage your energy and your health. Appreciate the interaction between your energy field and your physical body. Learn how to cut from negative people and heal adverse situations. Meditation and easy exercises that will help you feel brighter and more balanced and that will ease pain and reduce stress.

❏ *Ignite your Spirit – Centres of Consciousness*

This is a fascinating, inspired yet practical opportunity to learn more about your own energy anatomy and spirit.

Learn how we are interconnected with all of life through energy centres. Experience powerful guided healing meditations, and let your energy be replenished through wonderful transmissions of light and grace. Discover how to anchor more vitality and healing capacity, and have some fun as our teachers share their warmth, humour and personal stories of transformation. As you practise, your own energy will be enhanced – something you are likely to notice straight away, with continuing changes in the weeks ahead.

Discover more powerful ways to heal the mind and body, and safe effective use of light and sound for healing. Perceive the unique shape of your own energy field.

❏ *Yoga of the Mind*

The mind is an instrument of our soul, and when we learn to connect with our soul our consciousness transforms. Yoga means union and can be used to help us to attain peace and enlightenment. Yoga of the Mind is a companion to Ignite Your Spirit and helps us learn to still our minds, using ancient techniques to erase negative thought patterns, fears and self-defeating beliefs and ideas. Astounding changes in consciousness frequently occur during the seminar, and life changes afterwards are often profound. Break free of old grudges and negative habits and put in place new healthy foundations. Learn more about how to care for your developing energy body and add more healing techniques to your repertoire.

❏ *Dimensions of Wealth*

In Dimensions of Wealth we teach the art of Natural Manifesting. This is a method which aligns us with Universal design, which is Benevolence and Abundance. Wealth is both tangible and intangible. It includes having enough money to do whatever we want, as well as having the capacity to enjoy the earth, care for our families, have great friends, and a real sense of who I am and why I am here.

In this seminar we look at the way in which we either attract or repel good things in our lives. We learn potent affirmations to change our reality, study the five dimensions of wealth as well

as spiritual laws that bind us, whether we like it or not. Knowing them makes life a lot easier to understand.

Activations of the base chakra, learning how to self-assess our individual capacity to manifest wealth, and exercises to improve wealth creation are imparted.

❑ *Empowering Relationships Emotional Liberation*

Being empowered to have great relationships is an important key to a fulfilling life. Learn about your eight core needs and how to beat co-dependence. Experience an amazing healing meditation that you can practise any time. See how your mind, your energy, your soul and your speech can all become assets to anchor more love, joy, peace and intimacy, trust and security in ourselves and in our relationships. This transformative and experiential seminar will bring relief and freedom as well as a raft of ways to turn around difficult relationships and make good ones even better.

❑ *Empowering Relationships from Conflict to Connection*

It is easy in the honeymoon stage, but how do you keep the energy high and stay committed, retaining the zing and the intimacy? Rediscover the golden flow of deep togetherness. Learn simple ways to handle conflict, be more assertive and experience greater love. Find out how to gracefully transition relationships from one form to another, so that peace and authenticity, respect and trust are possible even when they may not have been in evidence till now. Practical and inspiring, we help you let go of old wounds, heal the past and get your energy into present time. Attain peace and happiness even in challenging relationships.

❒ *Empowering Relationships Spirit and Soul*

We live in a relational universe. Relationships are a portal for self-realisation and can be utilised as vehicles for the transformation of our consciousness. Rather than being stuck in old, habituated patterns, we can lift ourselves and our relationships into new paradigms. In this class, we learn tools of the spirit and soul for this exact transformation. You will be astounded by how liberating and transformative this is, and by how much freedom, light, love, clarity, and connection you can create in your life.

❒ *Spiritual Mastery Laws of the Soul*

Learn the rules of the game of Life!

The twelve spiritual laws are part of the fabric of creation itself. We cannot avoid them, so we need to learn to understand and embrace them. When we start to work with the Law of the Universe, the Universe starts to work with us and then anything is possible!

Spiritual Mastery –Hallmarks of Awakening

Explore 12 hallmarks of Spiritual Masters, with practical examples to help understand how Mastery can be lived. What should we be aspiring towards? What will bring us the greatest change internally and externally?

Measure your own progress in each of the 12 Hallmarks of Awakening. For each hallmark, you will clearly understand what we are seeking to attain, as well as how to avoid the pitfalls on the path. Practices which support each hallmark of spiritual mastery are explained and vibrant spiritual energy helps us to absorb the teachings to transform our experience of life.

❒ *Living Truth and Purpose by Gayatri Anderson*

Introducing Shakti Durga's daughter, Dr Gayatri has been living the Path of Ease and Grace, healing and teaching spirituality since her teenage years. Her program Living Truth and Purpose is part of the Path of Ease and Grace seminar series.

Everyone has a spark inside that yearns to be expressed. When we are in touch with the essence in the world, we feel alive, uplifted and inspired. We feel motivated even in the face of challenges.

When we are not in touch with that essence, we can feel like the spark inside has gone out. We can feel like the world is grey; like life is repetitive and boring. We can feel a sense of not being enough, even if we are hitting all our targets. We know deep inside that there is more to who we are, but we don't know how to find it. In Living Truth and Purpose, we will be exploring the multi-dimensional nature of purpose and soul-identity. We will be exploring soul-based, mental, emotional and physical techniques to connect with and live the truth of who we are.

ABOUT THE AUTHOR

Shakti Durga

Shakti Durga (Kim Fraser) is a mystical yogi, spiritual teacher and healer, sacred musician and a seeker of the Eternal Wisdom from both Eastern and Western sources.

She established the energy healing modality Ignite Your Spirit and Shanti Mission, a School for the Soul, in Australia. Shanti Mission now also operates in the USA, UK and India. Shanti means peace and the mission is to find peace within. Only then will we start to develop more peace in our world.

Shakti Durga's courses and seminars teach practical, grounded tools and approaches to resolving conflicts, financial issues, health issues and feelings of emptiness. Because she teaches beyond the mind, and helps students release and let go of blocks to creating better lives, people's lives transform rapidly. Common spiritual concepts and practical tools suddenly become much easier.

Prior to commencing her vocation in spirituality, Shakti Durga was a practising lawyer. She has two grown children and lives with her life partner in Cooranbong, north of Sydney in NSW, Australia

Imagine if work was joy

Relationships were bliss

And education developed the soul

As well as the mind and body?

What if hospitals were temples of healing

And prosperity was for everyone?

The Shanti vision becomes real.

Each of us holds tremendous, untapped power

To transform our world.

We have forgotten how to use it.

Come and find yourself,

Ignite your spirit and

Discover your Path of Ease and Grace.